SUPER
NATURE

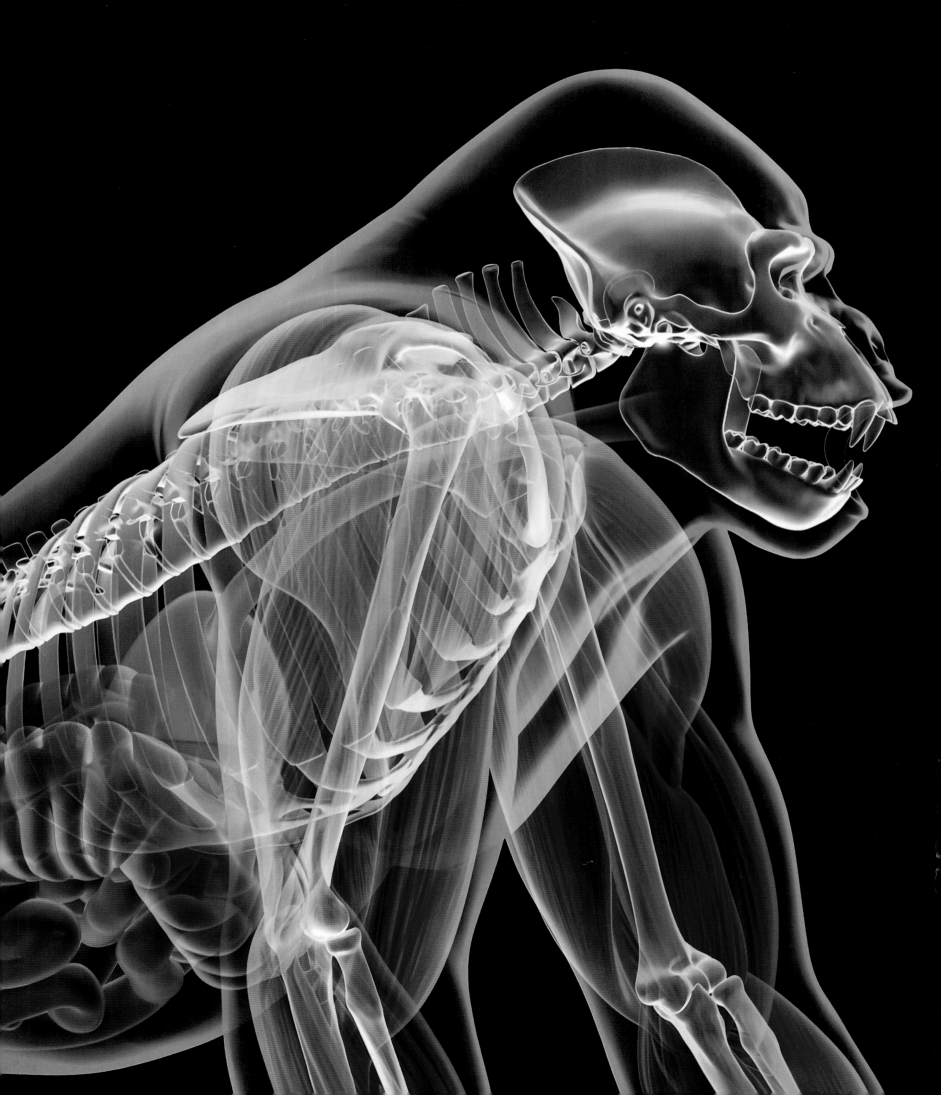

SUPER NATURE

THE 100 BIGGEST, *FASTEST*, DEADLIEST CREATURES ON THE PLANET

Derek Harvey

CONTENTS

STRONGEST BITE PAGE 18

FASTEST SPRINTER PAGE 118

DK LONDON

Senior Designer
Ina Stradins

Senior Editor
Angeles Gavira

Designers
David Ball, Alison Gardner,
Anna Hall, Peter Laws,
Fiona Macdonald, Francis Wong

Editors
Kim Bryan, Jemima Dunne,
Wendy Horobin, Janet Mohun,
Steve Setford, Laura Wheadon

DK Picture Library
Liz Moore

Editorial Assistant
Lili Bryant

Jacket Designers
Laura Brim, Silke Spingies

Jacket Editor
Manisha Majithia

Production Controllers
Erika Pepe, Alice Sykes

Production Editor
Victoria Khroundina

**LONDON, NEW YORK, MELBOURNE,
MUNICH, AND DELHI**

Managing Art Editor
Michelle Baxter

Managing Editor
Camilla Hallinan

Art Director
Philip Ormerod

Publisher
Sarah Larter

**Associate Publishing
Director**
Liz Wheeler

Publishing Director
Jonathan Metcalf

DK INDIA

Senior Art Editor
Devika Dwarkadas

Senior Editor
Soma B. Chowdhury

Art Editors
Suhita Dharamjit, Parul Gambhir,
Rakesh Khundongbam,
Vaibhav Rastogi

Editors
Suefa Lee, Neha Pande

Managing Editors
Rohan Sinha,
Alka Thakur Hazarika

DTP Designers
Rajesh Singh Adhikari,
Arvind Kumar, Tanveer Zaidi

Production Manager
Pankaj Sharma

Consultant Art Director
Shefali Upadhyay

DTP Manager
Balwant Singh

MOST CARING MOTHER PAGE **214**

SILENT FLYER PAGE **234**

LIFE STORIES

SUPERNATURAL SENSES

ILLUSTRATORS

Medi-Mation   Raj Doshi, Arran Lewis

Dotnamestudios   Andrew Kerr

Peter Minister

Peter Bull

First published in Great Britain in 2012
by Dorling Kindersley Limited
80 Strand, London WC2R 0RL
Penguin Group (UK)

2 4 6 8 10 9 7 5 3 1
001 – 183047– Sep/2012

A CIP catalogue record for this book is available
from the British Library

ISBN 978-1-4093-7651-4

Printed and bound in China by Leo Paper Products

Discover more at **www.dk.com**

LIVING PLANET

Life began in Earth's oceans about 3.5 billion years ago. It has since spread, in a spectacular number of different forms, to every corner of the planet. Among the host of animals that inhabit land and sea there are some true superstars of nature that boast amazing abilities, incredible bodies, and fascinating lifestyles.

▶ SAVANNA

Tropical savanna grassland is hot all year round, but there are distinct dry and wet seasons. A few trees and shrubs offer some shade. On the African savanna, grazing animals such as wildebeest and zebra follow the rains in search of fresh grass, preyed on by lions and other carnivores.

▶ POLAR ICE

The polar regions – the Arctic Ocean around the North Pole, and Antarctica around the South Pole – are mostly covered by thick ice. Many polar animals use thick layers of fur, feathers, or fat to keep out the cold, while some fish have antifreeze in their blood.

▶ TROPICAL FOREST

The lush, evergreen forests near the Equator are home to at least half of the world's plant and animal species. Often called "jungles", these forests are always warm and wet. Their flowers, fruits, and leaves are a rich source of food. Animals live at every level, from the tops of the tallest trees to the dark forest floor.

BOREAL FOREST

The dense forests of the far north are made up mainly of conifer trees. In the short summer there is plenty to eat, but food is scarce in the long, cold winter. Some animals hibernate in winter, others migrate south.

8.5%

CULTIVATED LAND

Nearly one-tenth of Earth's land area is used for farming. Cultivated land supports plant crops and domesticated animals, together with wild species that have managed to survive alongside humans.

9.5%

10%

11%

17%

The world's biomes

Biologists divide the world into "biomes", regions with similar landscapes, climates, and wildlife. The figures below show how much of Earth's land surface each biome occupies.

7%

6%

6%

5.5%

19.5%

TEMPERATE FOREST

Broadleaved, deciduous trees flourish in mild (temperate) climates. Summers are warm, winters cool, and rain falls year-round. Birds, bears, deer, and small mammals thrive in such forests.

TEMPERATE GRASSLAND

Cooler than savanna, temperate grasslands also have less rainfall and so cannot support trees or shrubs. They are home to large grazing animals such as bison and antelope.

OCEAN LIFE

71%

29%

Earth is a watery world, with vast oceans covering nearly three-quarters of its surface. Shallow seas near land, especially around coral reefs, are rich in wildlife. Animals that live out in the open ocean must be strong swimmers to move around in the currents. In the deepest ocean, up to 11 km (7 miles) below the surface, animals must cope with total darkness, very cold temperatures, and pressures that would crush a human.

MEDITERRANEAN ◄

Regions with a Mediterranean-style climate have short, wet, mild winters and long, dry summers. Shrubs, short trees, and cacti and other drought-resistant plants grow on their rugged landscapes. Animals include wild goats, lynx, jackals, boar, and vultures.

TUNDRA ◄

The flat, treeless tundra lands surrounding the Arctic are free of ice, but below the surface layer the soil is always frozen. The tundra comes alive with flowers and insects in summer, and many birds and mammals migrate there to feed and breed.

DESERT ◄

Places with less than 25 cm (10 in) of rain a year are called deserts. They are usually hot – up to a scorching 50°C (120°F) by day – and either rocky or covered with shifting sand. Desert animals can survive on very little water. Many are active at night, when it is cooler.

ALL SHAPES AND SIZES

The world is bursting with animals. We know of more than 1.5 million different species of living animals, in all shapes and sizes imaginable. In fact, there are so many that a whole branch of biology – taxonomy – is devoted to classifying them into groups based on shared features.

SPINELESS INVERTEBRATES

About two-thirds of all known animal species are invertebrates. Invertebrate groups include cnidarians, molluscs, echinoderms, sponges, worms, and arthropods. These animals have few features in common, apart from the fact that they all lack a backbone, or vertebral column. Familiar invertebrates include worms, arthropods such as insects, crabs, and spiders, and snails, which are molluscs. However, many invertebrates are so inconspicuous or tiny that we never notice them. A lot are found only in the sea. Others, such as insects, live on land and are common worldwide.

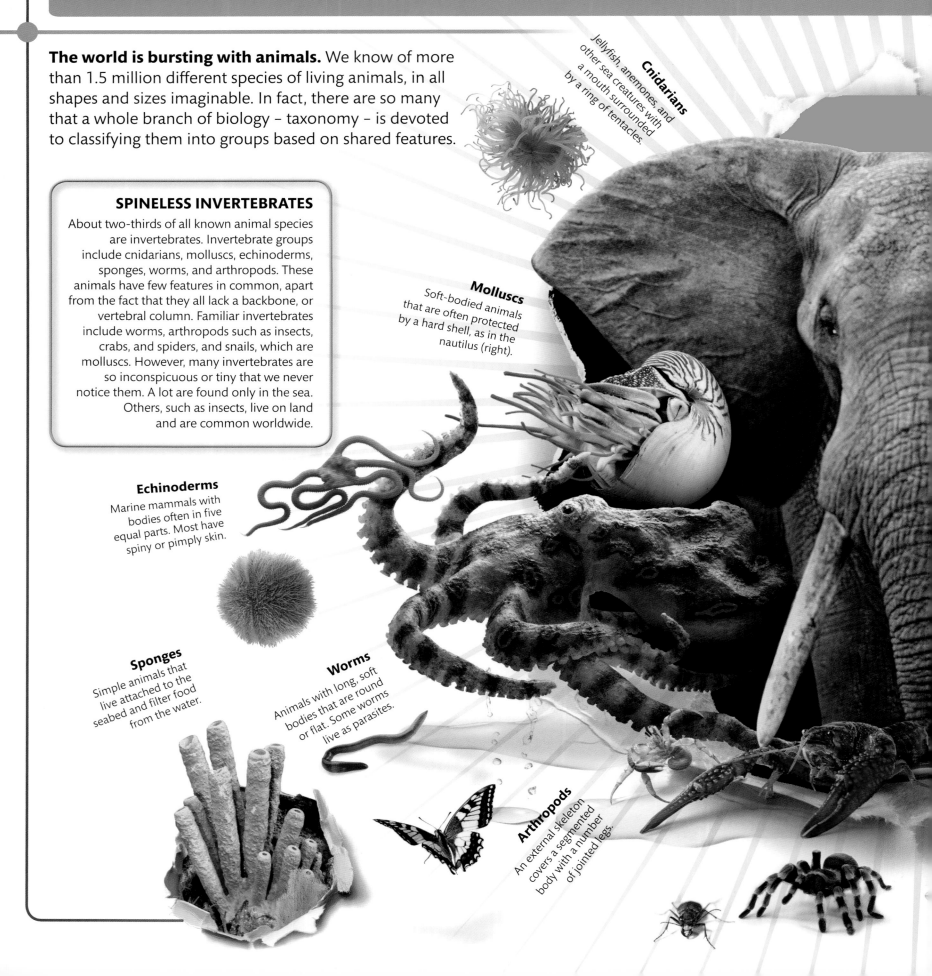

Cnidarians
Jellyfish, anemones, and other sea creatures with a mouth surrounded by a ring of tentacles.

Molluscs
Soft-bodied animals that are often protected by a hard shell, as in the nautilus (right).

Echinoderms
Marine mammals with bodies often in five equal parts. Most have spiny or pimply skin.

Sponges
Simple animals that live attached to the seabed and filter food from the water.

Worms
Animals with long, soft bodies that are round or flat. Some worms live as parasites.

Arthropods
An external skeleton covers a segmented body with a number of jointed legs.

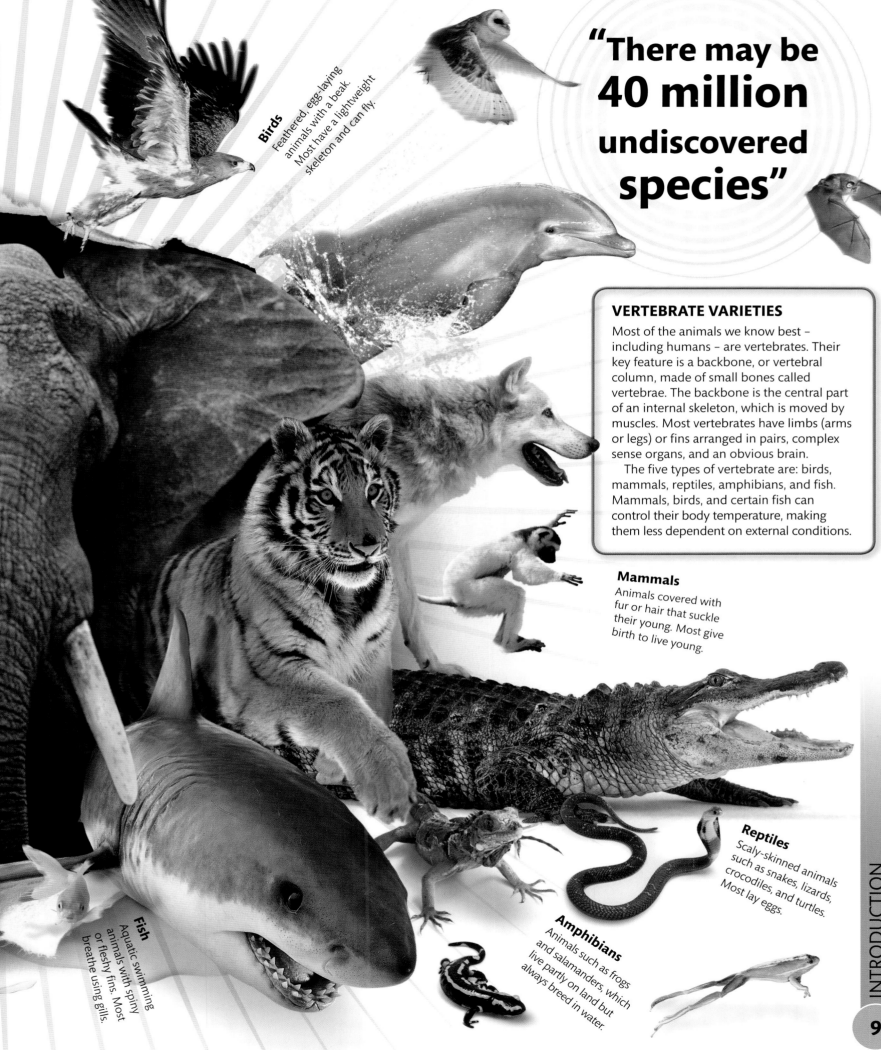

Birds
Feathered, egg-laying animals with a beak. Most have a lightweight skeleton and can fly.

"There may be 40 million undiscovered species"

VERTEBRATE VARIETIES

Most of the animals we know best – including humans – are vertebrates. Their key feature is a backbone, or vertebral column, made of small bones called vertebrae. The backbone is the central part of an internal skeleton, which is moved by muscles. Most vertebrates have limbs (arms or legs) or fins arranged in pairs, complex sense organs, and an obvious brain.

The five types of vertebrate are: birds, mammals, reptiles, amphibians, and fish. Mammals, birds, and certain fish can control their body temperature, making them less dependent on external conditions.

Mammals
Animals covered with fur or hair that suckle their young. Most give birth to live young.

Reptiles
Scaly-skinned animals such as snakes, lizards, crocodiles, and turtles. Most lay eggs.

Amphibians
Animals such as frogs and salamanders, which live partly on land but always breed in water.

Fish
Aquatic swimming animals with spiny or fleshy fins. Most breathe using gills.

EVER-CHANGING ANIMALS

Nothing stays the same for long in nature. Over many generations living things gradually change, or adapt, so that they are better suited to their surroundings. Those that fail to adapt become extinct – they die out. This process of slow change is called evolution, and it has produced the amazing variety of animals that we see today.

Zebras

A striped coat is a useful characteristic for zebras. It helps them to recognize and bond with their own kind – an important ability for herd animals.

HOW EVOLUTION WORKS

Young animals tend to look like their parents because characteristics are copied from parents to offspring. But this copying process is not exact, and sometimes the young develop new characteristics. If a new characteristic is useful – such as a coat colour that provides better camouflage – the animal is likely to live a longer and more successful life, producing more offspring that will also have the helpful trait.

Barapasaurus measured 18 m (59 ft) from its head to the tip of its tail

Body was bulky and heavy

SUPERSIZED MAMMALS

Major events, such as vast volcanic eruptions or meteorite strikes, can change animals' surroundings so rapidly that they cannot adapt quickly enough and many species die out. This is called a mass extinction.

After a mass extinction 65 million years ago wiped out the dinosaurs, large mammals evolved to take their place. They included a giant rhinoceros, 5.5 m (18 ft) tall, and giant sloths, beavers, and armadillos.

Flexible tail helped to balance the long neck

Giant armadillo

Glyptodon, a distant relative of modern armadillos, lived from around 5 million to 10,000 years ago.

Thick, scaly skin

Pillar-like legs

Sauropods walked on the tips of their toes

Modern armadillo is much smaller

Barapasaurus – a loser

Sauropod dinosaurs, such as this *Barapasaurus*, were among the many losers of the mass extinction 65 million years ago. The sauropods included the largest and heaviest animals ever to have lived on land.

"99.9% of all animal species that have ever lived are now extinct"

Short, deep head

Long neck allowed dinosaur to reach leaves high up in trees

Broad teeth for grinding up plant food

Bare skin on head and neck

Powerful bill for tearing meat

Vulture – a winner

When you look at a vulture, you are looking at one of evolution's winners. The scaly skin and reptilian eyes are a reminder that birds are descended from dinosaurs.

LOSERS AND WINNERS

We think of dinosaurs as being long-extinct, but that is not strictly true – their descendants are still with us today. The therapods were a group of dinosaurs that walked on two legs. They included the well known *Tyrannosaurus* and *Velociraptor.* About 160 million years ago, some smaller theropods grew feathers, perhaps as a way of keeping warm. Later, they began using their feathered forelimbs to glide or fly. Eventually, these feathered therapods evolved into birds. When the dinosaurs died out after a huge meteorite collided with Earth around 65 million years ago, the birds survived.

Simple feathers

Three-fingered hands

Thick bones supported the dinosaur's huge weight

Stubby feet like those of an elephant

Talons on three-toed feet

Bird ancestor

About the height of a human, the therapod *Guanlong* was a smaller relative of *Tyrannosaurus*. *Guanglong* had a large crest on its head, and its skin may have been covered with simple feathers.

BODY MATTERS

Animal bodies are made up of cells, which are grouped together to form tissues such as muscle and bone, and organs such as brains, kidneys, eyes, and skin. The arrangement of tissues and organs in animal bodies varies enormously, but it tends to be similar in closely related kinds of animal. It is almost always the best arrangement for each species' unique way of life.

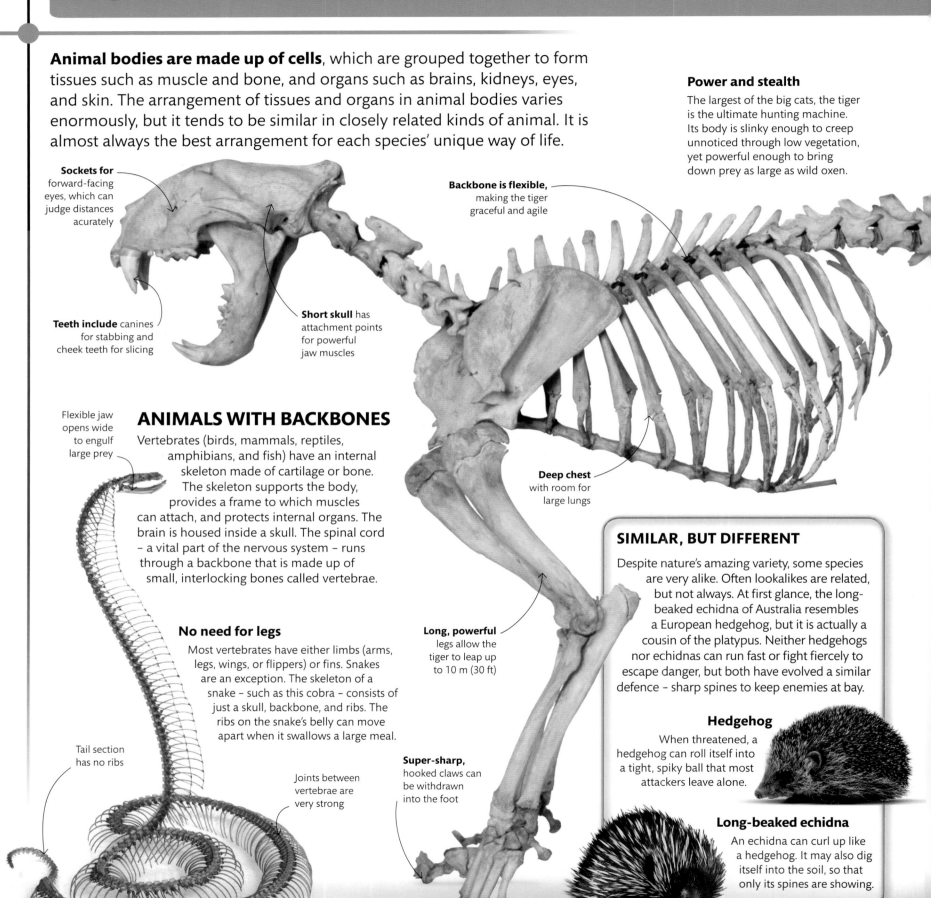

Sockets for forward-facing eyes, which can judge distances acurately

Teeth include canines for stabbing and cheek teeth for slicing

Short skull has attachment points for powerful jaw muscles

Backbone is flexible, making the tiger graceful and agile

Deep chest with room for large lungs

Power and stealth

The largest of the big cats, the tiger is the ultimate hunting machine. Its body is slinky enough to creep unnoticed through low vegetation, yet powerful enough to bring down prey as large as wild oxen.

ANIMALS WITH BACKBONES

Vertebrates (birds, mammals, reptiles, amphibians, and fish) have an internal skeleton made of cartilage or bone. The skeleton supports the body, provides a frame to which muscles can attach, and protects internal organs. The brain is housed inside a skull. The spinal cord – a vital part of the nervous system – runs through a backbone that is made up of small, interlocking bones called vertebrae.

Flexible jaw opens wide to engulf large prey

No need for legs

Most vertebrates have either limbs (arms, legs, wings, or flippers) or fins. Snakes are an exception. The skeleton of a snake – such as this cobra – consists of just a skull, backbone, and ribs. The ribs on the snake's belly can move apart when it swallows a large meal.

Tail section has no ribs

Joints between vertebrae are very strong

Long, powerful legs allow the tiger to leap up to 10 m (30 ft)

Super-sharp, hooked claws can be withdrawn into the foot

SIMILAR, BUT DIFFERENT

Despite nature's amazing variety, some species are very alike. Often lookalikes are related, but not always. At first glance, the long-beaked echidna of Australia resembles a European hedgehog, but it is actually a cousin of the platypus. Neither hedgehogs nor echidnas can run fast or fight fiercely to escape danger, but both have evolved a similar defence – sharp spines to keep enemies at bay.

Hedgehog

When threatened, a hedgehog can roll itself into a tight, spiky ball that most attackers leave alone.

Long-beaked echidna

An echidna can curl up like a hedgehog. It may also dig itself into the soil, so that only its spines are showing.

MADE-TO-MEASURE ARMOUR

Arthropods – such as crabs, insects, millipedes, and spiders – have a jointed external skeleton that fits like a perfect suit of armour. Called an exoskeleton, or cuticle, it covers the animal's entire body, including the mouthparts and eyes. It is made of a light, flexible material called chitin and strengthened with minerals. An exoskeleton gives excellent support and protection, but it limits movement and growth.

Tough case

In some large arthropods, such as this land crab, the exoskeleton is reinforced with a chalky substance called calcium carbonate, which makes it extremely hard.

Body is long and narrow, perfect for moving through dense forest

Narrow hips suited for running and jumping rather than climbing

Vertebrae have interlocking shapes

ROOM TO GROW

Unlike the internal skeleton of a vertebrate, the exoskeleton of an arthropod does not grow with the animal, so it has to be shed, or moulted, and regrown regularly. This Ecuadorian brown velvet tarantula spider will be soft and vulnerable for a few hours after moulting. It will hide in a safe place and wait for its new, roomier exoskeleton to harden.

MANAGING WITHOUT A SKELETON

Invertebrates that do not have an external skeleton support their bodies in a variety of ways. Most worms hold their shape by internal liquid pressure (a bit like a balloon full of water), while starfish and sea urchins grow a chalky shell immediately under their skin. Many molluscs, including clams and oysters, have a tough chalky or pearly shell. Others, such as squid and octopuses, rely mainly on the support of the water in which they live.

Reduced shell, or pen

Digestive system

Large eye

Muscular arms used for handling prey

Gill

Extendable tentacles used for attack and defence

Long thigh bones are embedded in some of the tiger's largest muscles

Squidgy squid

A squid has no skeleton, but some squid do possess an internal shell called a pen, which protects the animal's rear. The muscular body relies on the support of sea water, and some species can grow to enormous sizes.

Ankle joints raised off the ground act as shock absorbers

Long tail aids balance when running and climbing

Tigers walk on four toes on each foot

"A large lobster may moult up to 100 times during its life"

ANIMAL LIFESTYLES

All animals share the same basic characteristics – they are all able to grow, feed, reproduce, move, sense the world around them, and communicate at some level. But the ways in which animals do these things differ enormously, giving rise to a spectacular variety of animal lifestyles and behaviours.

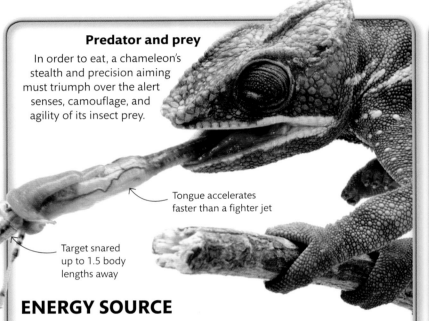

Predator and prey

In order to eat, a chameleon's stealth and precision aiming must triumph over the alert senses, camouflage, and agility of its insect prey.

Tongue accelerates faster than a fighter jet

Target snared up to 1.5 body lengths away

ENERGY SOURCE

Plants get their energy from sunlight, but animals have to obtain the energy they need to live and grow by eating other living things, or their remains. Plant-eating animals are called herbivores, and meat-eaters are carnivores. Tigers and most other carnivores are predators – hunters that kill other animals (known as prey) to get fresh meat. A few carnivores, including vultures, are scavengers; they do not kill but feed on animal remains. The least fussy eaters are omnivores, such as rats; they consume a wide variety of foods.

Tongue-twister

The giraffe, a herbivore, is a browser, meaning that it eats leaves that it plucks from trees. Its flexible tongue can work around even the sharpest thorns. Other herbivores have different feeding habits. Grazers, for example, eat grass, and gramnivores munch seeds.

SENSITIVE CREATURES

Senses are vital to an animal's survival, helping it to avoid danger and to find food or a mate. Like humans, most animals can detect light and touch, have a chemical sense such as taste or smell, and can detect sound waves or other vibrations. Some animals possess extra senses very different from our own, such as the way migrating birds can find their way using Earth's magnetic field.

Seeing the invisible

Honeybees can detect ultraviolet light, which human eyes are unable to see. Flowers often have ultraviolet markings, invisible to us, that direct bees to their pollen and nectar.

Light collectors

Most nocturnal animals have large eyes to gather as much light as possible. The spectral tarsier's eyes are bigger than its brain!

Bald eagle landing
Flight uses up a lot of energy, but it offers birds such as this bald eagle great rewards – including the ability to cover large distances rapidly.

"**Blue whale calls** can be **heard halfway** round the **world**"

SENDING SIGNALS

Animals have many ways of communicating with each another, including visual signals, sounds, and chemical messages. The messages are usually simple – a scent deposit to mark out territory, a warning cry or a mother's call to find her young, or a display to show aggression or attract a mate. Communication also helps social animals such as wolves and bees to live and work in groups.

Dazzling display
When a male peacock spreads out his tail fan, his shimmering plumage says "I am fit and strong" to potential mates. He also rattles his feathers to gain the female's attention.

ANIMALS IN MOTION

Most animals live in ever-changing environments, and they often need to move around to find new food sources, places to live, and others of their kind in order to breed. Even animals that live attached to one spot as adults – such as barnacles – are usually mobile when young. More active animals include walkers, runners, jumpers, crawlers, climbers, swimmers, gliders, and flyers. Travelling uses energy, so animal bodies are usually shaped to make a particular style of movement as effortless as possible.

Long-distance call
Wolves howl to let other pack members know where they are, and to tell rival packs to stay out of their territory. In the open, their calls carry for up to 16 km (10 miles).

Dive! Dive! Dive!
Like many swimming animals, penguins have streamlined bodies. They use their muscular flippers to achieve startling speeds, and their feet as steering rudders. They sometimes leap clear of the water – a stunt known as "porpoising".

AMAZING ANATOMY

Animals come in all shapes and sizes. There are big ones, small ones, hairy ones, and scaly ones. Some are super strong or ultra tough; others can stick to walls or deliver a nasty bite. Dive in and discover the ones that stand out from the crowd.

STRONGEST MAMMAL BITE
TASMANIAN DEVIL

Although scarcely bigger than a year-old bear cub, the Tasmanian devil has the strongest bite in relation to its size of any mammal. Its jaws can snap bones. It's an efficient scavenger of carrion, capable of eating a whole carcass, fur and all. It occasionally turns into a fearless killer, even attacking venomous snakes.

AT A GLANCE

- **SIZE** Head and body 53–80 cm (21–32 in) long, plus tail 23–30 cm (9–12 in) long
- **HABITAT** Heathland and forest
- **LOCATION** Tasmania
- **DIET** Carrion, living animals, and sometimes plant material

Bold white chest marking

PROTECTIVE MARKINGS

The white chest patch of a Tasmanian devil is particularly distinctive – although a small number of animals are born without it. The patch may act as a flag to draw aggressive bites from other devils away from the more vulnerable face.

Short legs give a slow, rolling gait

CARCASS COMPETITION

Most Tasmanian devils are not aggressive unless threatened or competing with another devil for food. When more than one animal is drawn to the same carcass, a noisy squabble might develop, but only rarely does it escalate into a fight. At times like this, growls, snorts, snarls, and screeches can be heard a very long distance away.

Broad head with large jaw muscles

Large pink ears with rounded tips

Coarse, blackish brown fur

Nocturnal hunter

The Tasmanian devil is a stocky, carnivorous marsupial that spends the day in hollow logs or burrows made by other animals, such as wombats. It emerges at night to search for food, relying mostly on its good sense of smell.

STATS AND FACTS

11.8
KG
MAXIMUM WEIGHT

Tasmanian devils can eat the equivalent of up to 10% of their body weight in meat a day. When well fed, they store fat in their tails in case food becomes scarce.

TOP SPEED

11
KM/H

BITE STRENGTH

	55 (domestic cat)		418	
N	200	400		600

PREY WEIGHT

			0.1–40 kg		
lb	20	40	60	80	
kg	15	30		45	

DISTANCE

		3.2–16 km (travelled at night)			
miles	2	4	6	8	10	12
km	5	10	15		20

"A Tasmanian devil's sneeze can be a sign of aggression"

COSY START

A female Tasmanian devil produces a litter of two to four tiny babies. They spend just over three months in her pouch, suckling and growing before they are moved to a den. The father sometimes helps keep the babies clean, and when they are old enough, the parents take turns carrying them around piggy-back fashion.

WARMEST COAT
SEA OTTER

The coat of a sea otter is as cosy as a winter duvet. There are more hairs in a square centimetre of its incredibly thick fur than there are on a whole human head. The sea otter certainly needs it. It lives in the cold waters along the north Pacific coastlines, but lacks the layer of fatty blubber under its skin that other sea mammals use as insulation. Instead, it relies on its dense coat to trap warm air close to its body. When floating, it holds its paws above the water to stop them getting too cold.

"There can be **800 million hairs** in an adult otter's coat"

AT A GLANCE

Dark fur on body, white on head

- **SIZE** Head and body 1–1.2 m (3¼–4 ft) long, plus tail 25–37 cm (10–14½ in) long
- **HABITAT** Shoreline and shallow ocean waters, within 1 km (0.6 miles) of coast
- **LOCATION** Japan and western coastal North America
- **DIET** Slow-swimming fishes, sea urchins, crabs, and molluscs

STATS AND FACTS

45 KG RECORD WEIGHT

The thickest part of the sea otter coat is the underfur that is closest to the skin, helping the animal stay warm when diving in icy water.

DENSITY OF HAIR

200 (human)   150,000

| hair/sq cm | 100,000 | 200,000 |

DIVE

40 m (depth)   97 m (record depth)

| ft | 100 | 200 | 300 |
| m | 30 | 60 | 90 | 120 |

265 sec. (record duration)

| sec. | 50 | 100 | 150 | 200 | 250 | 300 |

52–90 sec. (duration)

TEMPERATURE

1–15°C (surrounding water)

| °F | 50 | 75 | 100 |
| °C | 10 | 20 | 30 | 40 |

37°C (body temperature, same as human)

TOP SWIMMING SPEED

9 KM/H

DENSEST FUR

LAID-BACK DRIFTERS

Sea otters rest by floating in the water on their backs – and usually sleep this way, wrapping themselves in seaweed so they don't drift out to sea. They even use their bellies as dinner tables, balancing a rock on their chest as an anvil to crack open clam shells.

TALLEST ANIMAL

GIRAFFE

The tallest giraffe could easily look through a second-floor window without even stretching. A combination of long legs and long neck means the giraffe can not only eat leaves from high branches, but it can spot danger further away, too.

Tongue is about 50 cm (20 in) long

Horns are bony outgrowths of the skulll

Ligament helps hold head and neck up

Neck bones have ball-and-socket joints that give greater flexibility

Neck muscles are strong to support heavy bones

TONGUE TWISTER

A giraffe can reach even further into its favourite acacia trees with its long tongue. The tongue is extremely flexible so it can wrap around the acacia's thorny shoots to pluck the succulent leaves. A coating of sticky saliva blankets any thorns that end up being swallowed.

GETTING IT IN THE NECK

Male giraffes frequently do battle with one another by swinging their necks and bashing rivals with their heads. This helps more dominant males keep their authority within the herd. Battles are usually gentle, but if a female is around, things may escalate and a male might even be knocked unconscious.

STATS AND FACTS

WEIGHT OF HEART

0.3 kg (human)   3   6   9   11 kg
lb   10   20   12
kg

HEARTBEATS

bpm   60 (giraffe when resting)   1 min
bpm   75 (human)   1 min

RECORD HEIGHT

6 METRES

Special blood vessels in the head stop blood rushing to it when the giraffe stoops to drink.

SPRINTING SPEED

68 KM/H

"Every step a giraffe takes is 4.5 m (15 ft) long"

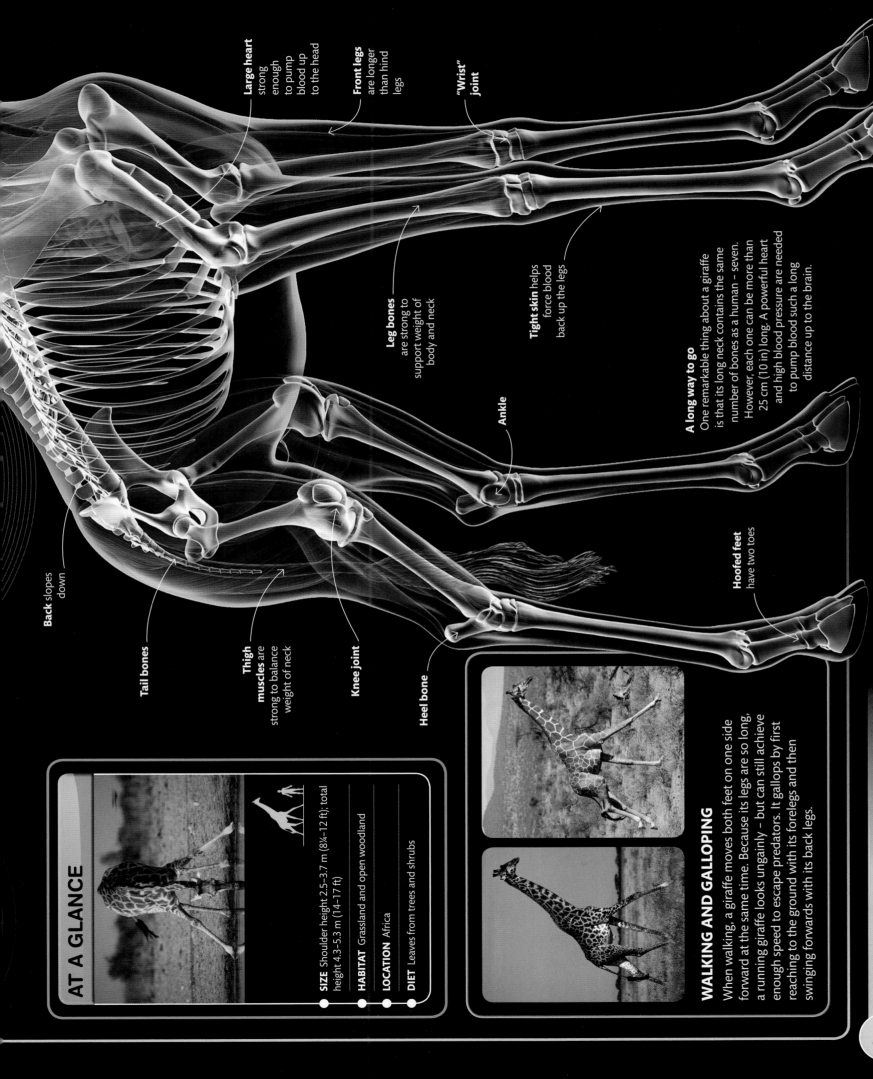

Large heart strong enough to pump blood up to the head

Front legs are longer than hind legs

"Wrist" joint

Leg bones are strong to support weight of body and neck

Tight skin helps force blood back up the legs

Ankle

A long way to go
One remarkable thing about a giraffe is that its long neck contains the same number of bones as a human – seven. However, each one can be more than 25 cm (10 in) long. A powerful heart and high blood pressure are needed to pump blood such a long distance up to the brain.

Hoofed feet have two toes

Back slopes down

Tail bones

Thigh muscles are strong to balance weight of neck

Knee joint

Heel bone

AT A GLANCE

SIZE Shoulder height 2.5–3.7 m (8¼–12 ft); total height 4.3–5.3 m (14–17 ft)

HABITAT Grassland and open woodland

LOCATION Africa

DIET Leaves from trees and shrubs

WALKING AND GALLOPING

When walking, a giraffe moves both feet on one side forward at the same time. Because its legs are so long, a running giraffe looks ungainly – but can still achieve enough speed to escape predators. It gallops by first reaching to the ground with its forelegs and then swinging forwards with its back legs.

AMAZING ANATOMY

ICE-COLD KILLER
POLAR BEAR

Polar bears are the largest animals to prowl the icy wastes of the Arctic Circle. Size is important in a place that is well below freezing for much of the year: a giant body generates warmth and a thick coat traps it inside. Its size also means that a polar bear can overpower and kill large prey.

LARGEST **LAND** CARNIVORE

STATS AND FACTS

1,002 KG
MAXIMUM WEIGHT

Polar bears prefer to hunt by stalking seals, but they can run fast enough over short distances to bring down a caribou.

TEETH

	55 (bite strength of domestic cat)	1,200 (bite strength)	
N	500	1,000	1,500
in	1	2	
cm	2	4	6
	0.5 cm (canine length of domestic cat)		4–5 cm (canine length)

PREY WEIGHT

		10–1,200 kg	
lb	1,000	2,000	3,000
kg	500	1,000	1,500

49 KM/H
TOP SPEED ON LAND

Mighty Arctic bear

The polar bear has thick layers of fur and blubber to keep warm – it is so well insulated that it could overheat if the weather becomes too warm. This bear is also at home in the cold Arctic waters, where it dives and swims, using its rear end as a rudder.

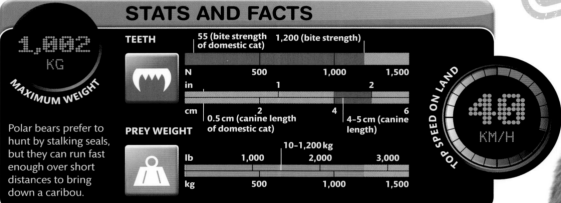

Sharp claws for extra grip

Fur stops feet slipping

FURRY FEET

The polar bear has huge hairy feet, with small pads, to help it grip on the slippery ice. Its large round feet also make excellent paddles when swimming. A polar bear uses its front paws to catch and kill its prey – these are so powerful they can crush the biggest seals and the strongest caribou.

Feet act like snow shoes

Distinctive
dark eye

Fur-covered
ears

SHARP SENSES

Polar bears have good
eyesight and hearing.
However, a bear relies mainly
on its nose and excellent sense of
smell to locate its prey, and can sniff out
young seals in dens below the ice.

White fur
helps the
bear hide
in the snow

Curved claws
help the bear
dig through ice

AT A GLANCE

- **SIZE** Head and body 2–2.5 m (6½–8¼ ft) long, plus tail 8–13 cm (3¼–5 in) long

- **HABITAT** Arctic pack ice and tundra

- **LOCATION** Coastlines and islands of the Arctic region

- **DIET** Seals, seabirds, caribou, fishes, and sometimes vegetation

AMAZING ANATOMY

LARGEST CAT

WARM COAT

In the cold forests of far eastern Siberia – where winter temperatures plummet far below freezing – tigers are kept warm by a coat that grows three times longer than that of tropical Asian tigers.

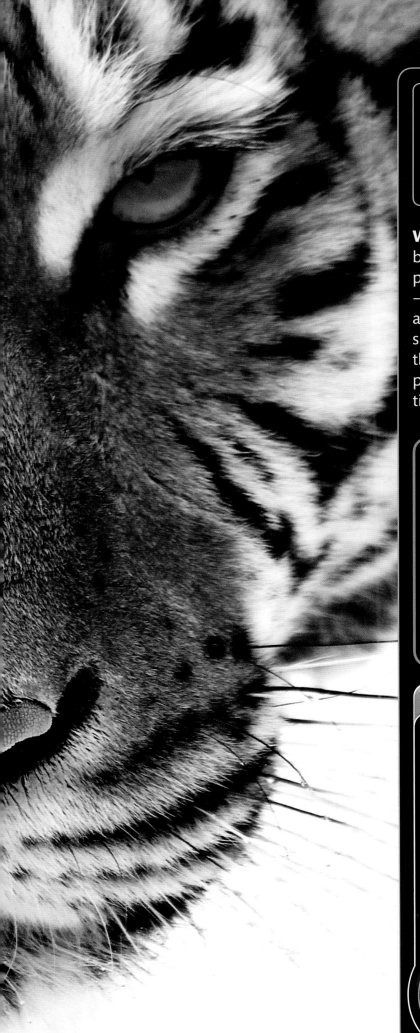

FELINE GIANT
SIBERIAN TIGER

With a neck-breaking bite and the strength to kill the biggest stag, the Siberian tiger is one of the largest land predators. A tiger catches prey by stalking and pouncing – it gets close to its quarry without being seen, then leaps at its neck. It clamps its jaws around its victim's throat to suffocate it, or bites the back of the neck to fatally sever the spinal cord. Long, dagger-like canine teeth grip the prey and shearing cheek teeth slice through its flesh, but tiger teeth are too fragile to crack bones.

AT A GLANCE

- **SIZE** Head and body 1.7–2.1 m (5½–7 ft) long, plus tail 84–100 cm (33–39 in) long
- **HABITAT** Cold coniferous and broad-leaved forests
- **LOCATION** Eastern Russia and some in northern China
- **DIET** Deer and smaller prey, such as rabbits and hares

STATS AND FACTS

15 YEARS
MAXIMUM LIFESPAN

The massive skull of a Siberian tiger supports powerful jaw muscles. They allow the tiger to throttle a big animal, such as a deer, within minutes.

PREY WEIGHT

0.5 kg (hare)–320 kg (deer)

lb	200	400	600	800
kg	100	200	300	400

BITE STRENGTH

55 (domestic cat)   1,500

N	500	1,000	1,500	2,000

FOOD CONSUMPTION

10 kg meat required per day

20–40 kg can be consumed at one go

MAXIMUM SPEED
68 KM/H

SMALLEST CARNIVORE

LEAST WEASEL

STATS AND FACTS

WEIGHT	oz	50	100
	g	1,000	2,000	3,000

25–250 g (weasel)

	oz	50	100
	g	1,000	2,000	3,000

10–2,000 g (prey)

12–15 (to reach adult size)

5 (gestation period)

TIME	weeks	5	10	15	20

6–8 (to wean)

LIFESPAN IN CAPTIVITY
18 YEARS

The least weasel is active throughout the year and even breeds in winter.

MAXIMUM WEIGHT
458 GRAMS

Size can be deceptive – the least weasel is so small that it could squeeze through a hole the diameter of a man's finger. It usually hunts mice, but can kill much bigger prey, such as rabbits. Least weasels have lightning-quick reflexes, and live life at a fast pace too. Within 6 months, newborn weasels have grown into miniature killers, fully capable of looking after themselves.

ARMED TO KILL

A least weasel has an elongated skull and a short face. The eye sockets are large and it has long, sharp canine teeth to puncture the head or neck of prey and break its bones. Like all mammal carnivores, there are special cheek teeth called carnassials on each side of the upper and lower jaws that are used for cutting through hide, flesh, and bone.

Long braincase

Carnassial teeth

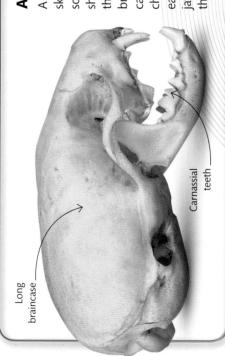

SMALL AND LIGHT

Weasels vary a lot in size across their geographic range and females are always smaller than males. Both sexes have a brown upper coat that provides them with some camouflage – but over most of their range they turn completely white in the winter to match the snow. Only in the far south, where it is warmer, do they stay brown.

"Kills prey 10 times its own body weight"

Fast and athletic

The long, sinuous body and short legs of the least weasel allow it to bolt down narrow burrows in search of prey. Long-distance jumps and fast chases make the weasel tricky to catch but it also keeps close to cover to avoid being seen by predators.

Soles of feet are furred in winter

AT A GLANCE

SIZE Head and body 12–26 cm (4¾–10 in) long, plus tail 2–8 cm (¾–3¼ in) long

HABITAT Woodland, grassland, and tundra

LOCATION North America, Europe, and Asia

DIET Mostly rodents; sometimes bigger prey such as rabbits

Chestnut brown coat with white underparts

Sharp claws

Short tail

RAPID GROWTH

Weighing only 5 g (¼ oz) at birth, a least weasel kit grows very quickly.

It reaches adult size in about 15 weeks. Females mature first and can produce their own kits when only three months old.

PINT-SIZE PREDATOR

Least weasels take on prey much larger than themselves. Because the males can be twice the weight of the females, they are more likely to hunt rabbits, but will also take hares and birds as large as capercaillies. Females mostly go after mouse-like rodents or baby rabbits.

ARMED FOR COMBAT

Antlers are covered in velvety skin. This "velvet" contains blood vessels that nourish the growing bone underneath. It is rubbed off during the autumn, exposing the bony weaponry used by males during combat.

FASTEST-GROWING BONES
MOOSE

The world's largest deer grows the heaviest antlers in record time. A male moose regrows its antlers every year since they fall off at the end of each breeding season – an achievement that is equivalent to growing an adult human skeleton in just a few months. As in other kinds of deer, antlers are used for combat: males use them for shoving each other when they compete for females.

AT A GLANCE

- **SIZE** Body length 2.4–3.2 m (7¾–10 ft) , plus 5–12 cm (2–4¾ in) tail length
- **HABITAT** Marshes, and open woodland that is snow covered in winter
- **LOCATION** North America and northern Eurasia
- **DIET** Shoots, stems, and roots of woody and aquatic plants

"Large antlers can be **1.8 m** (6 ft) across"

STATS AND FACTS

KG
RECORD ANTLER WEIGHT

An additional 10–20% nutrition is required to grow antlers each year. The calcium and phosphorus needed for bone growth come from the plants a moose eats.

ANTLERS GROW IN

GROWTH RATE OF ANTLERS

days	5 kg	28 kg	32 kg	35 kg
	25	50	75	100

DAILY FOOD CONSUMPTION

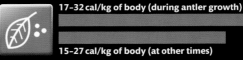

17–32 cal/kg of body (during antler growth)

15–27 cal/kg of body (at other times)

HOME RANGE

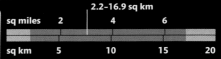

2.2–16.9 sq km

sq miles	2	4	6
sq km	5	10	15	20

GIANT-JAWED GRAZER
HIPPOPOTAMUS

FIGHT, NOT BITE

The longest teeth in a hippopotamus's mouth are its pointed canines, at 60 cm (23½ in) tall. These are used for fighting rather than grazing – instead it uses its horny lips to crop grass low to the ground.

The hippopotamus is a huge animal, equally at home in water or on land. It also has the biggest mouth. Despite being a vegetarian, the hippo's mouth is equipped with strong tusk-like teeth for fighting rivals. This – as well as the fact that it can easily outrun a human – makes it extremely dangerous. Hippos spend most of their day in water, but leave it at night to graze on land plants.

AT A GLANCE

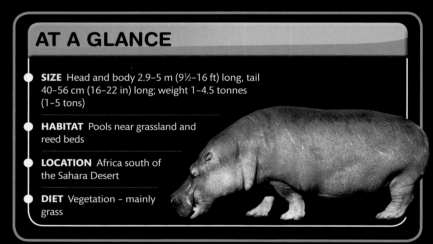

- **SIZE** Head and body 2.9–5 m (9½–16 ft) long, tail 40–56 cm (16–22 in) long; weight 1–4.5 tonnes (1–5 tons)

- **HABITAT** Pools near grassland and reed beds

- **LOCATION** Africa south of the Sahara Desert

- **DIET** Vegetation – mainly grass

STATS AND FACTS

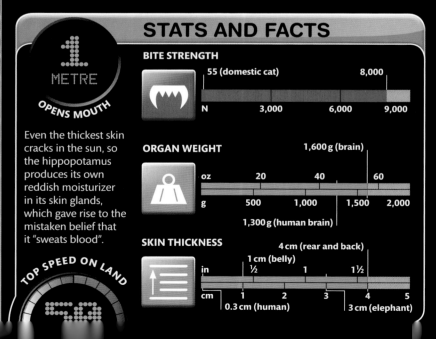

1 METRE
OPENS MOUTH

Even the thickest skin cracks in the sun, so the hippopotamus produces its own reddish moisturizer in its skin glands, which gave rise to the mistaken belief that it "sweats blood".

TOP SPEED ON LAND

BITE STRENGTH

55 (domestic cat)			8,000	
N	3,000	6,000	9,000	

ORGAN WEIGHT

1,600 g (brain)

oz	20	40	60
g	500	1,000	1,500	2,000

1,300 g (human brain)

SKIN THICKNESS

4 cm (rear and back)
1 cm (belly)

in	½	1	1½
cm	1	2	3	4	5

0.3 cm (human)
3 cm (elephant)

WIDEST
MOUTH
ON LAND

LARGEST PRIMATE
GORILLA

The biggest gorilla weighs as much as four men. But this heavyweight primate is actually a vegetarian – it never eats meat and has a specially big stomach to help it digest the toughest plant material. A gorilla spends most of its time on the ground and does sometimes stand up on two feet. Males, in particular, stand upright to make their chest-thumping displays look more impressive.

LONG BONES

Although the gorilla can stand on two legs, its skeleton is not built to stay this way for long. Its legs are shorter for its body size than in humans and have to support a large body with a wide chest. Seen upright, the extra-long arms reach way down past the knees. Long upper arms and big hands are good for grasping.

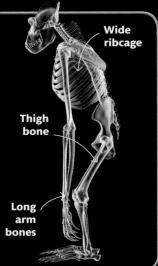

Wide ribcage

Thigh bone

Long arm bones

AT A GLANCE

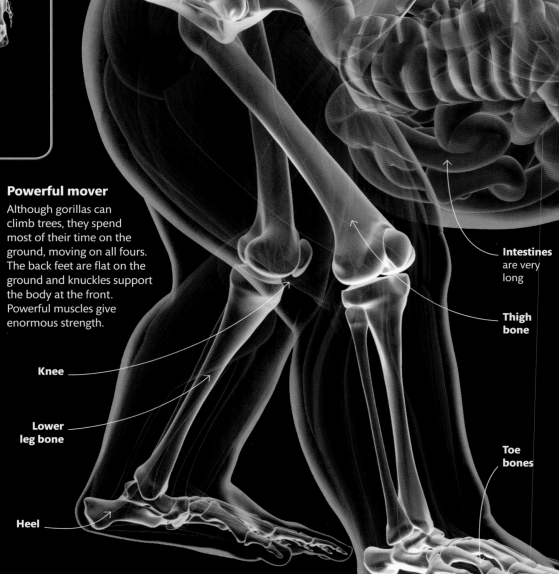

SIZE Height on two feet 1.25–1.75 m (4–5¾ ft).

HABITAT Rainforest

LOCATION Central and East Africa

DIET Leaves, shoots, and stems of plants, especially bamboo; sometimes flowers and fruit

Powerful mover

Although gorillas can climb trees, they spend most of their time on the ground, moving on all fours. The back feet are flat on the ground and knuckles support the body at the front. Powerful muscles give enormous strength.

Spine

Pelvis

Intestines are very long

Thigh bone

Knee

Lower leg bone

Toe bones

Heel

Shoulder blades at back allow large range of movement

Skull

Jaw bone

Upper arm bone

Muscles are larger and much stronger than those of humans

Large stomach to digest plant food

Forearm bone

Knuckle supports the massive weight

Wrist bone

"The biggest is as strong as five men"

CHEWING IT OVER

Gorillas may spend up to 14 hours a day eating. About 85 per cent of their diet is made up of leaves, shoots, and stems – all of which they collect with their hands. They can get through up to 25 kg (55 lb) of plant material in a day. Despite their large size, gorillas are gentle giants and will even leave helpless birds' nests well alone when searching for food.

STATS AND FACTS

50 YEARS
MAXIMUM LIFESPAN

Compared with humans, the gorilla has a relatively small brain – about a third of the size of a human brain. But the gorilla's heart is bigger to enable it to pump blood round the much larger body.

MAXIMUM WEIGHT
275 KG

ARM SPAN

ft		4		8	2–2.75 m	12
m	1	2	3			4

1.5–2 m (human)

ORGAN WEIGHT

365 g (heart)
465–540 g (brain)

oz		15	25	35	45
g	300	600	900	1200	1500

300 g (human heart)
1,300 g (human brain)

DISTANCE

ft		20	40	60
m	5	10	15	20

18 m (covered on two legs)

FAMILY LIFE

Gorillas live in groups led by a dominant male (a silverback). The group will often have an immature male (a blackback), a few females, and several youngsters. The silverback may lead the group for many years before his son takes over.

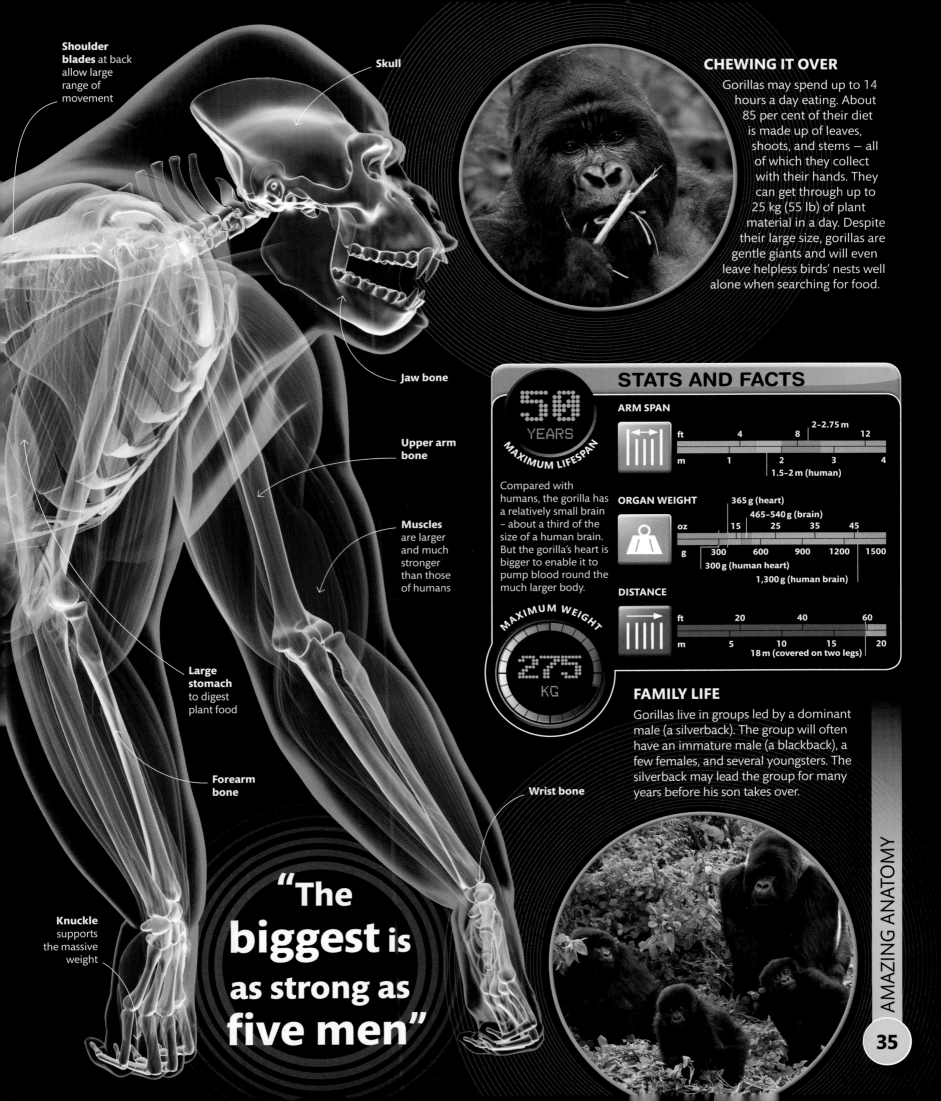

"At sea, elephant seals spend 90% of their time underwater"

BEACH BULLDOZER
SOUTHERN ELEPHANT SEAL

The biggest carnivore that breeds on land, the male southern elephant seal is up to ten times heavier than a polar bear. The males also weigh five times more than the females. Elephant seals spend up to eight months out in the open sea, travelling huge distances in search of food. During fishing dives, they can hold their breath for up to two hours – the longest for any marine mammal.

AT A GLANCE

- **SIZE** 2–6 m (6½–20 ft) long; 360–5,000 kg (790–11,025 lb) in weight (males much longer and heavier than females)

- **HABITAT** Stony beaches and adjoining seas

- **LOCATION** Islands around the Antarctic and southern tip of South America

- **DIET** Fishes and squid

STATS AND FACTS

5,000 KG
RECORD WEIGHT

When elephant seals dive in cold water their heart rate drops to concentrate circulating blood around vital organs. This dive reflex happens in humans too, but is less effective.

SWIMMING SPEED
25 KM/H

DIVE

miles	¼	½	¾	1	1¼

1.4 km (record depth)

km	0.5	1	1.5	2

120 (record duration)

min		60	120	180

HEARTBEATS

bpm	60 (resting on land)	1min

bpm	30 (during dive)	1min

BREATHING RATE

10 (resting on land) 16 (human)

breaths/min	10	20

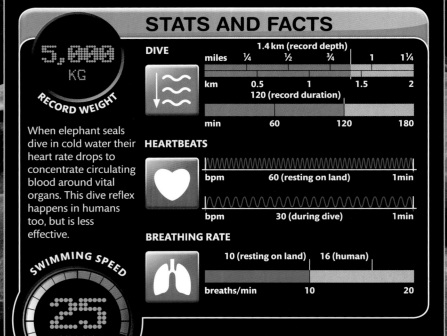

LARGEST SEAL

BRUISING BATTLES

In September, southern elephant seals come ashore to breed. Males fight for groups of females, roaring and lunging at each other with their canine teeth. The male's long nose helps to resonate their roars and makes them even louder. Pups may get squashed in the struggle.

LARGEST RODENT
CAPYBARA

South American swamps are home to a rodent the size of a pig. The capybara, which means "master of grasses" in the local language, is a social animal that lives in herds. On land, it runs like a horse and in water it swims like a beaver. When grazing, the capybara uses its front incisor teeth to crop grass close to the ground. Its intestines are long to aid digestion and, like the cattle that may mingle with them, the capybara sometimes regurgitates partially digested grass to give it a second chew.

AT A GLANCE

- **SIZE** 1–1.3 m (3¼–4¼ ft) long and up to 50 cm (20 in) high at the shoulder
- **HABITAT** Flooded grassland and riverside forest
- **LOCATION** South America east of the Andes
- **DIET** Mainly grasses and aquatic plants, but also grain and melons

STATS AND FACTS

18 YEARS
LIFESPAN

Like many bigger herbivores, such as cattle, the enormous gut of a capybara contains a rich soup of microbes that helps it to digest tough plant material.

RECORD WEIGHT
91 KG

INCISOR LENGTH
2.4 cm

in	½	1	1½
cm	1	2	3	4

HOME RANGE AREA
0.1–2 sq km

sq miles	½	1
sq km	1	2	3

HERD SIZE
20–100 individuals

0	25	50	75	100	125

"Chisel-edged **incisor teeth** grow throughout a capybara's life"

SAFETY IN NUMBERS
Living in herds, capybara have many pairs of eyes on the lookout for predators, such as jaguars. If danger threatens, they flee into the water and swim away using their partially webbed feet as paddles.

PRICKLE POWER
CRESTED PORCUPINE

It's a bad idea to get on the wrong side of a porcupine. With sharp quills to defend themselves, porcupines have been known to take on attackers as dangerous as lions and hyenas. An angry porcupine charges backwards, jabbing its spikes in the direction of an enemy. An infected quill wound can even kill.

AT A GLANCE

- **SIZE** Head and body 60–85 cm (23 1/2–34 in) long, plus tail 8–15 cm (3 1/4–6 in) long

- **HABITAT** Grassland, open woodland, and forest

- **LOCATION** Mediterranean, Africa

- **DIET** Roots, fruit, bark; sometimes small animals

Coat is coarse and bristly

SPIKIEST
HAIR

SHARP TEETH

Porcupines have chisel-like front teeth and powerful jaw muscles. Though they are mainly vegetarian, their burrows are sometimes littered with bones as porcupines gnaw on them for calcium and to sharpen their teeth.

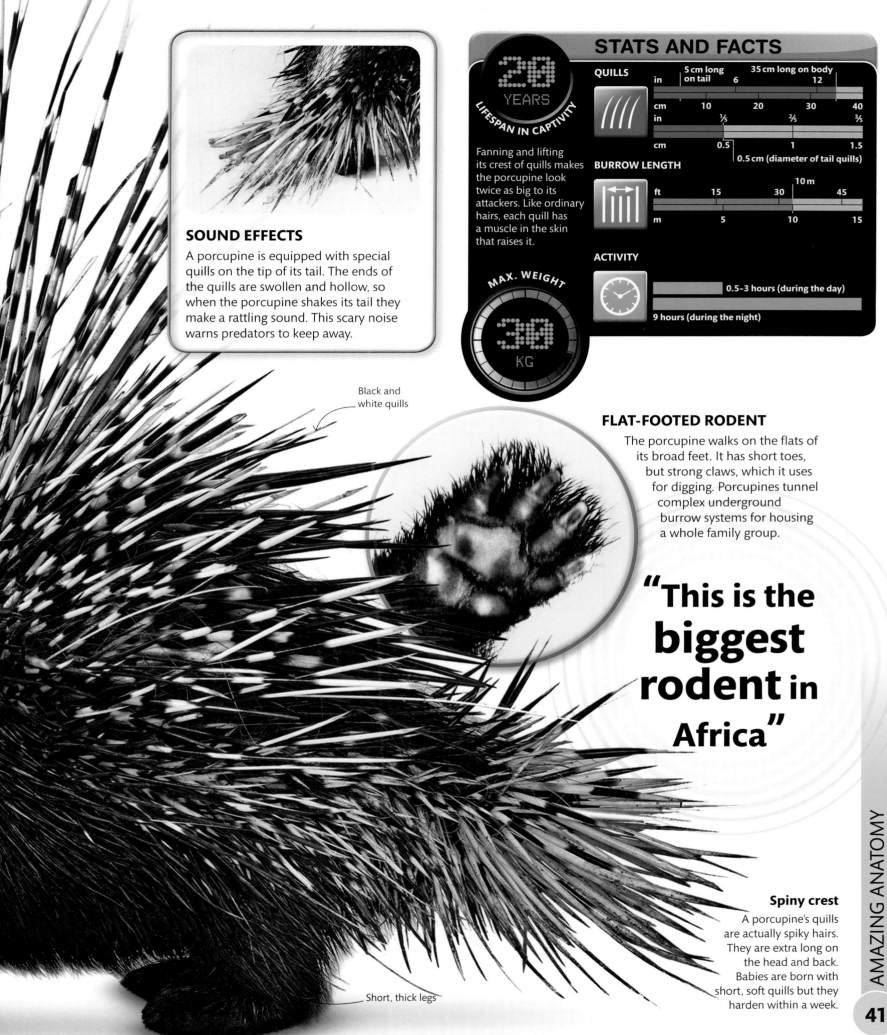

SOUND EFFECTS

A porcupine is equipped with special quills on the tip of its tail. The ends of the quills are swollen and hollow, so when the porcupine shakes its tail they make a rattling sound. This scary noise warns predators to keep away.

STATS AND FACTS

20 YEARS LIFESPAN IN CAPTIVITY

Fanning and lifting its crest of quills makes the porcupine look twice as big to its attackers. Like ordinary hairs, each quill has a muscle in the skin that raises it.

MAX. WEIGHT 30 KG

QUILLS

		5 cm long on tail		35 cm long on body	
in			6		12
cm	10	20		30	40
in		⅓		⅔	⅗
cm	0.5		1		1.5

0.5 cm (diameter of tail quills)

BURROW LENGTH

			10 m	
ft	15	30		45
m	5	10		15

ACTIVITY

0.5–3 hours (during the day)

9 hours (during the night)

Black and white quills

FLAT-FOOTED RODENT

The porcupine walks on the flats of its broad feet. It has short toes, but strong claws, which it uses for digging. Porcupines tunnel complex underground burrow systems for housing a whole family group.

"This is the biggest rodent in Africa"

Spiny crest

A porcupine's quills are actually spiky hairs. They are extra long on the head and back. Babies are born with short, soft quills but they harden within a week.

Short, thick legs

AMAZING ANATOMY

41

BIGGEST BAT
LARGE FLYING FOX

The large flying fox is a nocturnal fruit eater that roosts by day in trees and flies out at dusk to sniff out food. A noisy troop of flying foxes gathered in their favourite fruiting tree can be heard squabbling over territory from half a mile away.

NO TABLE MANNERS

Flying foxes are messy eaters. They squeeze fruit to get at the juice – and then throw away the pith and seeds, which soon accumulate at the base of the tree. Only very soft fruit is swallowed after chewing.

Ears are small and pointed

STATS AND FACTS

1.1 KG
RECORD WEIGHT

Flying foxes split into groups or family units of up to 50 bats when feeding, but roost in much bigger flocks during the day.

WINGS

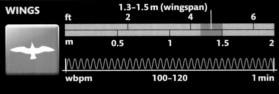

1.3–1.5 m (wingspan)

| ft | 2 | 4 | 6 |
| m | 0.5 | 1 | 1.5 | 2 |

wbpm   100–120   1 min

COLONY SIZE

2,000–15,000

0   5,000   10,000   15,000   20,000

FLYING SPEED
40 KM/H

Brain

Strong chest muscles power wings

Second digit

Wrist connects fingers to forearm

Forearm

Fifth digit stretches membrane out from body

Fourth digit

JUICE EXTRACTOR

The fox-like head is quite unlike that of smaller insect-eating bats. Flying foxes have a long pointed muzzle and large sockets for big eyes. Unlike smaller insect-eating bats (which hunt by echolocation), flying foxes find food by sight, even at night. The roof of the mouth is ridged – the bat crushes fruit against these ridges with its tongue to suck out the juice.

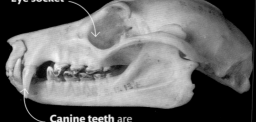

Eye socket

Canine teeth are grooved on inside

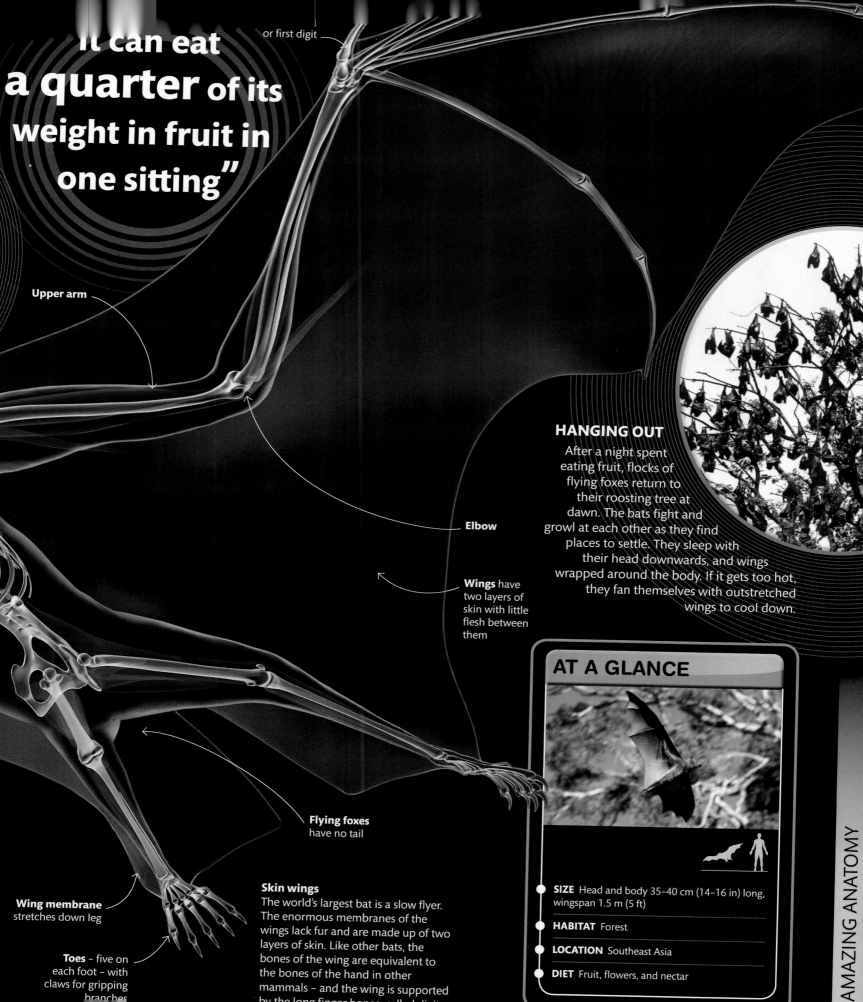

"It can eat **a quarter** of its weight in fruit in one sitting"

or first digit

Upper arm

Elbow

Wings have two layers of skin with little flesh between them

Flying foxes have no tail

Wing membrane stretches down leg

Toes – five on each foot – with claws for gripping branches

Skin wings
The world's largest bat is a slow flyer. The enormous membranes of the wings lack fur and are made up of two layers of skin. Like other bats, the bones of the wing are equivalent to the bones of the hand in other mammals – and the wing is supported by the long finger bones, called digits.

HANGING OUT
After a night spent eating fruit, flocks of flying foxes return to their roosting tree at dawn. The bats fight and growl at each other as they find places to settle. They sleep with their head downwards, and wings wrapped around the body. If it gets too hot, they fan themselves with outstretched wings to cool down.

AT A GLANCE

SIZE Head and body 35–40 cm (14–16 in) long, wingspan 1.5 m (5 ft)

HABITAT Forest

LOCATION Southeast Asia

DIET Fruit, flowers, and nectar

"Its **blood vessels** are so wide you could **swim** along **them**"

ACCORDION MOUTH

This whale is called a rorqual, meaning "furrow whale", because its throat is marked by lots of grooves. These allow the throat to expand so that the whale can take more water into its mouth when collecting krill

MARINE SUPERGIANT
BLUE WHALE

This huge whale is nearly twice the size of the next-biggest living animal – the fin whale. But this giant feeds on some of the world's smallest animals – shrimp-like crustaceans known as krill. It gulps mouthfuls of seawater as it swims, straining it through bristle-edged mouth arches called baleen plates, which trap the food.

AT A GLANCE

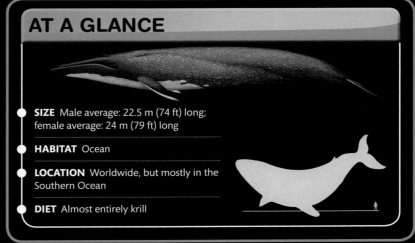

- **SIZE** Male average: 22.5 m (74 ft) long; female average: 24 m (79 ft) long
- **HABITAT** Ocean
- **LOCATION** Worldwide, but mostly in the Southern Ocean
- **DIET** Almost entirely krill

STATS AND FACTS

188 TONNES
RECORD WEIGHT

MAXIMUM SPEED
50

During the southern summer, blue whales migrate close to Antarctica, where the sea is rich with krill. At other times they live further north and mostly survive on stored body fat.

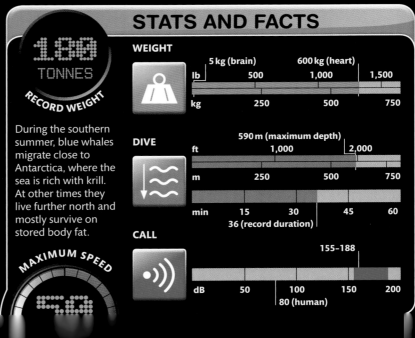

WEIGHT

	5 kg (brain)	600 kg (heart)	
lb	500	1,000	1,500
kg	250	500	750

DIVE

	590 m (maximum depth)		
ft	1,000	2,000	
m	250	500	750
min	15 30	45	60

36 (record duration)

CALL

		155–188	
dB	50 100	150	200

80 (human)

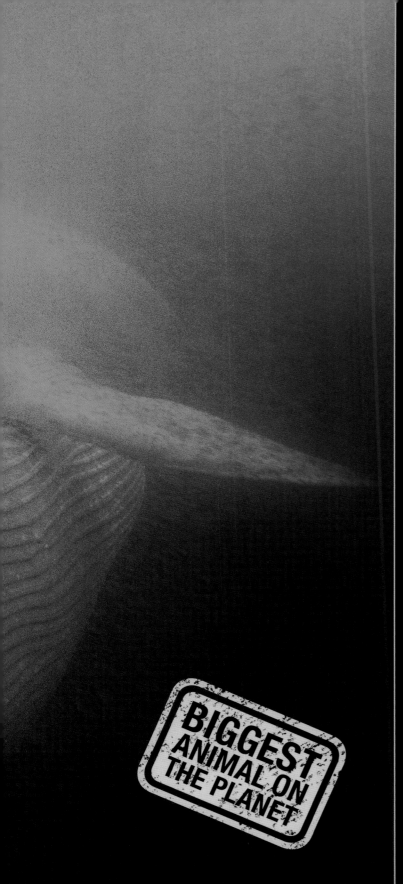

BIGGEST ANIMAL ON THE PLANET

SIZE 1.75–2.75 m (5¾–9 ft) long (males are bigger than females)

HABITAT Grassland, desert, and open woodland

LOCATION Africa

DIET Grasses, seeds, and leaves; sometimes small animals

TALLEST BIRD

OSTRICH

This extraordinary flightless bird is the world's biggest and it also lays the world's largest egg. Even so, the ostrich egg is only a fraction of the size of the bird that laid it. One female can lay up to 10 eggs and, remarkably, other lower-ranking females add to her nest so it may hold up to 30 eggs.

FLIGHTLESS FEATHERS

Ostrich feathers are soft and fluffy as the individual barbs are not held together by hooks as they are in the feathers of birds that can fly. Ostriches also have no oil gland so their feathers are not waterproof and become sodden when it rains.

Head and neck are covered with thin down

Flexible neck has 17 vertebrae

Back is shorter than neck

Huge wings with a span of up to 2 m (6½ ft) provide balance when running

Thigh is the shortest leg bone

Ovaries and reproductive system of female

Barbs are separated

Ribcage protects body organs

Heart is bigger than a human's

Knee cap

BIG TOES

This is the only bird with two-toed feet – the inner one being the biggest. This helps minimize contact with the ground when it's running, which combined with its powerful leg muscles and massive stride, makes this bird a top sprinter.

Inner toe is the only one with a toenail

Powerful toes can kick enemies and injure them

Legs are featherless

Ankle joint

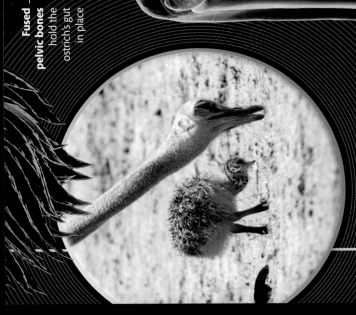

Big bird

The tallest and heaviest bird, the flightless ostrich is well adapted to life on the African grasslands. Its long legs and neck give it height so it can spot predators easily. Although it has a small head, its eyes are the biggest of any land vertebrate.

Powerful muscles enable ostrich to outrun predators

Long legs give the bird height

"Ostriches can run faster than any other bird"

Fused pelvic bones hold the ostrich's gut in place

CARING PARENTS

Ostrich chicks leave the nest within three days of hatching then follow their parents everywhere for four to five months. In hot weather they shelter under mum or dad's enormous wings. If a predator threatens, one parent mounts a diversion while the other takes the chicks to safety.

COMMUNAL NEST

An ostrich "nest" is a small pit in the ground. While other females lay eggs in the nest, only the dominant female and her mate incubate them – the pale earth-coloured female sits by day, and the black-feathered male sits at night. The eggs take 42 to 46 days to hatch.

STATS AND FACTS

TOP SPEED

72 KM/H

MAXIMUM WEIGHT

156 KG

This enormous bird has a tiny brain and a big heart. The newly hatched chicks are cared for in large multi-family crèches.

ORGAN WEIGHT

| lb | 0.04 kg (brain) | 0.5 | 1 kg (heart) | 1 | 2 | 3 |
| kg | | 0.3 kg (human heart) | | 1.3 kg (human brain) | | 1.5 |

WEIGHT OF EGG

| lb | 0.05 kg (chicken egg) | 0.5 | 1.4 kg | 1 | 2 | 3 |
| kg | | | | | | 1.5 |

47

AMAZING ANATOMY

BEAKIEST BIRD
AUSTRALIAN PELICAN

Pelicans have the largest bills in the animal kingdom, and the Australian pelican has the biggest bill of all. Its enormous bill has a very practical purpose – to catch fish. A huge pouch of skin hangs from the lower part of the beak. While swimming, the pelican sweeps its pouch below the surface, where it acts like a fishing net, trapping fishes near the surface. The bird catches dozens of fishes at a time, then lifts its catch to drain the water and gulp its prey down whole.

"A pelican can **live** from **10** to **25** years in the **wild**"

AT A GLANCE

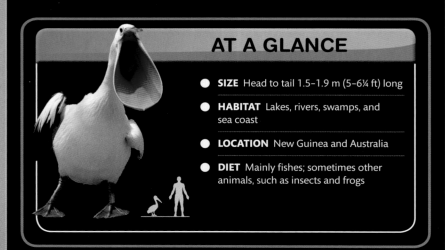

- **SIZE** Head to tail 1.5–1.9 m (5–6¼ ft) long
- **HABITAT** Lakes, rivers, swamps, and sea coast
- **LOCATION** New Guinea and Australia
- **DIET** Mainly fishes; sometimes other animals, such as insects and frogs

STATS AND FACTS

58 CM
LENGTH OF BILL

During their time in the nest, juvenile Australian pelicans pile on the weight. They start to lose it as they begin to move about after fledging.

TOP FLYING SPEED
56

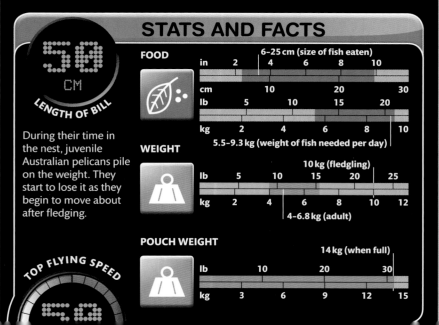

FOOD

6–25 cm (size of fish eaten)

in	2	4	6	8	10
cm		10		20		30
lb	5	10	15	20
kg	2	4	6	8	10

5.5–9.3 kg (weight of fish needed per day)

WEIGHT

10 kg (fledgling)

lb	5	10	15	20	25
kg	2	4	6	8	10	12

4–6.8 kg (adult)

POUCH WEIGHT

14 kg (when full)

lb		10	20	30
kg	3	6	9	12	15

BIGGEST BILL

TAKING A BREATHER

Pelicans have large, powerful wings for soaring and gliding, and strong legs with webbed feet. Between fishing trips, they rest on exposed hot places, and flutter their pouch to keep themselves cool.

FEATHERIEST FLYER

TUNDRA SWAN

No swan breeds further north than the tundra swan. Its dense winter plumage has the highest feather count of any bird, which is needed to trap in body warmth. It nests within the Arctic Circle and makes the most of the brief Arctic summer to do it. Its eggs hatch more quickly and its chicks mature in half the time of other swans'. Within three months the family is ready to fly south.

AT A GLANCE

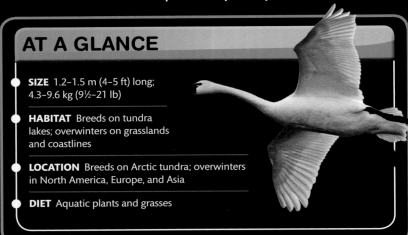

- **SIZE** 1.2–1.5 m (4–5 ft) long; 4.3–9.6 kg (9½–21 lb)

- **HABITAT** Breeds on tundra lakes; overwinters on grasslands and coastlines

- **LOCATION** Breeds on Arctic tundra; overwinters in North America, Europe, and Asia

- **DIET** Aquatic plants and grasses

STATS AND FACTS

20 YEARS
MAXIMUM LIFESPAN

Tundra swans migrate north in spring as the Arctic ice retreats. Once they have raised their young, they migrate south again to avoid the worst of the severe Arctic winter.

FEATHERS IN WINTER

SURROUNDING TEMPERATURE

3–14°C (summer)

°F		40		50		60	
°C	3	6	9	12	15	18

°F		40		50		60	
°C	3	6	9	12	15	18

4–10°C (winter)

DISTANCE COVERED DAILY

33–140 km (during migration)

miles	30	60	90	120	150
km	50	100	150	200	250

WINGS

2.1 m (wingspan)

ft		3	6	9	12	15
m	1	2	3	4	5

wbpm		120		1min

ALL IN A FLAP

Tundra swans spend most of the winter on water, even sleeping afloat. They need a lot of space to take off and land, madly flapping their wings as they go. Their other name of "whistling" swan comes

"Migrating tundra swans **fly** as high as **8 km** (5 miles)"

TOUGHEST HEADBANGER

WOODPECKER

It's a wonder that woodpeckers never get headaches. They spend most of the day hammering holes in trees with ten times the force needed to knock out a human. All this headbanging has a purpose – to find food, to create a safe place to nest and raise young, and to communicate with other woodpeckers.

INSECT EXTRACTOR

The tongue of a woodpecker is so long it has to wrap around inside the skull when not in use. It has muscles that stiffen it when it's poked into tree holes. Sharp, sticky barbs at its tip help grip insects as it pulls them out. Some woodpeckers drink the tree sap, too.

Tongue wraps around skull to cushion the brain against the impact

SHOCK ABSORBERS

A woodpecker's skull is made of spongy bone that absorbs vibrations from the impact. Its brain sits very tightly inside the skull to stop it bouncing off the bone when the bill strikes. Dense muscles in the neck also help divert the impact away from the brain.

Special cells at tip repair any damage to bill

Bill is so strong it does not bend or break

Inner eyelid closes a millisecond before impact to prevent injury

Stiff tail feathers brace the bird against the tree

Feel the beat

Woodpeckers proclaim their territory by their loud, rhythmic drum rolls – and each type of woodpecker has its own distinctive beat. The pileated woodpecker – the largest living in North America – does two short drum rolls a minute, each lasting just a couple of seconds.

Claws dig into bark

HOLD ON TIGHT

Woodpeckers have strong feet and claws for climbing tree trunks. When perched, two toes face forwards and two back – but when scaling a trunk, one of the hind toes is extended sideways to give a better grip so that the bird holds firm, even when hammering.

Toe muscles contract to lock them onto trunk

"Woodpeckers can even make holes in concrete"

STATS AND FACTS

DRUMMING RATE

times/sec	18–22	1 sec
drums	4,000	8,000	12,000	16,000

8,000–12,000/day

HAMMERING STRENGTH

30 (force of impact)

N	10	20	30	40	50	60

DRUMMING SPEED
KM/H

MAXIMUM LIFESPAN
YEARS

It takes a pair of woodpeckers around a month to hammer out a hole for a nest, which is lined with the wood chips.

GIANT PARROT
KAKAPO

The kakapo is so heavy that it cannot fly. Although it has wings, it lacks the large breastbone that other birds have for supporting wing muscles, and the feathers are soft and downy, rather than stiff for flying. The world's only flightless parrot is a slow, owl-faced plant-eater that sleeps all day and ventures out at night. If threatened, it stands still and tries to blend into the background. However, this makes it an easy target for predatory rats and cats, and it is now critically endangered.

"Kakapos use their wings for **balance**, not flying"

AT A GLANCE

- **SIZE** Body length 64 cm (25 in); weight 0.85–3.6 kg (1¾–8 lb)

- **HABITAT** Mossy forest and grassy meadows

- **LOCATION** Three islands off New Zealand

- **DIET** Leaf buds, roots, stems, nuts, fruit, bark, moss, and fungi. It is particularly fond of the fruit of the rimu tree.

STATS AND FACTS

120 YEARS
MAXIMUM LIFESPAN

Males attract females by making a loud booming call that can travel several kilometres. After mating, a female retires to her nest in a burrow to raise her brood alone.

NUMBER OF KAKAPOS
131

WINGSPAN

in	10	20	30	90 cm
cm	20	40	60	80	100

JOGGING SPEED

2 km/h

mph	1	2
km/h	1	2	3	4	5

EGGS LAID IN A CLUTCH

1–4

| 0 | 1 | 2 | 3 | 4 | 5 |

BIGGEST PARROT

MOONLIGHT FORAGER

A kakapo walks several kilometres every night in its search for food. It has strong claws for clambering through thickets and "whiskers" for sensing its surroundings in the dark. A keen sense of smell helps it find its favourite leaves, which it strains through its beak to suck out the juices.

"One bird travelled **6,000 km** **(3,700 miles) in** **12 days**"

LOVELY TO SEE YOU AGAIN

Albatrosses are devoted partners. A male and a female will pair up for life, only meeting to breed every two years. They rear a single chick, which remains in the nest for nine months. Once it has fledged it will not return to land for another six years.

SUPER-SOARING SEABIRD
WANDERING ALBATROSS

Carried by the world's longest wings, the wandering albatross soars above the southern oceans, hardly flapping its wings at all. It rarely returns to land, except to breed. Its wings lock when fully extended and the bird relies on rising air currents to gain height above the waves, dropping only 1 m (3 ft) for every 22 m (72 ft) it glides.

AT A GLANCE

- **SIZE** Body length 1.07–1.35 m (3½–4½ ft); weight 5.9–12.7 kg (13–28 lb)
- **HABITAT** Open ocean and oceanic islands
- **LOCATION** Southern oceans and islands around Antarctica
- **DIET** Squid, fishes, and carrion

STATS AND FACTS

500 METRES
LONGEST GLIDE

Gliding flight is not strenuous, so the bird's heartbeat rate is only slightly different when it is flying to when it is resting. It needs a lot more energy for takeoff and landing.

TOP SPEED
40

WINGS

3.7 m (wingspan)

ft		5	10		15
m	1	2	3	4	5

wbpm 15 (concentrated in first 6 sec) 1 min

DISTANCE TRAVELLED IN A DAY

200–500 km

miles	100	200	300	
km	100	200	300	400	500	600

HEARTBEATS

60 (resting)–80 (gliding)

bpm 1 min

bpm 150 (takeoff and landing) 1 min

LARGEST WINGSPAN

FEATHERY SHOW-OFF
KING OF SAXONY BIRD OF PARADISE

The King of Saxony bird of paradise is so bizarre that when people in Europe first heard of it, they didn't think it could be real. Males have two long head feathers – each with a row of flag-like plates running along the length – that are like nothing else in any other bird. The males use these extraordinary feathers in courtship dances, to attract a mate.

Putting on a show

One head feather can be more than twice the length of the bird's body, but muscles at their base are strong enough to raise them up for a display. The male chooses a good position before bobbing up and down with his feathers held high.

Colourful aqua-blue mouth

Brightly coloured yellow breast

Head feathers look like a row of bunting

AT A GLANCE

SIZE 22 cm (9 in) long

HABITAT Mountain rainforest

LOCATION New Guinea

DIET Fruit and insects

MOST UNUSUAL **FEATHER**

STATS AND FACTS

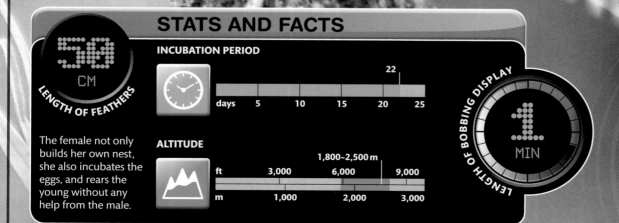

58 CM
LENGTH OF FEATHERS

The female not only builds her own nest, she also incubates the eggs, and rears the young without any help from the male.

INCUBATION PERIOD

| days | 5 | 10 | 15 | 20 | 22 | 25 |

ALTITUDE

1,800–2,500 m

| ft | 3,000 | 6,000 | 9,000 |
| m | 1,000 | 2,000 | 3,000 |

1 MIN
LENGTH OF BOBBING DISPLAY

"Females **raise** their **young** alone"

TINY ATHLETE
AMETHYST WOODSTAR

SIZE 6–7 cm (2¼–2¾ in) long

HABITAT Rainforest, open woodland, and grassland

LOCATION South America

DIET Nectar and insects

The heart of a flying hummingbird can beat as many times per hour as a human heart beats in a whole day. These tiny birds are fuelled by nectar, and can visit as many as a thousand flowers in a day just to get enough food to keep going. One of the smallest of all birds, the amethyst woodstar has a body that ticks over like a tiny revving engine, and burns up five hundred times more energy than a human just to stay alive.

Wings beat quickly so bird can hover

Deep sleepers
When awake, the amethyst woodstar has to drink plenty of nectar to fuel its hectic lifestyle. At night, however, it can't feed, so it has to take desperate measures to save energy. Its body temperature plummets and it enters a state of "mini-hibernation".

Long bill to reach nectar in flowers

"Hummingbird nests are the size of a golf ball"

STATS AND FACTS

PER MIN

WINGBEATS

This tiny bird has a very strong heart. Rapid beating delivers plenty of oxygen to power the hovering wing muscles.

HEARTBEATS

200 (resting)

bpm .... 1 min

bpm   1,200 (in flight)   1 min

DAILY FOOD CONSUMPTION

14 cal/g of body

0.026 cal/g of body (human)

TOP FLYING SPEED

KM/H

FASTEST METABOLISM

AMAZING ANATOMY

COLOSSAL COBRA
KING COBRA

The world's longest venomous snake can be so fierce that even other snakes fear it. The king cobra has the strength and the venom to kill and eat small pythons, ratsnakes, and even other cobras. But this predator has a caring side, too. Unlike other snakes, the female builds a nest for her eggs and keeps guard until they hatch, attacking anything that comes close.

AT A GLANCE

- **SIZE**: 3–4 m (9¾–13 ft) long
- **HABITAT** Forests
- **LOCATION** India and Southeast Asia
- **DIET** Other snakes

Sharp fangs

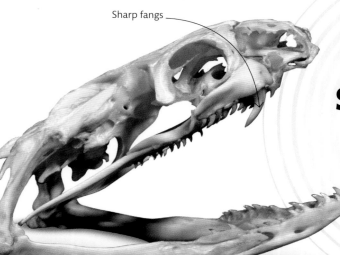

*"This snake's **strike** range is up to **2m** (6½ ft)"*

KING COBRA SKULL

The needle-sharp fangs of a king cobra are positioned at the front of the mouth. Although many other snakes have stronger venom, the king cobra injects a greater amount to maximize its effect.

Hooded snake

When cobras feel threatened, they raise their head and flatten their neck to form a hood. This makes them appear bigger – and they can strike an enemy from this position too.

STATS AND FACTS

5.5 METRES
RECORD LENGTH

The king cobra's venom attacks the nervous system. The poison first paralyses the body then kills by stopping the heart and lungs.

FANG LENGTH

		1.5 cm	
in	¼	½	¾
cm	0.5	1	1.5	2

VENOM

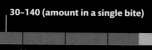

30–140 (amount in a single bite)

| drops | 30 | 60 | 90 | 120 | 150 |

20 (minimum amount to kill a human)

STRIKE SPEED

2 M/SEC

Keen eyesight for spotting prey

HATCHLINGS

After guarding her eggs for two or three months, a mother king cobra will abandon them once they start hatching – perhaps so she is not tempted to treat them as prey and eat them. Unlike their parents, hatchlings have a stripy pattern, but already have dangerous venom.

Fully extended hood

SCALY SKIN

The scales of an adult king cobra are smooth, shiny, and dark olive-brown in colour. Adults shed their skin four to six times per year.

LONGEST VENOMOUS SNAKE

SLOBBERY STALKER

There are so many bacteria in the saliva of a Komodo dragon that bites quickly become septic. This weakens prey too big to bring down by force. The saliva is also known to contain a mild venom. After biting, a dragon will stalk its victim by tracking it with its tongue, waiting for its prey to drop dead.

LARGEST LIZARD

"Eats 80% of its body weight in **one** meal"

MONSTER LIZARD
KOMODO DRAGON

On Komodo Island giant dragons rule the land with long claws and saw-like teeth. A Komodo dragon eats meat – and finds it by "tasting" the air with a flicking tongue. Dead pigs and deer are smelt half an island away, but living animals, such as wild pigs and deer, are also targeted by this surprisingly fast-moving reptile. These are knocked down by a swipe of its powerful tail and killed with a bite to the throat. Small prey is swallowed whole. Indigestible horns, hair, and teeth are later spewed back up in a slimy pellet.

AT A GLANCE

- **SIZE** Up to 3.1 m (10 ft) long, including a tail as long as the body
- **HABITAT** Tropical grassland and dry forest up to 700 m (2,300 ft) above sea level
- **LOCATION** Komodo and four neighbouring islands in Indonesia, Southeast Asia
- **DIET** Carrion and almost any living animal

STATS AND FACTS

166 KG
RECORD WEIGHT

A stretchy stomach allows the Komodo dragon to eat every part of its prey.

MAXIMUM SPEED
20

SMELL DETECTION

				4 km	
miles		1	2		3
km	1	2	3	4	5

BITE

2.5 cm (length of tooth)

in	½	1	1½
cm	1	2	3	4

40–100 (bite strength)

N	20	40	60	80	100	120

55 (bite strength of domestic cat)

SUPER SQUEEZER
GREEN ANACONDA

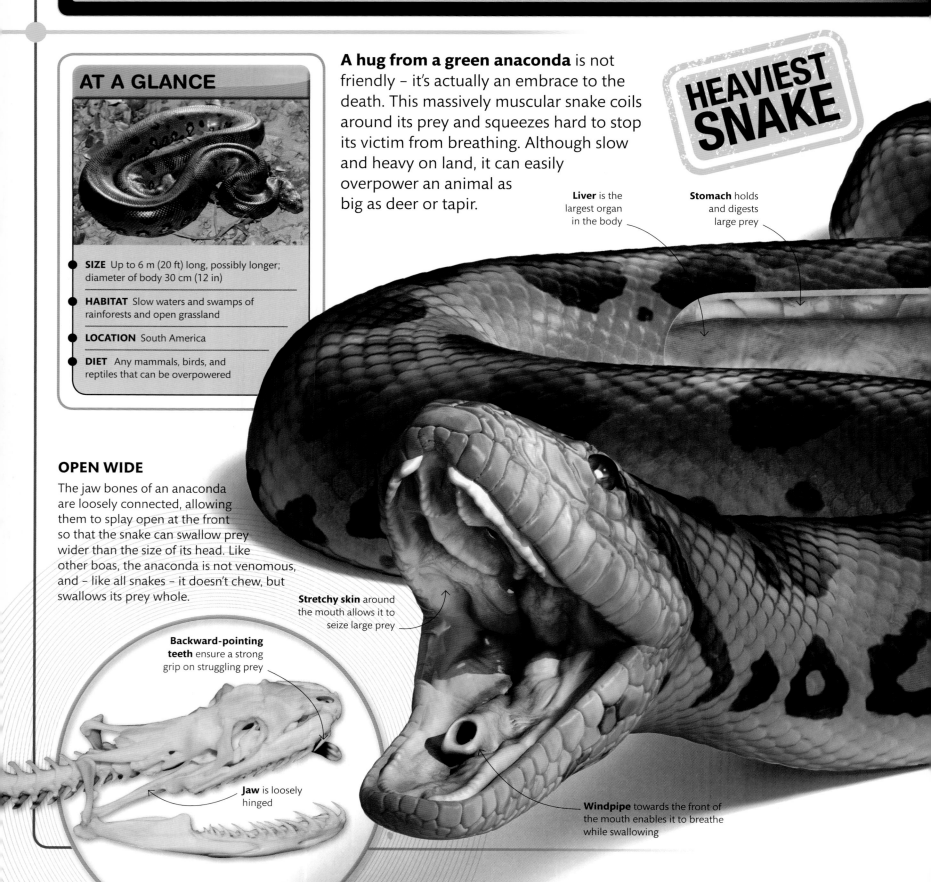

A hug from a green anaconda is not friendly – it's actually an embrace to the death. This massively muscular snake coils around its prey and squeezes hard to stop its victim from breathing. Although slow and heavy on land, it can easily overpower an animal as big as deer or tapir.

HEAVIEST SNAKE

AT A GLANCE

SIZE Up to 6 m (20 ft) long, possibly longer; diameter of body 30 cm (12 in)

HABITAT Slow waters and swamps of rainforests and open grassland

LOCATION South America

DIET Any mammals, birds, and reptiles that can be overpowered

Liver is the largest organ in the body

Stomach holds and digests large prey

OPEN WIDE

The jaw bones of an anaconda are loosely connected, allowing them to splay open at the front so that the snake can swallow prey wider than the size of its head. Like other boas, the anaconda is not venomous, and – like all snakes – it doesn't chew, but swallows its prey whole.

Stretchy skin around the mouth allows it to seize large prey

Backward-pointing teeth ensure a strong grip on struggling prey

Jaw is loosely hinged

Windpipe towards the front of the mouth enables it to breathe while swallowing

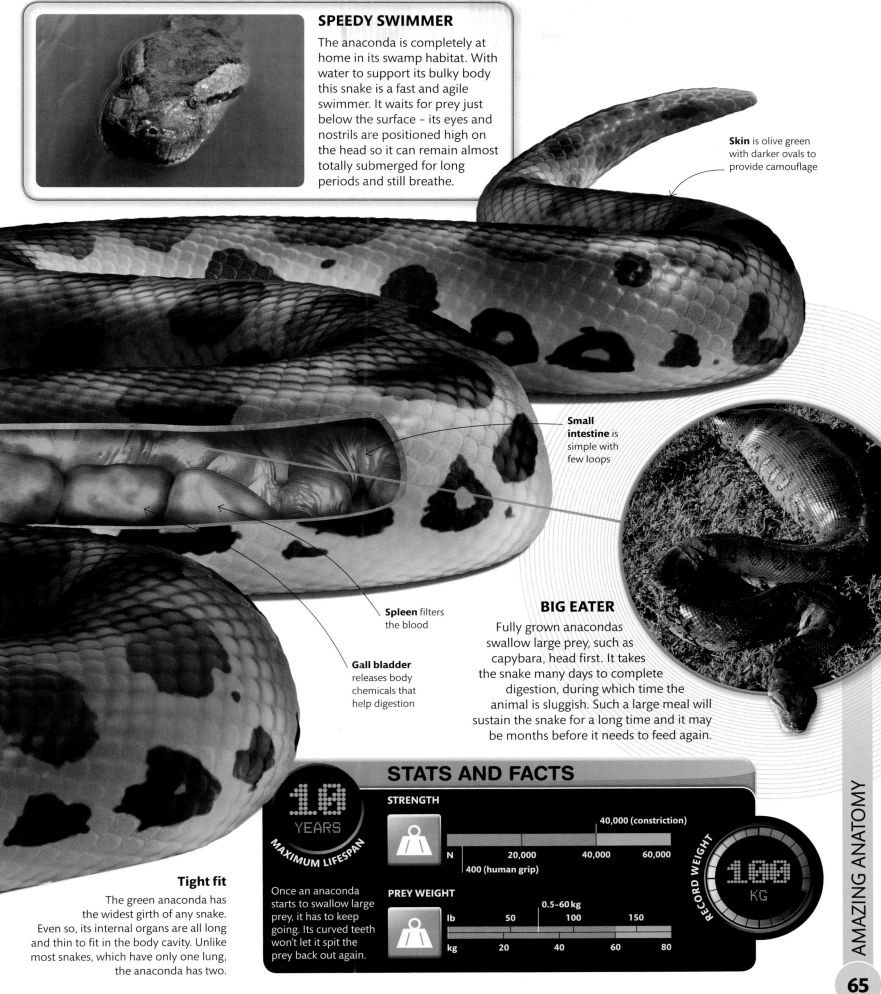

SPEEDY SWIMMER

The anaconda is completely at home in its swamp habitat. With water to support its bulky body this snake is a fast and agile swimmer. It waits for prey just below the surface – its eyes and nostrils are positioned high on the head so it can remain almost totally submerged for long periods and still breathe.

Skin is olive green with darker ovals to provide camouflage

Small intestine is simple with few loops

Spleen filters the blood

Gall bladder releases body chemicals that help digestion

BIG EATER

Fully grown anacondas swallow large prey, such as capybara, head first. It takes the snake many days to complete digestion, during which time the animal is sluggish. Such a large meal will sustain the snake for a long time and it may be months before it needs to feed again.

Tight fit

The green anaconda has the widest girth of any snake. Even so, its internal organs are all long and thin to fit in the body cavity. Unlike most snakes, which have only one lung, the anaconda has two.

STATS AND FACTS

10 YEARS
MAXIMUM LIFESPAN

STRENGTH

Once an anaconda starts to swallow large prey, it has to keep going. Its curved teeth won't let it spit the prey back out again.

			40,000 (constriction)	
N	20,000	40,000	60,000	
400 (human grip)				

PREY WEIGHT

		0.5–60 kg		
lb	50	100	150	
kg	20	40	60	80

RECORD WEIGHT
100 KG

FANG-TASTIC BITER
GABOON VIPER

A bite from a Gaboon viper is potentially fatal, especially if left untreated. This giant viper is found in forests and grassland across Africa, where it preys on birds and mammals up to the size of a dwarf antelope. Unlike smaller vipers, which retreat after biting to allow the venom to work, the Gaboon viper has the strength to hold on until its victim is dead.

LIGHTNING STRIKER

This viper's strike is one of the fastest of all snakes and a bite from the long, hinged fangs is very painful. In spite of its scary appearance, the Gaboon viper will only attack when provoked – it is not usually agressive.

"Produces **more venom** than any other snake"

Fangs

SKULL

The lower jaw of a snake is only loosely attached to its skull. It can even stretch apart at the front to allow the snake to swallow large animals.

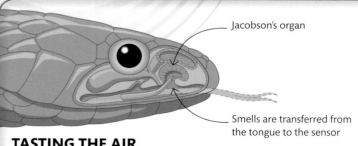

Jacobson's organ

Smells are transferred from the tongue to the sensor

TASTING THE AIR

Like other snakes, the Gaboon viper has a sensor called the Jacobson's organ in the roof of its mouth for detecting smells. After tasting the air, the snake inserts its tongue into the organ pit, where its smell sensors analyse the scent particles from its prey.

AT A GLANCE

- **SIZE** 1.2–1.5 m (4–5 ft) long
- **HABITAT** Forest and open scrubland
- **LOCATION** Central Africa
- **DIET** Mammals and birds large enough to swallow comfortably

LONGEST FANGED SNAKE

Strike force

The large triangular head of the Gaboon viper is highly distinctive, with two small horns between its nostrils. If disturbed by an intruder, this viper inflates its body and hisses loudly before striking. It rises up as it attacks, injecting its venom deep into its victim.

Forked tongue used to collect smells

BLENDING IN

Boldly patterned with patches of brown, black, and cream, the Gaboon viper's skin provides an excellent disguise against a leaf litter background. It can sit motionless for hours, waiting for prey to come close.

STATS AND FACTS

16 KG
RECORD WEIGHT

2 M/SEC
STRIKE SPEED

The Gaboon viper has highly moveable eyes and can fix its focus on prey with deadly accuracy to ensure a successful strike.

FANG LENGTH

in		1	5 cm	2
cm	2	4		6

VENOM

100–180 drops in single bite

0	50	100	150	200

3–20 drops can kill a human

PREY WEIGHT

30 g (mouse)–2,000 g (rabbit)

oz	20	40	60	80
g	500	1,000	1,500	2,000	2,500

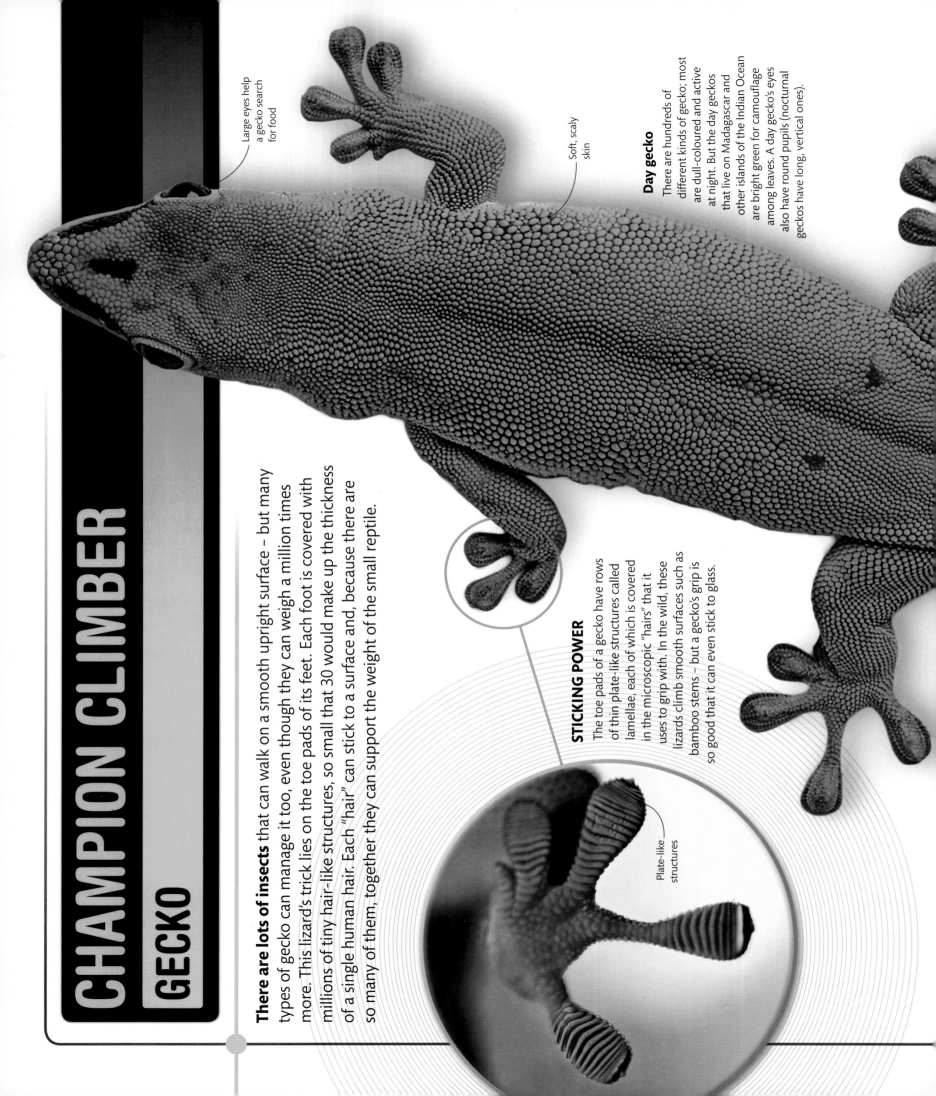

CHAMPION CLIMBER

GECKO

There are lots of insects that can walk on a smooth upright surface – but many types of gecko can manage it too, even though they can weigh a million times more. This lizard's trick lies on the toe pads of its feet. Each foot is covered with millions of tiny hair-like structures, so small that 30 would make up the thickness of a single human hair. Each "hair" can stick to a surface and, because there are so many of them, together they can support the weight of the small reptile.

Large eyes help a gecko search for food

Soft, scaly skin

Day gecko

There are hundreds of different kinds of gecko; most are dull-coloured and active at night. But the day geckos that live on Madagascar and other islands of the Indian Ocean are bright green for camouflage among leaves. A day gecko's eyes also have round pupils (nocturnal geckos have long, vertical ones).

STICKING POWER

The toe pads of a gecko have rows of thin plate-like structures called lamellae, each of which is covered in the microscopic "hairs" that it uses to grip with. In the wild, these lizards climb smooth surfaces such as bamboo stems – but a gecko's grip is so good that it can even stick to glass.

Plate-like structures

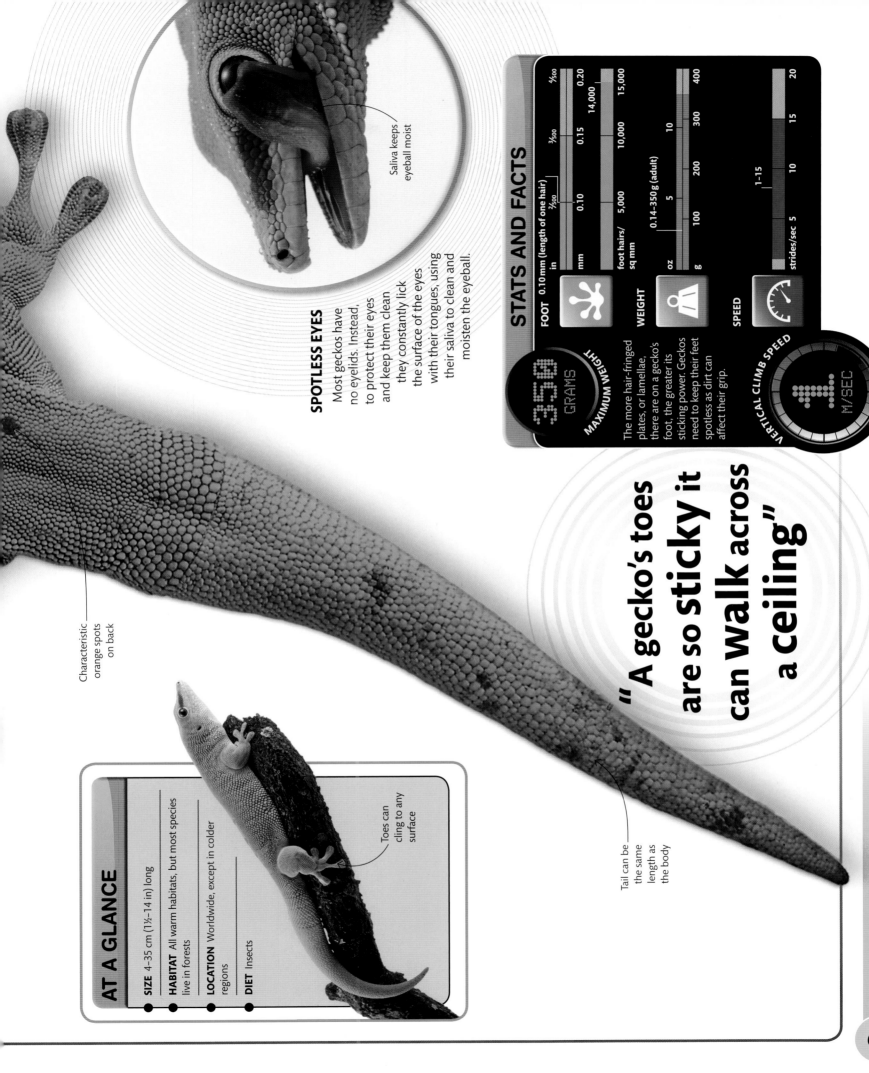

SPOTLESS EYES

Most geckos have no eyelids. Instead, to protect their eyes and keep them clean they constantly lick the surface of the eyes with their tongues, using their saliva to clean and moisten the eyeball.

Saliva keeps eyeball moist

STATS AND FACTS

FOOT 0.10mm (length of one hair)

in	²/₅₀₀	³/₅₀₀	⁴/₅₀₀
mm	0.10	0.15	0.20

WEIGHT

foot hairs/ sq mm	5,000	10,000	14,000	15,000

0.14–350g (adult)

oz	5	10
g	100	200	300	400

SPEED

1–15

strides/sec	5	10	15	20

350 GRAMS

MAXIMUM WEIGHT

The more hair-fringed plates, or lamellae, there are on a gecko's foot, the greater its sticking power. Geckos need to keep their feet spotless as dirt can affect their grip.

VERTICAL CLIMB SPEED

4 M/SEC

"A gecko's toes are so sticky it can walk across a ceiling"

Characteristic orange spots on back

Tail can be the same length as the body

AT A GLANCE

SIZE 4–35 cm (1½–14 in) long

HABITAT All warm habitats, but most species live in forests

LOCATION Worldwide, except in colder regions

DIET Insects

Toes can cling to any surface

SWAMP MONSTER
SALTWATER CROCODILE

Not much can escape the jaws of a crocodile. Weighing as much as a small car, the saltwater croc is a top predator of large mammals, including humans. It prefers freshwater swamps but often swims out to sea.

Eyes on top of head so it can see above water while body is submerged

Teeth are strong and sharp

AT A GLANCE

- **SIZE** Males up to 7 m (23 ft) long; females are around half this size
- **HABITAT** Rivers, estuaries, and salt water
- **LOCATION** India, Southeast Asia, New Guinea, and Australia
- **DIET** Animals up to the size of a water buffalo

CROC TEETH

The long toothy snout of a saltwater crocodile acts like a vice for clamping down on struggling prey. The fourth lower tooth fits into a notch in the upper jaw – which is how you can tell a crocodile from an alligator.

Feet are webbed for swimming

Heart has four chambers to deliver oxygen to muscles

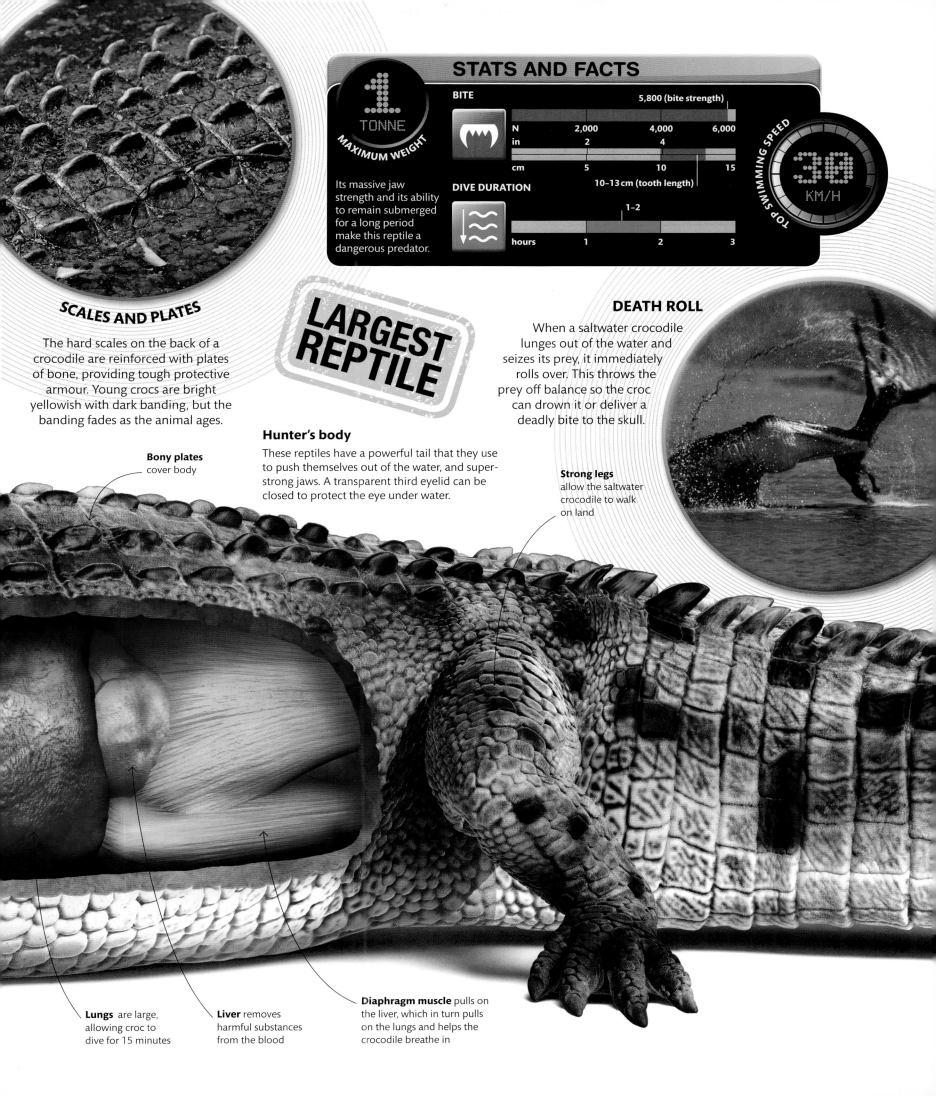

1 TONNE

MAXIMUM WEIGHT

Its massive jaw strength and its ability to remain submerged for a long period make this reptile a dangerous predator.

BITE

5,800 (bite strength)

N		2,000		4,000		6,000
in			2		4	
cm		5		10		15

10–13 cm (tooth length)

DIVE DURATION

1–2

| hours | | 1 | | 2 | | 3 |

TOP SWIMMING SPEED

38 KM/H

SCALES AND PLATES

The hard scales on the back of a crocodile are reinforced with plates of bone, providing tough protective armour. Young crocs are bright yellowish with dark banding, but the banding fades as the animal ages.

LARGEST REPTILE

DEATH ROLL

When a saltwater crocodile lunges out of the water and seizes its prey, it immediately rolls over. This throws the prey off balance so the croc can drown it or deliver a deadly bite to the skull.

Hunter's body

These reptiles have a powerful tail that they use to push themselves out of the water, and super-strong jaws. A transparent third eyelid can be closed to protect the eye under water.

Bony plates
cover body

Strong legs
allow the saltwater crocodile to walk on land

Lungs are large, allowing croc to dive for 15 minutes

Liver removes harmful substances from the blood

Diaphragm muscle pulls on the liver, which in turn pulls on the lungs and helps the crocodile breathe in

FASTEST TONGUE
CHAMELEON

The fastest tongue in the forest belongs to the chameleon – a bizarre tree-living reptile with feet that grasp like hands and eyes that swivel independently of one another. Chameleons are expert at catching fast-moving insect prey. They shoot out their incredibly long tongue, a fleshy sucker on the end sticks to the target, and within a fraction of a second it's pulled into the mouth.

AT A GLANCE

- **SIZE** 4–65 cm (1½–25 in) long
- **HABITAT** Mostly forest
- **LOCATION** Mediterranean, Africa, Madagascar, and India
- **DIET** Insects

Ridge of spines on belly

GRASPING TAIL

Like other tree-living chameleons, the panther chameleon has a long tail that can grasp and acts like a fifth leg. The tail provides extra grip as the chameleon moves through branches.

Bright colours of body change with mood

Tail tends to curl up when not gripping branches

"The **tongue** is often **longer** than the body"

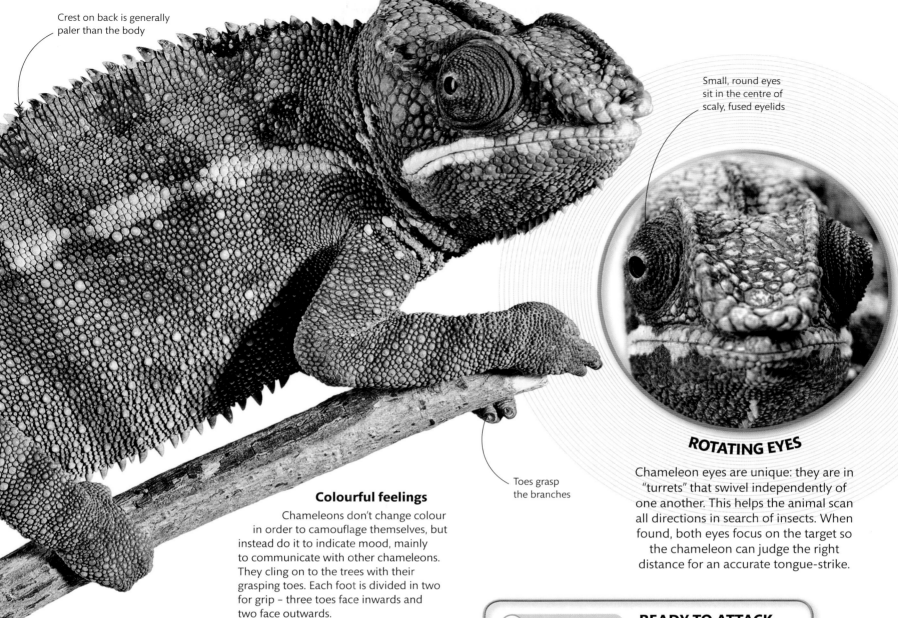

Crest on back is generally paler than the body

Small, round eyes sit in the centre of scaly, fused eyelids

Toes grasp the branches

Colourful feelings

Chameleons don't change colour in order to camouflage themselves, but instead do it to indicate mood, mainly to communicate with other chameleons. They cling on to the trees with their grasping toes. Each foot is divided in two for grip – three toes face inwards and two face outwards.

ROTATING EYES

Chameleon eyes are unique: they are in "turrets" that swivel independently of one another. This helps the animal scan all directions in search of insects. When found, both eyes focus on the target so the chameleon can judge the right distance for an accurate tongue-strike.

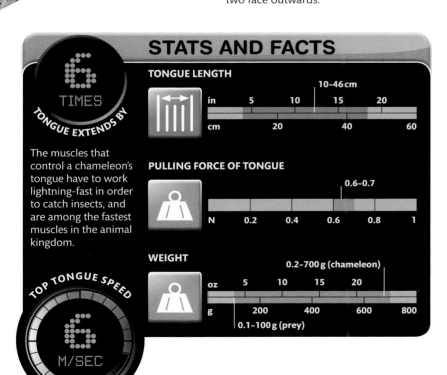

STATS AND FACTS

6 TIMES
TONGUE EXTENDS BY

The muscles that control a chameleon's tongue have to work lightning-fast in order to catch insects, and are among the fastest muscles in the animal kingdom.

6 M/SEC
TOP TONGUE SPEED

TONGUE LENGTH

10–46 cm

in		5	10		15	20	
cm			20		40		60

PULLING FORCE OF TONGUE

0.6–0.7

N	0.2	0.4	0.6	0.8	1

WEIGHT

0.2–700 g (chameleon)

oz		5	10	15	20	
g		200	400	600	800	

0.1–100 g (prey)

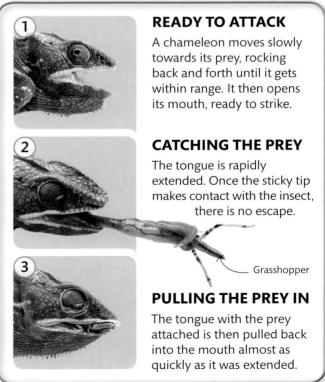

READY TO ATTACK

1 A chameleon moves slowly towards its prey, rocking back and forth until it gets within range. It then opens its mouth, ready to strike.

CATCHING THE PREY

2 The tongue is rapidly extended. Once the sticky tip makes contact with the insect, there is no escape.

Grasshopper

PULLING THE PREY IN

3 The tongue with the prey attached is then pulled back into the mouth almost as quickly as it was extended.

STAYING ALIVE

A soft-bodied frog (especially one smaller than a coin) can dry up and die very quickly, so it needs damp surroundings to survive. The Amau frog is only active at dawn and dusk, when it makes high-pitched chirps that sound more like those of an insect than a frog.

MINIATURE FROG
AMAU FROG

Because it is so very small, the Amau frog could sit comfortably on a human thumbnail and still have room to spare. It lives among the wet leaves that carpet the floor of the Papua New Guinea rainforest, where it is perfectly camouflaged against predators. Here it can complete its entire life cycle – laying soft, wet eggs on moist ground that bypass the tadpole stage and hatch into even tinier versions of the adults. For this tiny frog, even the smallest insect that creeps along the forest floor makes a filling meal.

AT A GLANCE

SIZE Head and body 7–8 mm (about ¼ in) long

HABITAT Leaf litter of rainforest floor

LOCATION Papua New Guinea

DIET Small insects and mites

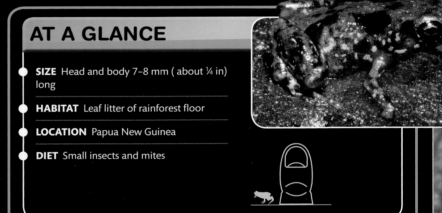

STATS AND FACTS

8 MM
MAXIMUM SIZE

In the noisy rainforest, frogs call out with distinctive patterns of notes to communicate.

YEAR OF DISCOVERY

SIZE

in		⅛		¼	
mm	2	4		6	8

4 mm (lower leg length)

3 mm (head width)

CALL

8.4–9.4 (pitch)

kHz	20	40	60	80	100

min	1	2	3	4

1–3 (duration)

BEST REGENERATOR

SCIENTIFIC WONDER

The wild axolotl is rare and found in only two small lakes on the outskirts of Mexico City. Its ability to regenerate its body is of great interest to scientists – it can make transplanted organs from other axolotls work properly again, and can even regrow some areas of its brain.

FOREVER YOUNG
AXOLOTL

Imagine being able to grow a new limb. The axolotl – a type of aquatic salamander – can do just that. If an axolotl is injured, its body responds by regrowing the lost part instead of forming a scar. This is a handy trick when you've just had a close encounter with a heron – the axolotl's main predator. Although they live for 10–15 years, axolotls also never really grow up. Other amphibians have gills when young and develop air-breathing lungs when they mature, but axolotls keep their branch-like gills as they grow bigger – and only lose them if their habitat dries up.

AT A GLANCE

- **SIZE** Up to 30 cm (12 in) head to tail
- **HABITAT** Freshwater lakes and drainage channels
- **LOCATION** Lakes Xochimilco and Chalco in Mexico
- **DIET** Algae when young, aquatic insects and other small animals when older

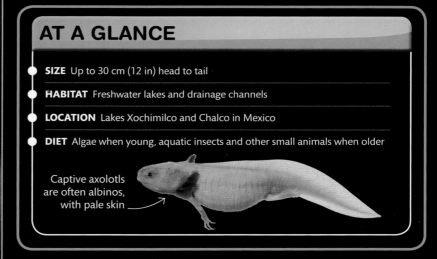

Captive axolotls are often albinos, with pale skin

STATS AND FACTS

15 YEARS
AVERAGE LIFESPAN

Like all cold-blooded amphibians, axolotls become more active and grow faster as the temperature rises.

GROWS NEW LIMB IN

GROWTH

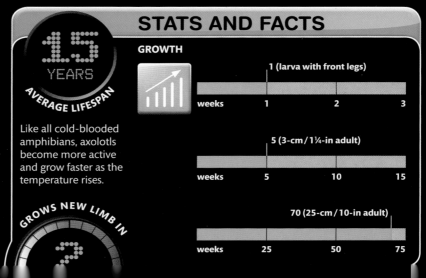

1 (larva with front legs)

| weeks | 1 | 2 | 3 |

5 (3-cm / 1¼-in adult)

| weeks | 5 | 10 | 15 |

70 (25-cm / 10-in adult)

| weeks | 25 | 50 | 75 |

BIGGEST TOAD
CANE TOAD

This is one of the largest toads in the world. The cane toad may look harmless, but it's packed with a powerful foul-tasting poison, which it releases to drive away an attacking predator. In its native South America few animals try to eat it, and when the cane toad was introduced to control pests in Australia, it became a problem itself – preying on the native wildlife.

AT A GLANCE

Ear just behind eye

● **SIZE** 10–24 cm (4–9½ in) long

● **HABITAT** Everywhere from forests to open fields

● **LOCATION** Native to South America, but introduced to many parts of the world

● **DIET** Insects, worms, and other small animals

*"*It can **eat** a **rodent** or small **snake**"

Skin colour provides camouflage

WEBBED HIND FEET

Many frogs and toads have broad webbed feet for swimming in water, but the cane toad's feet are only partially webbed. It spends most of its time on drier grasslands and only goes in water to breed.

Translucent webbing between long toes

Large, bulging eyes

STATS AND FACTS

15 YEARS
LIFESPAN IN CAPTIVITY

TIME

1–3 (eggs hatch)   21–140 (tadpole stage)

days   50   100   150

With few predators willing to tackle the cane toad, its numbers increased rapidly after it was introduced to Australia in 1935.

EGGS

8,000– 35,000 (produced at a time)

0   10,000   20,000   30,000   40,000

RECORD WEIGHT **2.65 KG**

Adult cane toad

This toad is almost indestructible. Both adults and tadpoles are poisonous and taste foul to most predators, and the warty skin of the males develops sharp spines in the breeding season. Its mouth is big enough to swallow small mammals.

Breathes through nostril

Ear protected by thin membrane

SHARP SENSES

The cane toad relies more on its sense of smell to find food than other toads. It also has a good sense of hearing, which allows it to hear the calls of other toads. Many amphibians use their skin to help them breathe but the cane toad relies more on its nostrils and lungs.

POISON GLANDS

The poison of a cane toad is packaged in two large glands found towards the back of its head, one on each side. The foul-tasting poison is released when the toad is stressed or the glands are squeezed by an unsuspecting predator.

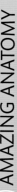

AMAZING ANATOMY

MOST POISONOUS ANIMAL
GOLDEN POISON FROG

This bright-yellow frog is scarcely the size of your thumb but it is extremely dangerous. It lives on the rainforest floor, where it feasts on insects caught with its sticky tongue. Some of these insects contain a poison that the frog then stores in its skin. The frog is unaffected by it, as are its tadpoles. They ride on their father's back until he finds a tiny pool of water to drop them into.

AT A GLANCE

- **SIZE** Up to 4.7 cm (1¾ in) long, from nose to bottom
- **HABITAT** On the ground among the leaf litter in rainforests. Tadpoles are deposited in pools of water that have collected in the leaf rosettes of bromeliad plants.
- **LOCATION** Foothills of the Andes Mountains, Colombia (South America)
- **DIET** Insects and other small invertebrates

STATS AND FACTS

3 YEARS
LIFESPAN IN THE WILD

The golden poison frog produces 20 times more poison than other South American poison frogs. This poison paralyses the predator's muscles and ultimately stops its heart beating.

ONE FROG CAN KILL
10 PEOPLE

POISON

½₀th of drop can kill 1,000 mice
¹⁄₁₀th of drop can kill one human

0   Poison in one frog = 1 drop

FOOD CONSUMPTION

33% (ants)   33% (beetles)   33% (other invertebrates)

0   100%

PITCH OF CALL

1.8

kHz   20   40   60   80   100
0.12 (human)

"**Just touching** its skin could **kill** you"

WARNING COLOURS

Young frogs are black with gold stripes and become completely golden when several months old. The colour warns predators that they are deadly. Native hunters in the rainforest use the frogs to poison the tips of their blow-gun darts.

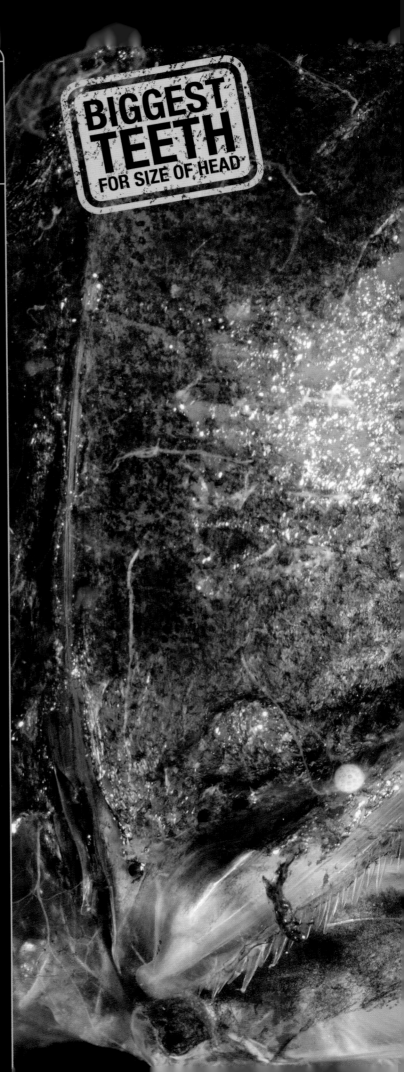

TOOTHY TERROR
SLOANE'S VIPERFISH

At the bottom of the ocean lurks a fish whose teeth are the stuff of nightmares. In deep, dark water food is difficult to find, so predators need to be sure of a catch. The viperfish does this by enticing prey with a light-emitting lure on its dorsal fin, then quickly snapping its mouth shut so its target has no time to escape. The viperfish's long, needle-like fangs hold the struggling victim securely while it relaxes its throat to allow even the biggest prey to slip down easily.

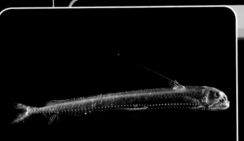

AT A GLANCE

- **SIZE** 20–35 cm (8–14 in) long
- **HABITAT** Deep sea
- **LOCATION** Tropical and subtropical oceans around the world
- **DIET** Any animals that can fit into the mouth – mainly shrimps, squid, crabs, and small fishes

STATS AND FACTS

1,000 METRES
DEPTH FOUND AT

Food is so scarce in the deep ocean that viperfish stock up whenever possible. The stomach can stretch to twice its normal size when food is plentiful.

SWIMMING SPEED
1.5 KM/H

PREY SIZE — 12–22 cm (63% of viperfish's length)

in	2	4	6	8
cm	5	10	15	20	25

TEETH — 8 (upper jaw)   10–18 (lower jaw)

	0	4	8	12	16	20
in	¼	½	¾	1	1¼	1½
cm		1	2	3	4

1.25 cm (maximum length of tooth)

HEAD LENGTH

in	½	1	1½	2	2½	3
cm		2	4	6	8

2.5 cm

BIGGEST TEETH FOR SIZE OF HEAD

FORMIDABLE FANGS
Extra-long teeth are good for snagging prey, but the viperfish has to open its mouth almost vertically to grab its catch. The transparent teeth can't be seen in the dark – ideal for trapping the unwary.

STRONGEST BITE
GREAT WHITE SHARK

The great white shark is the most terrifying fish in the sea. Its scary reputation comes from its preference for large, warm-blooded prey – seals, seabirds, and occasionally humans. Powerful muscles warm its blood, giving it speed to chase down prey or ram it from below. A single bite from a great white can inflict terrible wounds – even in the most thickly blubbered skin.

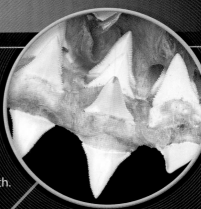

RAZOR SHARP

Each triangular tooth has a serrated edge as sharp as a kitchen knife. There are more than 300 of them arranged in rows within the mouth.

Sensitive snout

Teeth set in jaw of cartilage

FEELING THE BUZZ

As well as the usual five, sharks have an extra sense – they can detect the electrical activity given off by all living animals. The tiny detectors sit inside jelly-filled pores around the head of the fish.

Pectoral fin used for steering

Powerful jaw muscles give the bite its strength

Gill arches support the gills

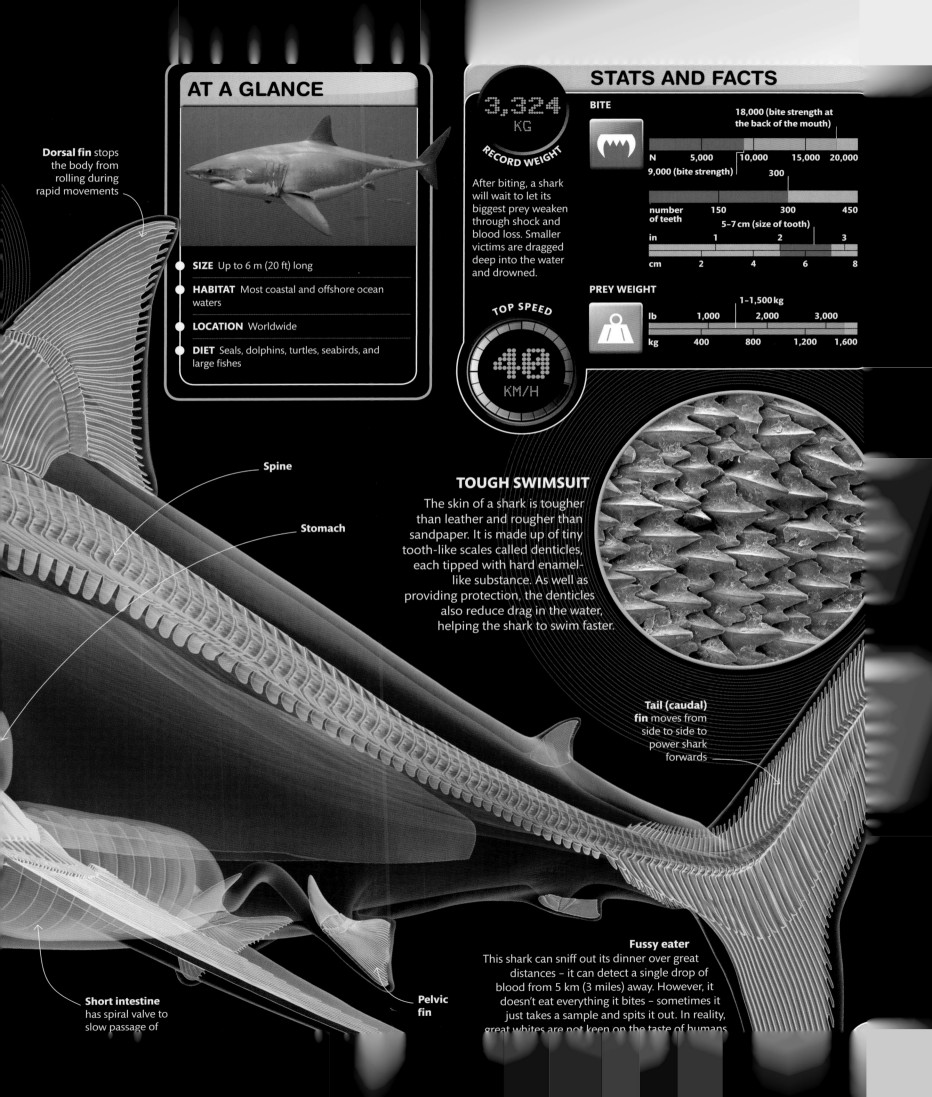

Dorsal fin stops the body from rolling during rapid movements

AT A GLANCE

SIZE Up to 6 m (20 ft) long

HABITAT Most coastal and offshore ocean waters

LOCATION Worldwide

DIET Seals, dolphins, turtles, seabirds, and large fishes

Spine

Stomach

Short intestine has spiral valve to slow passage of

Pelvic fin

STATS AND FACTS

3,324 KG
RECORD WEIGHT

After biting, a shark will wait to let its biggest prey weaken through shock and blood loss. Smaller victims are dragged deep into the water and drowned.

TOP SPEED
48 KM/H

BITE

N	5,000	10,000	15,000	20,000

18,000 (bite strength at the back of the mouth)

9,000 (bite strength)

number of teeth	150	300	450

300

in	1	2	3

5–7 cm (size of tooth)

cm	2	4	6	8

PREY WEIGHT

1–1,500 kg

lb	1,000	2,000	3,000

kg	400	800	1,200	1,600

TOUGH SWIMSUIT

The skin of a shark is tougher than leather and rougher than sandpaper. It is made up of tiny tooth-like scales called denticles, each tipped with hard enamel-like substance. As well as providing protection, the denticles also reduce drag in the water, helping the shark to swim faster.

Tail (caudal) fin moves from side to side to power shark forwards

Fussy eater

This shark can sniff out its dinner over great distances – it can detect a single drop of blood from 5 km (3 miles) away. However, it doesn't eat everything it bites – sometimes it just takes a sample and spits it out. In reality, great whites are not keen on the taste of humans

MEGAMOUTH
WHALE SHARK

While slowly cruising the sunlit ocean surface, a whale shark feeds on vast quantities of tiny floating animals called plankton. It has about 4,000 small teeth but these are useless for eating. Instead its giant mouth and gill arches are covered with small prickles that strain the plankton from the water – a process known as filter feeding. Every minute the whale shark passes gallons of water through its mouth and out via its gill slits and any trapped plankton is swallowed.

AT A GLANCE

- **SIZE** 9.7 m (32 ft) long
- **HABITAT** Surface waters of the open ocean
- **LOCATION** Warm and tropical oceans around the world
- **DIET** Plankton (including krill – shrimp-like animals of open water), small fishes, and squid

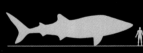

STATS AND FACTS

100 YEARS ESTIMATED LIFESPAN

One of the biggest animals preys on some of the smallest. The whale shark prefers plankton-rich surface waters – but can dive deeper than 1,000 m (3,280 ft).

DAILY FOOD CONSUMPTION

2–3 tonnes of plankton

ton	1	2	3	4
tonne	1	2	3	4	5

SIZE OF PLANKTON PREY

2–70 mm

in	1	2	3	
mm	20	40	60	80	100

DISTANCE COVERED PER DAY

30 km

miles	10	20	30
km	10	20	30	40	50

TOP SPEED

5.4 KM/H

"**This fish has a huge mouth, but a tiny throat**"

LARGEST FISH

THICK SKIN

At 15 cm (6 in) thick, the rough skin of the whale shark is thicker than that of any other animal. It protects this fish from all but the largest of predators. Suckerfish often hitch a ride on a whale shark – even entering the mouth.

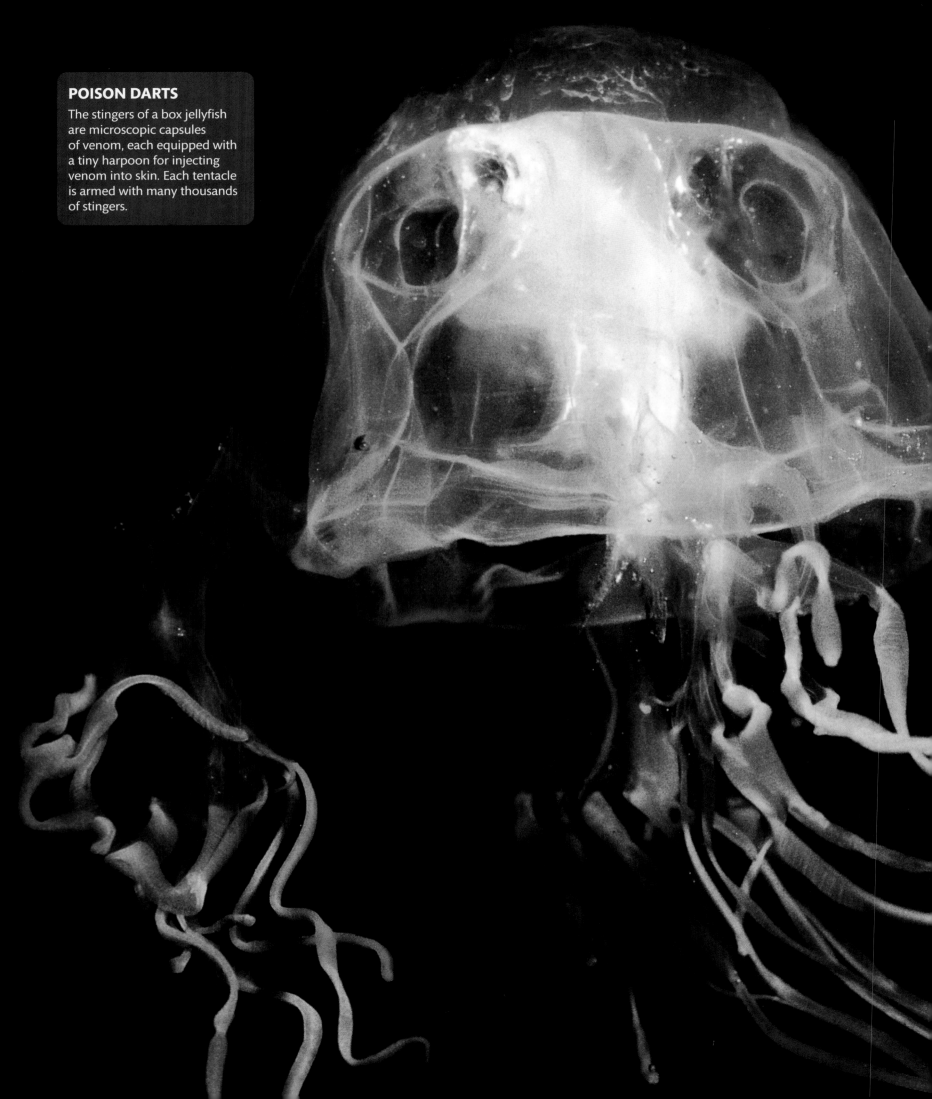

POISON DARTS

The stingers of a box jellyfish are microscopic capsules of venom, each equipped with a tiny harpoon for injecting venom into skin. Each tentacle is armed with many thousands of stingers.

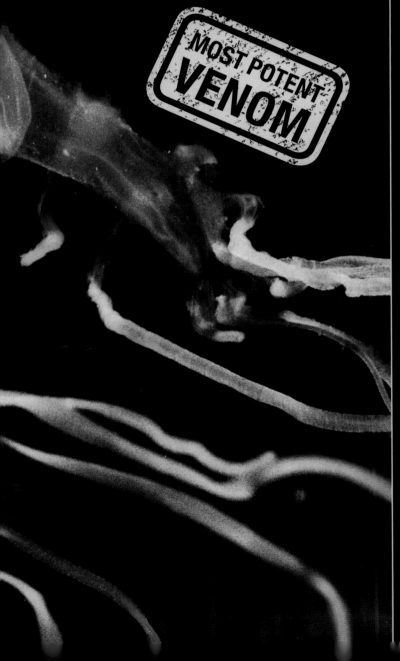

"The **shock** of its sting can stop a **heart beating**"

MOST POTENT **VENOM**

DEADLY SEA STINGER
BOX JELLYFISH

Box jellyfish can inflict one of the most painful of all stings: their venom is so strong that it can kill a human. They swim in tropical waters and sometimes come close to the shore – and to swimmers. Unlike other jellyfishes, they have clusters of eyes on their box-shaped swimming "bell" and powerful muscles that help them swim against the currents. Box jellyfish have transparent bodies, so they may not be noticed by swimmers until it is too late.

AT A GLANCE

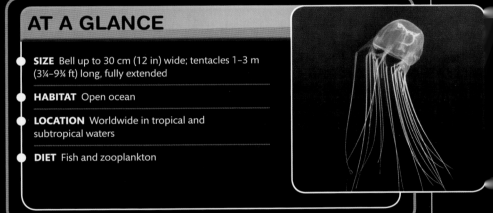

- **SIZE** Bell up to 30 cm (12 in) wide; tentacles 1–3 m (3¼–9¾ ft) long, fully extended
- **HABITAT** Open ocean
- **LOCATION** Worldwide in tropical and subtropical waters
- **DIET** Fish and zooplankton

STATS AND FACTS

2 KG
MAXIMUM WEIGHT

Box jellyfish swim faster than typical jellyfishes, and their painful stings can be so damaging, they can leave lasting scars.

TOP SWIMMING SPEED

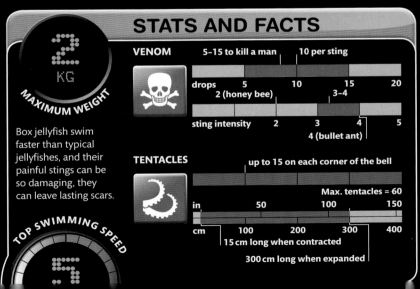

VENOM

drops	5–15 to kill a man		10 per sting	
	5	10	15	20

sting intensity	2 (honey bee)		3–4	
	2	3	4	5
			4 (bullet ant)	

TENTACLES

in	up to 15 on each corner of the bell		Max. tentacles = 60	
	50	100		150
cm	100	200	300	400

15 cm long when contracted

300 cm long when expanded

HOME TO BILLIONS
GREAT BARRIER REEF

BIGGEST ANIMAL-MADE STRUCTURE

The Great Barrier Reef is the world's biggest coral reef, and the single biggest structure made by animals. It is so big that it runs down half the coast of Australia and can be seen from space. It was formed over thousands of years by coral – an animal that grows as a colony of tiny anenome-like structures, called polyps. As the coral grows, it lays down a skeleton of chalky rock that forms the reef.

AT A GLANCE

- **SIZE** 2,600 km (1,610 miles) long
- **HABITAT** Coastal ocean waters
- **LOCATION** Off the north-eastern coast of Australia
- **DIET** Coral feeds on plankton; also sugars and nutrients made by algae living on the flesh of the coral

STATS AND FACTS

20,000 YEARS APPROXIMATE AGE

The coral forms the basis of the reef in the same way that trees form the basis of a forest. Thousands of other types of animals live and grow on and around the coral.

DISTANCE FROM COASTLINE

32–260 km

miles	40	80	120	160
km	50	100	150	200	250	300

COMPOSITION

1,500 (fish species)

400 (coral species)

species	400	800	1,200	1,600

TEMPERATURE OF WATER

21°C (winter)–28°C (summer)

°F	50	70	90	110
°C	10	20	30	40	50

LENGTH OF REEF

"5% of the world's fish species live here"

ALL SHAPES AND SIZES
Coral grows in an amazing variety of forms. The outer skeleton of hard coral forms rocky outcrops, but there are soft, fleshy corals growing among them too. Some even look like brains or fat fingers.

LARGEST SPIDER
GOLIATH SPIDER

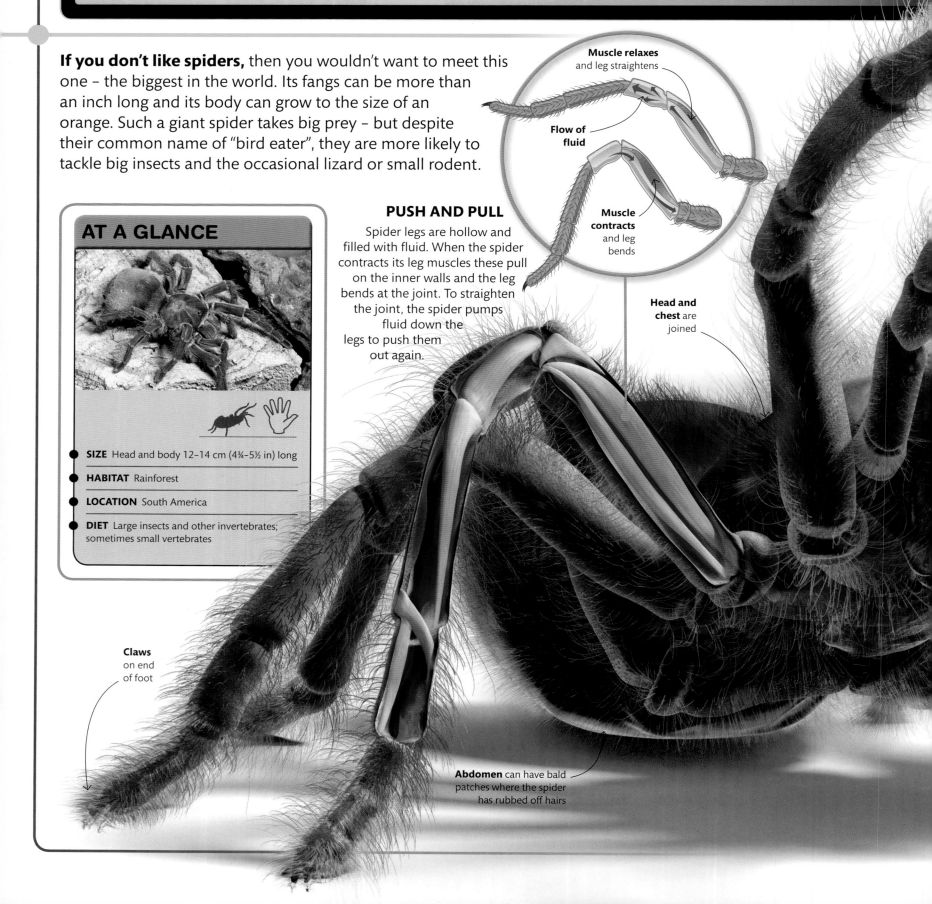

If you don't like spiders, then you wouldn't want to meet this one – the biggest in the world. Its fangs can be more than an inch long and its body can grow to the size of an orange. Such a giant spider takes big prey – but despite their common name of "bird eater", they are more likely to tackle big insects and the occasional lizard or small rodent.

Muscle relaxes and leg straightens

Flow of fluid

Muscle contracts and leg bends

PUSH AND PULL
Spider legs are hollow and filled with fluid. When the spider contracts its leg muscles these pull on the inner walls and the leg bends at the joint. To straighten the joint, the spider pumps fluid down the legs to push them out again.

Head and chest are joined

AT A GLANCE

SIZE Head and body 12–14 cm (4¾–5½ in) long

HABITAT Rainforest

LOCATION South America

DIET Large insects and other invertebrates; sometimes small vertebrates

Claws on end of foot

Abdomen can have bald patches where the spider has rubbed off hairs

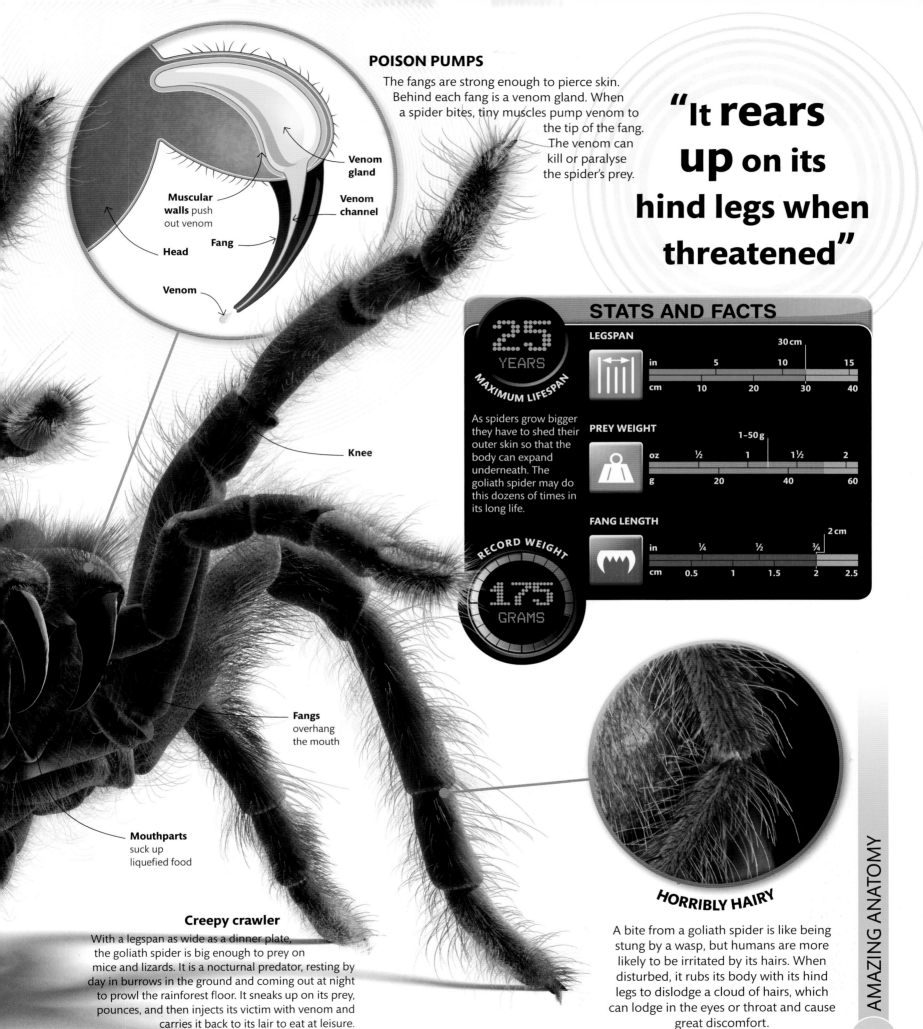

POISON PUMPS

The fangs are strong enough to pierce skin. Behind each fang is a venom gland. When a spider bites, tiny muscles pump venom to the tip of the fang. The venom can kill or paralyse the spider's prey.

Venom gland

Muscular walls push out venom

Venom channel

Head

Fang

Venom

"It rears up on its hind legs when threatened"

Knee

STATS AND FACTS

25 YEARS
MAXIMUM LIFESPAN

As spiders grow bigger they have to shed their outer skin so that the body can expand underneath. The goliath spider may do this dozens of times in its long life.

RECORD WEIGHT
175 GRAMS

LEGSPAN				30 cm	
in		5	10		15
cm	10	20	30		40

PREY WEIGHT		1–50 g			
oz	½	1	1½		2
g	20		40		60

FANG LENGTH				2 cm	
in	¼	½	¾		
cm	0.5	1	1.5	2	2.5

Fangs overhang the mouth

Mouthparts suck up liquefied food

Creepy crawler

With a legspan as wide as a dinner plate, the goliath spider is big enough to prey on mice and lizards. It is a nocturnal predator, resting by day in burrows in the ground and coming out at night to prowl the rainforest floor. It sneaks up on its prey, pounces, and then injects its victim with venom and carries it back to its lair to eat at leisure.

HORRIBLY HAIRY

A bite from a goliath spider is like being stung by a wasp, but humans are more likely to be irritated by its hairs. When disturbed, it rubs its body with its hind legs to dislodge a cloud of hairs, which can lodge in the eyes or throat and cause great discomfort.

AMAZING ANATOMY

93

REPELLING INTRUDERS

The male dung beetle's horns aren't just for pushing dung – they are also a powerful weapon against rivals. A male will lock horns with any intruder that invades his tunnel to steal his mate or his dung ball. Weaker males are simply pushed out of the way.

WEIGHTLIFTING WONDER
HORNED DUNG BEETLE

Imagine moving a pile of dung the size of a house and you have some idea of what a dung beetle can do. It is the muscles of the insect world, feeding itself and its young on dung. The horned dung beetle tunnels under dung pats, where a hornless female lays eggs on underground larders of dung. The male guards the entrance and uses brute force to repel any intruders.

AT A GLANCE

- **SIZE** 0.8–1 cm (⅓–½in) long
- **HABITAT** Open country on sandy soil
- **LOCATION** Mediterranean as far east as Turkey and Iran; introduced to Australia and the southern USA
- **DIET** Dung

STATS AND FACTS

3 MONTHS
ADULT LIFESPAN

The strongest males guard the tunnel entrances. However, their horns are a hindrance inside the tunnels, so more agile hornless males may slip by and mate with the female instead.

WEIGHT PULLED

		30 g (hornless male and unfed horned male)		
oz	1	2	3	4
g	30	60	90	120

100 g (well-fed horned male)

TUNNEL LENGTH

			20–30 cm		
in	3	6	9	12	15
cm	10	20	30	40

TIME TO RUN THROUGH TUNNEL

4–5 seconds (hornless male)

5–7 seconds (horned male)

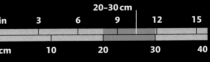
STRONGEST INSECT

MAX. WEIGHT PULLED
120 GRAMS

MEGABUG
LITTLE BARRIER GIANT WETA

Wetas are huge flightless crickets from New Zealand. The heaviest of them all, which weighs as much as a blackbird, lives only on a tiny island called Little Barrier. Whereas other wetas eat insects, the giant weta feeds on leaves. It is too big to jump so makes a hissing sound to scare off enemies. If that doesn't work, it can lash out with its spiny legs, causing a painful injury. They only bite humans if they are provoked.

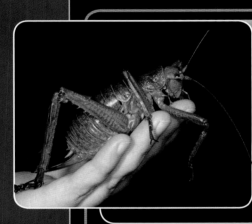

AT A GLANCE

- **SIZE** Body 10 cm (4 in) long
- **HABITAT** Forest; adults lives in trees, but females go to the ground to lay eggs
- **LOCATION** Little Barrier Island in New Zealand
- **DIET** Leaves

STATS AND FACTS

2 YEARS LIFESPAN

Wetas grow and breed slowly compared with most insects. They lay their eggs in warm, damp soil. As wetas grow they periodically shed their thick outer casing (exoskeleton) and grow a new one.

RECORD WEIGHT 71 GRAMS

GROWTH

0.5 cm (length when newly hatched)

in	1	2	3
cm	2	4	6	8	10

7–8 cm (length of adult)

0	5	10	15

10 (number of moults)

EGGS

0.7 cm (length)

in	¼	½
cm	0.5	1	1.5

in	1	2
cm	2	4	6

5 cm (depth at which buried)

LEGSPAN

20 cm

in	2	4	6	8
cm	5	10	15	20	25

"**Giant wetas can weigh** up to **71 g (2½ oz)**"

UGLY BUG

In the local Maori language, the giant weta's name *wetapunga* means "the god of ugly things". It is largely nocturnal, preferring to hide away during the day to avoid predators, but it often gives itself away by the large droppings (as big as a rat's) it leaves beneath its tree.

MOST SPECTACULAR WINGS
ATLAS MOTH

The large, papery wings of the Atlas moth are among the most colourful of all moths'. However, they are also fragile and only work well in calm conditions. The female is larger and heavier than the male with a wingspan that's as big as a bird's. Her sole function is to attract a male to mate with. Afterwards, she lays her eggs on the underside of a leaf and dies.

A giant among moths

Although some big moths have longer wings, the Atlas moth's wings cover a larger area. Adults lack mouthparts and cannot feed. They survive for a short time by living off the body fat they stored when they were caterpillars.

BIGGEST **MOTH** BY WING AREA

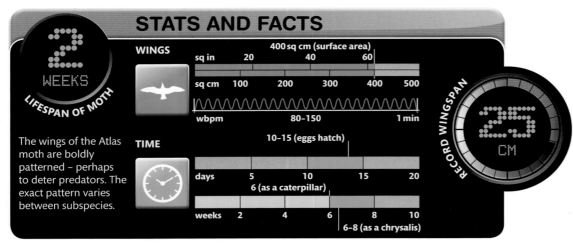

Wings are covered with tiny scales

AT A GLANCE

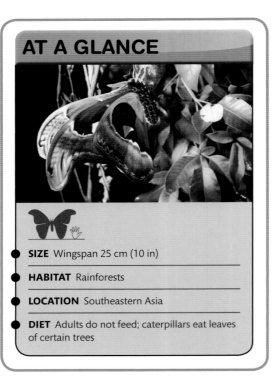

SIZE Wingspan 25 cm (10 in)

HABITAT Rainforests

LOCATION Southeastern Asia

DIET Adults do not feed; caterpillars eat leaves of certain trees

STATS AND FACTS

2 WEEKS LIFESPAN OF MOTH

The wings of the Atlas moth are boldly patterned – perhaps to deter predators. The exact pattern varies between subspecies.

WINGS

	400 sq cm (surface area)		
sq in	20	40	60
sq cm	100 200 300 400	500

wbpm 80–150 1 min

TIME

10–15 (eggs hatch)

days	5	10	15	20

6 (as a caterpillar)

weeks	2	4	6	8	10

6–8 (as a chrysalis)

RECORD WINGSPAN **25 CM**

FEATHERY ANTENNAE

The long, feathered antennae of the male Atlas moth are covered with sensor cells called chemoreceptors. They are so sensitive that they can pick up the scent of a female several kilometres away.

Patterning on wing tips looks like a snake's head

Antennae of females have less feathering

"Adult Atlas moths only **live** for **two weeks**"

Strongly scented chemicals are released from a gland at the tip of the female's abdomen

FEEDING STAGE

Most of an Atlas moth's life is spent as a caterpillar. It feeds voraciously, munching its way through the leaves of citrus trees until it's about 11.5 cm (4½ in) long and ready to pupate. It then spins a silk cocoon around itself and changes into an adult moth over about four weeks.

AMAZING ANATOMY

A NEW SUIT OF ARMOUR

The longer a spider crab lives, the bigger it gets, but over time, other animals such as sponges and anemones grow on its shell. These hitchhikers don't last: spider crabs must moult their shells to grow bigger. With such long legs, this can take around two hours to complete.

"This **crab** can **grow** to the size of **a small car**"

SEAFLOOR SCUTTLER

JAPANESE SPIDER CRAB

Picking its way slowly across the ocean floor is a crab that looks like a huge mechanical spider. Despite its long, gangly legs, the Japanese spider crab's body is scarcely the size of a basketball. Armed with strong claws for tearing apart its food, this crab is actually a gentle giant. It prefers to live by scavenging on the seafloor – its weight makes it too slow to chase after fast-moving prey.

AT A GLANCE

- **SIZE** Legspan 2.5–3.8 m (8¼–12 ft)
- **HABITAT** Coastal waters at depths down to 600 m (2,000 ft)
- **LOCATION** Northwestern Pacific off Japan and Taiwan
- **DIET** Smaller crabs, snails, and carcasses

STATS AND FACTS

1oo YEARS
RECORD LIFESPAN

A spider crab is a decapod – it has ten legs. Eight of these are used for walking and the other, shorter pair end in pincers that are used for feeding.

LENGTH

		1.5m (longest leg)		
ft	2	4	6	
m	0.5	1	1.5	2	2.5

DIAMETER

			40 cm (body)	
in	5	10	15	
cm	10	20	30	40	50

WEIGHT

		21 kg (record)		
lb	20	40	60	
kg	10	20	30	

15–20 kg (normal range)

RECORD LEGSPAN
3.8 METRES

MAGNIFICENT MOLLUSC
GIANT CLAM

Shelled giants of the ocean, these clams grow all their lives. The oldest can weigh as much as a dolphin. Unlike smaller clams, they can thrive in nutrient-poor waters because each giant clam has microscopic algae living in its flesh that make energy-rich sugars – just like plants – which they share with the clam. It also feeds on plankton, which it sucks out of the seawater.

AT A GLANCE

- **SIZE** Up to 1.2 m (4 ft) long
- **HABITAT** Shallow ocean waters
- **LOCATION** Tropical oceans, mostly of the Indo-Pacific
- **DIET** Plankton and food produced by live-in algae

STATS AND FACTS

100 YEARS
MAXIMUM LIFESPAN

The giant clam has powerful muscles to open and close its shell, but contrary to popular opinion, these work too slowly to trap human beings. Not all species can close completely.

RECORD WEIGHT
250 KG

STRENGTH

	4,500 (muscle strength to close shell)				
N	1,000	2,000	3,000	4,000	5,000

400 (human grip)

FOOD

65% (food made by algae)	35% (plankton)

young

65% (plankton)

old 35% (food made by algae)

DEPTH

2–20 m

ft	20	40	60	80
m	5	10	15	20	25

BIG-LIPPED BIVALVE

The main body of a clam consists of a thick, fleshy tissue called the mantle. In giant clams this is brightly coloured and contains the algae that provide the clam with food. When the clam is open, the mantle extends out over the shell to expose the maximum area to sunlight.

"Giant clams release **500 million eggs** in one go"

COCONUT SMASHER

Robber crabs are often seen climbing trees in search of food, such as bananas and coconuts. They dehusk a fallen coconut and then either haul it back up the tree to drop it and crack it open, or they simply smash or snip the tough shell with their claws.

TREE-CLIMBING COLOSSUS
ROBBER CRAB

You won't find these crabs hiding in a rock pool – they can't swim and they're not keen on water. Robber crabs are land-dwelling hermit crabs, and are so well adapted to life in air that they drown in the sea. However, this is a risk every female must take as she needs to release her eggs in the rising tides. These eggs hatch into larvae, which settle on the seafloor. As a soft-bodied juvenile, the crab lives in discarded snail shells and uses gills to breathe. When it leaves the water it starts to breathe air and its body hardens into a tough shell.

AT A GLANCE

- **SIZE** Head and body 40 cm (16 in) long; legspan 90 cm (35 in)

- **HABITAT** Coastal areas

- **LOCATION** Islands of the Indian Ocean and Western Pacific

- **DIET** Seeds, fruit, coconuts, and carrion

STATS AND FACTS

4.1 KG
RECORD WEIGHT

LARGEST LAND CRAB

Robber crabs find food using the highly sensitive smell sensors on their antennae.

MAXIMUM SIZE AT

HOME RANGE

		40–250 sq m		
sq ft	1,000	2,000		3,000
sq m	100	200		300

SMELL DETECTION

50 m (crab smells unripe banana)

ft	40	80	120	160	200
m		30			60

1 m (human smells food)

sensors	500	1,000	1,500	2,000

1,600–1,800 (smell sensors on each antenna)

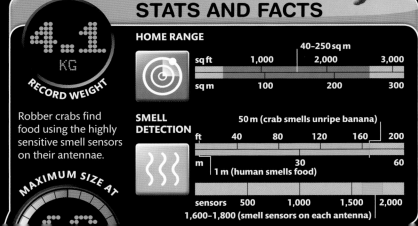

RECORD-BREAKERS

Animals have a staggering range of body shapes and sizes, from microscopic rotifers to gigantic whales. This breathtaking variety of forms depends on many factors, including whether an animal lives on land or in water, how it moves, the temperature of its habitat, and what it eats. Big animals can overpower competitors or their prey, while small animals can hide more easily from enemies. Each group of animals has its own record-breakers when it comes to unusual size and interesting body features.

"The duck-billed platypus is the most venomous mammal"

PLATYPUS

SUPER SNAKE

The longest snake is the reticulated python. The biggest one ever caught and measured was a whopping 10.2 m (33 ft). They usually average 3–6 m (10–20 ft) in the wild.

RETICULATED PYTHON

BONIEST ANIMAL

The snipe eel has the most bones of any animal, often with more than 750 bones in its spine. Its body is so thin that it is 75 times longer than it is wide.

BEE HUMMINGBIRD

HEAVIEST ANIMALS

Blue whale	180 tonnes (198 tons)
Whale shark	21.5 tonnes (23½ tons)
African savanna elephant	12.25 tonnes (13½ tons)
Colossal squid	495 kg (1,090 lb)
Saltwater crocodile	450 kg (990 lb)
Leatherback turtle	364 kg (800 lb)
Ostrich	156 kg (344 lb)
Giant salamander	64 kg (140 lb)
Goliath spider	170 g (5 oz)

AFRICAN ELEPHANT

TINIEST MINIBEASTS

Moss rotifer	0.05 mm (⅟₅₁₂ in)
Amau frog	8 mm (¼ in)
Paedocypris fish	1 cm (⅜ in)
Dwarf sphaero gecko	1.6 cm (½ in)
Bumblebee bat	4 cm (1½ in)
Bee hummingbird	5 cm (2 in)

BIGGEST AMPHIBIAN

The Chinese giant salamander is the biggest amphibian in the world. It can grow up to 1.8 m (6 ft) long and weigh up to 64 kg (140 lb), although large specimens are getting harder to find in their native habitat.

1.8 METRES

SMALLEST INSECT

The tiniest insects are fairy wasps at just 0.4 mm (⅟₆₄ in) long. Female fairy wasps lay their eggs on the eggs of other insects and when their eggs hatch, the larvae feed on the contents of the host egg.

0.4 MM

"The sting of a bullet ant feels as painful as walking on hot coals"

LARGE FLYING FOX

LION

GREATEST WINGSPANS

● Wandering albatross	3.7 m (12 ft)
● Andean condor	3.2 m (10 ft)
● Large flying fox	1.8 m (6 ft)
● Bornean giant dragonfly	15 cm (6 in)

MIGHTIEST MOTH

The insect with the longest wingspan – 28 cm (11 in) – is the white witch moth of Central and South America. Like most moths, this giant is active at night and is sometimes mistaken for a bat.

POISONOUS PUFFERS

Pufferfishes are the most poisonous creatures in the ocean. They give predators plenty of warning by inflating themselves into balls, which makes their sharp spines stick out.

28 CM

STRONGEST BITES

● Great white shark	9,000 newtons
● Saltwater crocodile	5,800 newtons
● Lion	1,770 newtons
● Spotted hyena	770 newtons
● Tasmanian devil	418 newtons

PUFFERFISH

"A blue whale's heart weighs up to 600 kg (1,300 lb) and is the size of a small car"

STRONGEST MAMMAL BITE

Mammals tend to have strong bites because of their powerful jaw muscles. The mightiest bite of any mammal is not that of a big predator, such as a lion or tiger, but the plant-eating hippopotamus!

8,000 NEWTONS

HIPPOPOTAMUS

AMAZING ANATOMY

107

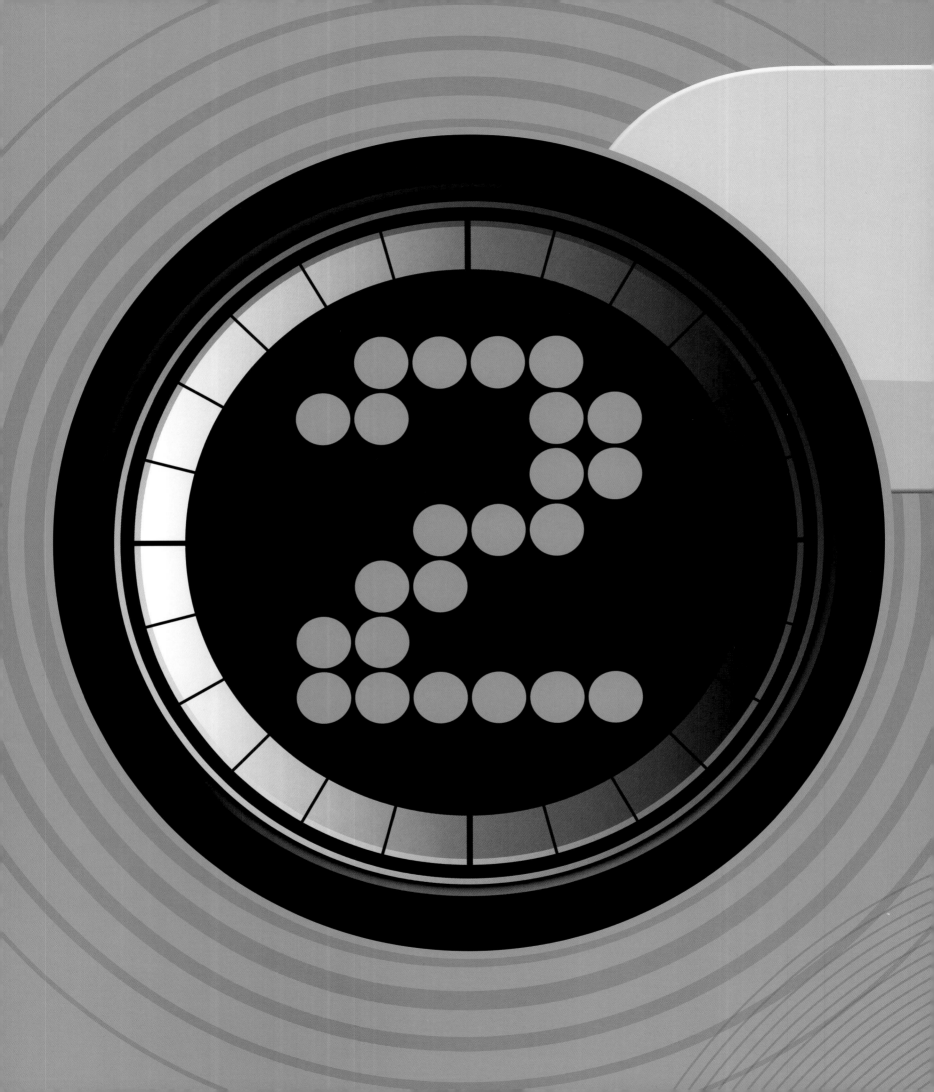

ANIMAL ATHLETES

However good a human is at running, jumping, or swimming, there is always an animal that can do it better. Animals have other spectacular talents, too, ranging from building and decorating to mimicry and walking on water. To an animal, these achievements are simply a way of life.

"Honey possums **depend on flowers** more than any other mammal"

FUSSIEST EATER
HONEY POSSUM

One of the tiniest of marsupials is devoted to flowers. The honey possum lives on Australian heathland, where it sups nectar from the blossoms. Lots of other mammals eat nectar, but most need protein in the form of insects. The honey possum, instead, gets protein from pollen, and so relies completely on flowers to survive. It has a long, bristle-tipped tongue for licking up its food – and is so attentive that it rarely misses a single bloom.

AT A GLANCE

- **SIZE** Head and body 7–9 cm (2¾–3½ in) long, plus tail 7–10 cm (2¾–4 in) long
- **HABITAT** Heathland and woodland
- **LOCATION** Southwestern Australia
- **DIET** Nectar and pollen

STATS AND FACTS

2 YEARS
MAXIMUM LIFESPAN

Newborn honey possums are the smallest of any mammal, but grow fast on energy-rich milk. They spend two months in their mother's miniature pouch.

TONGUE LENGTH

in	¼	½	1.8 cm ¾	1
cm		1	2	3

TIME

weeks	10	20	30	40

3–4 (gestation period)
10 (to wean)
32 (to reach adult weight)

WEIGHT

0.005 g (newborn)

7–16 g (adult)

FLOWERS VISITED

2,400

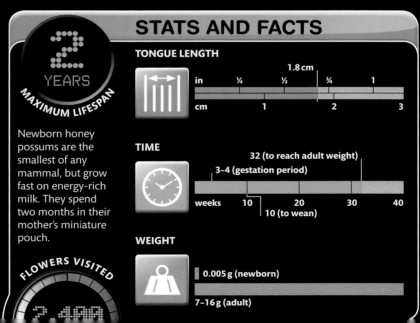

SURVIVAL STRATEGY

As the honey possum is so light, it can climb up slender stems and right into the flowers to feed. Its hands and feet are excellent for keeping a grip as it licks up the nectar, but this tiny animal has

BONE CRUSHER
HYENA

Little is left of a carcass once a hyena has finished with it. Its powerful jaws can crunch right through bone, which it swallows along with the marrow inside. Only the grass-filled stomachs of herbivores are left uneaten. Almost everything can be processed because its stomach has such powerful digestive juices.

Pointed ears can follow sound from any direction

NOSE FOR TROUBLE

A keen sense of smell is important for finding food and for communicating with other striped hyenas. Territorial boundaries are marked with a strong-smelling, yellow paste to warn off intruders.

Short, blunt muzzle

AT A GLANCE

- **SIZE** Head and body 95–160 cm (37–63 in) long, plus tail 27–47 cm (10½–18½ in) long

- **HABITAT** Grassland

- **LOCATION** Africa, Middle East, and eastern India

- **DIET** Carrion, living prey, and fruit

Front feet are larger than the hind feet, but all have four toes

Carnassial tooth is used for cutting through hide, flesh, and bone

BONE CRUSHERS

Carnivorous mammals have a cheek tooth on each side of the upper and lower jaws, called a carnassial. These teeth are extremely strong and with the powerful jaw muscles make the hyena's bite particularly good at crushing bones.

STATS AND FACTS

86 KG
MAXIMUM WEIGHT

The bite of a hyena is stronger than that of many animals of a similar size.

FOOD CONSUMPTION

	70% (live prey)	30% (carrion)
Spotted hyena		100%

20–40% (live prey and plant material)

Striped hyena		100%

60–80% (carrion)

BITE STRENGTH

55 (domestic cat)		550–770

N   200   400   600   800

TOP SPEED
64 KM/H

SPOTTED HYENA

The spotted hyena lacks the mane of the striped hyena and is redder in colour. This species kills more animals than it scavenges. A solitary spotted hyena tackles small prey, but by working in a pack, hyenas can hunt large animals and will spend up to two hours chasing a weak zebra to bring it down.

Mane is raised when excited or alarmed

Medium length, bushy tail

"Cubs fight so aggressively that 25% of them die"

Striped hyena

The hyena's strength is concentrated at the front of its body. Its shoulder and neck muscles are so powerful it can pull its own body weight in carrion. The back end is weaker – and the hind legs are shorter than the front legs so that the back slopes down towards the tail.

ANIMAL ATHLETES

CHAMPION LONG JUMPER
SNOW LEOPARD

In the cold, rocky mountains of Tibet, this sleek predator scales heights and clears chasms with such graceful agility that few highland animals can escape it. The snow leopard's long-haired coat keeps it warm, while a long thick tail – up to three-quarters its body length – helps it balance. When it sleeps, the tail doubles up as a blanket to protect its face and paws against freezing winds.

AT A GLANCE

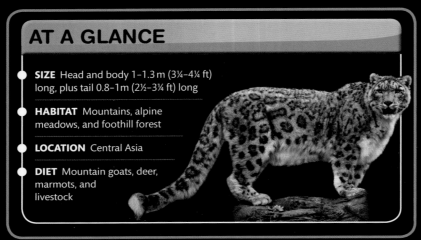

- **SIZE** Head and body 1–1.3 m (3¼–4¼ ft) long, plus tail 0.8–1m (2½–3¼ ft) long
- **HABITAT** Mountains, alpine meadows, and foothill forest
- **LOCATION** Central Asia
- **DIET** Mountain goats, deer, marmots, and livestock

STATS AND FACTS

17 METRES LONGEST JUMP

Thick fur insulates the snow leopard in the cold mountains. Its high-domed skull even has extra-large nose cavities to warm the chilled air when it breathes in.

TOP SPEED
60 KM/H

ALTITUDE
1,800 m (winter)

ft	6,000	12,000	18,000	24,000
m	1,500	3,000	4,500	6,000	7,500

6,000 m (summer)

TEMPERATURE
38°C (body)

°F	-100	-50	0	50	100
°C		-50		0		50

37°C (human)
-40–40°C (surroundings)

LENGTH OF HAIR
43 mm (belly)

in	½	1	1½	2	2½
mm		15	30	45	60

54 mm (back)

FURRY FEET
Wide paws with furry undersides give the snow leopard a sure footing on slippery slopes, and keep out the cold. Even so, it prefers to hunt on sun-warmed slopes where its coat provides better camouflage against the dappled grey rocks.

EXTREME SURVIVOR
BACTRIAN CAMEL

A Bactrian camel is well adapted to living in the desert. It can go for weeks without water, and when it finds some, it can gulp down half a bathful in just 10 minutes – it can even drink salty water if necessary. Contrary to popular opinion the camel's humps store fat, not water. The Bactrian camel's homeland in Central Asia, high above sea-level, gets little rainfall, and is either freezing cold or very hot. There are few animals as big as the Bactrian camel that can survive in such extremes.

AT A GLANCE

- **SIZE** 1.8–2.3 m (6–7½ ft) high at the shoulder

- **HABITAT** Desert and dry grassland

- **LOCATION** Central Asia, including the Gobi Desert

- **DIET** Any plant matter; it will even eat carrion when very hungry

"It can go three weeks without water"

Belly does not need sun protection so coat is thinner

FASTEST DRINKER

Feet adapted for any terrain

TREADING THE SAND

The Bactrian camel's feet each have two toes and one very wide, tough padded sole, which can be as large a dinner plate. This means that the camel can cope equally well with walking over sharp stony ground, very hot soft sand, or compacted winter snow.

TWO TOES

TOUGH PADDED SOLE

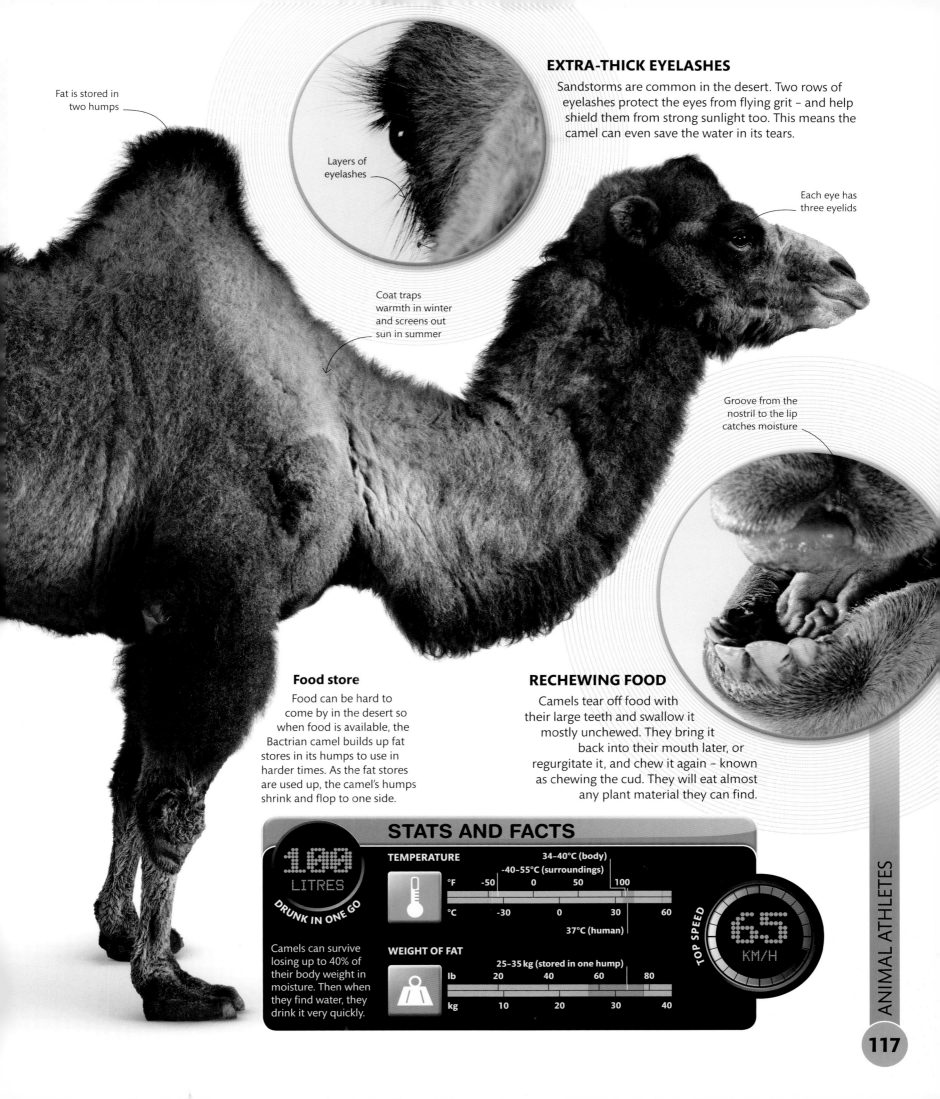

Fat is stored in two humps

EXTRA-THICK EYELASHES

Sandstorms are common in the desert. Two rows of eyelashes protect the eyes from flying grit – and help shield them from strong sunlight too. This means the camel can even save the water in its tears.

Layers of eyelashes

Each eye has three eyelids

Coat traps warmth in winter and screens out sun in summer

Groove from the nostril to the lip catches moisture

Food store

Food can be hard to come by in the desert so when food is available, the Bactrian camel builds up fat stores in its humps to use in harder times. As the fat stores are used up, the camel's humps shrink and flop to one side.

RECHEWING FOOD

Camels tear off food with their large teeth and swallow it mostly unchewed. They bring it back into their mouth later, or regurgitate it, and chew it again – known as chewing the cud. They will eat almost any plant material they can find.

STATS AND FACTS

100 LITRES
DRUNK IN ONE GO

Camels can survive losing up to 40% of their body weight in moisture. Then when they find water, they drink it very quickly.

TEMPERATURE

34–40°C (body)
-40–55°C (surroundings)

°F	-50	0	50	100
°C	-30	0	30	60

37°C (human)

WEIGHT OF FAT

25–35 kg (stored in one hump)

lb	20	40	60	80
kg	10	20	30	40

TOP SPEED

65 KM/H

FASTEST SPRINTER
CHEETAH

Never try to outrun a cheetah – when it comes to fast acceleration, nothing on two or four legs can beat it. Although its slimline physique is too light to ambush heavy-bodied prey, its astonishing speed allows it to outpace nimble animals, like gazelles. It trips its victim mid-sprint, and kills it with a bite to the throat.

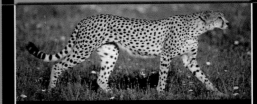

AT A GLANCE

SIZE Up to 2.3 m (7½ ft) long, plus tail 65–85 cm (26–34 in) long

HABITAT Mainly savanna but also semi-desert and dense bush

LOCATION Southern and eastern Africa

DIET Small hoofed mammals

Skull is small and made of thin bone

Neck is long

Skeleton is lightweight

AN EYE FOR DETAIL
Forward-facing eyes help the cheetah to see detail several kilometres away and judge distance for a chase. Black "tear" marks make its face look fiercer when it snarls to scare larger predators.

Heart is large, pumping blood around the body fast to cope with muscle demand for oxygen

FAST TWITCH
Cheetahs have lots of "fast-twitch" fibres in their muscles. These are good for reaching high speeds but tire quickly. This means the cheetah can only run for a short time (about 20–60 seconds) over a maximum of 500 m (550 yds) before needing to rest so these muscles can recover.

Claws only partially pull back, giving extra grip

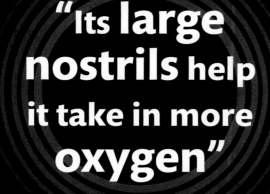

"Its large nostrils help it take in more oxygen"

Spine is extremely flexible

Fast-twitch fibres are concentrated in powerful leg muscles

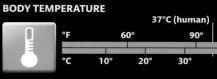

STATS AND FACTS

8 YEARS MAXIMUM LIFESPAN

BODY TEMPERATURE

	37°C (human)	39°C
°F	60° 90°	120°
°C	10° 20° 30° 40°	50°

Running at speed puts the cheetah's body under strain. Its temperature rises so fast that it has to rest before eating its prey. Rapid breathing allows maximum oxygen supply to muscles.

BREATHING RATE

16 (resting)   150 (sprinting)

breaths/min   50   100   150   200

10–20 (human while resting)   up to 100 (human while exercising)

TOP SPEED

114 KM/H

HEARTBEATS

bpm   250 (maximum)   1 min

bpm   100 (resting)   1 min

"This cat can reach 64 km/h (40 mph) in three seconds"

Cut to the chase
High-speed chases use a lot of energy. To be sure of success, the cheetah must stalk its prey very closely before rushing from cover.

Tail is long to help the cheetah balance in tight turns

Legs are long to maximize stride length

SUPER-FLEXY SPINE

The cheetah has the longest spine in proportion to the rest of its body of any cat. It is also very flexible and is alternately straightened and flexed when the animal is galloping, to maximize stride length for greater speed. This movement is controlled by powerful back muscles that make up half the body's muscle weight. The spine curves so much that it allows the back feet to move in front of the forefeet. Extended claws give the cat grip as it hurtles along. It then reaches as far as it can before curling itself up for the next stride.

STRAIGHTENED

FLEXED

ANIMAL ATHLETES

ENDURANCE CHAMPION
PRONGHORN

The pronghorn has lungs like bellows and a powerful heart, which together can deliver large amounts of oxygen to its leg muscles over a long period of time. This lightweight grassland animal can leap distances of six metres (20 ft), too. Only the very young, ill, or injured are in danger from predators because even the swiftest meat eater tires out long before a pronghorn does.

AT A GLANCE

- **SIZE** Head and body 1–1.5 m (3¼–5 ft) long, plus tail 8–18 cm (3¼–7 in) long (males are bigger than females)

- **HABITAT** Grassland and desert

- **LOCATION** Eastern and central North America

- **DIET** Grasses, cacti, and other low vegetation

STATS AND FACTS

12 YEARS
LIFESPAN IN CAPTIVITY

Although a champion runner and long-jumper, the pronghorn cannot jump very high and prefers to go under obstacles, rather than over them.

TOP SPEED
100 KM/H

WEIGHT OF HEART 340–660 g (pronghorn)

oz	10	20	
g	250	500	750

oz	10	20	
g	250	500	750

120–470 g (goat)

SPEED 48 km/h (cruising)

mph	20	40	60
km/h 20	40	60	80	100

65–85 km/h (fast run)

DISTANCE COVERED 5–6 km (in fast run)

miles	1	2	3	4
km	2	4	6	8

FASTEST ANIMAL OVER A LONG DISTANCE

DANGER SIGNAL

A pronghorn needs to be able to spot predators in time to make a speedy escape. It has very large eyes for its size, which are ever watchful for danger. If a predator is spotted, a pronghorn raises its white rump hairs, making the patch more visible to the animals around it. The whole herd will then flee at speed.

FASTEST DRUMMER
AYE-AYE

The strange-looking aye-aye from Madagascar likes nothing better than a juicy grub. But the best insects live hidden inside trees, so to find them the aye-aye uses its drumming skills and exceptional hearing. It taps at the bark and listens carefully for the tell-tale sign of a hollow tunnel. Then it gnaws a hole and uses its special twig-like middle finger to hook out the grub inside.

AT A GLANCE

- **SIZE** Head and body 36–44 cm (14–17 1/2 in) long, plus tail 50–60 cm (20–23 1/2 in) long
- **HABITAT** Rainforest
- **LOCATION** Madagascar
- **DIET** Insect larvae, seeds, and nectar

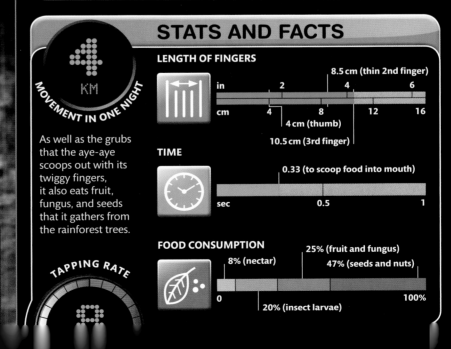

STATS AND FACTS

MOVEMENT IN ONE NIGHT
KM

As well as the grubs that the aye-aye scoops out with its twiggy fingers, it also eats fruit, fungus, and seeds that it gathers from the rainforest trees.

TAPPING RATE

LENGTH OF FINGERS

in	2	4	6
cm	4	8	12	16

8.5 cm (thin 2nd finger)
4 cm (thumb)
10.5 cm (3rd finger)

TIME

0.33 (to scoop food into mouth)

sec	0.5	1

FOOD CONSUMPTION

8% (nectar)
25% (fruit and fungus)
47% (seeds and nuts)
20% (insect larvae)

0		100%

NIGHT VISION

The aye-aye is nocturnal, so has big eyes and ears for sensing its way through the dark forest – sometimes leaping from tree to tree. It spends its days resting in

EXPERT ENGINEERS
BEAVER

No animal, except a human, alters its habitat quite like a group of beavers. These big rodents are the lumberjacks of the natural world. They have powerful jaws and use their chisel-like teeth to fell small trees, which they use to dam a stream or river and build a lodge. Here, they can raise a family safely out of the reach of predators.

AT A GLANCE

- **SIZE** Head and body 60–80 cm (23½–32 in) long, plus tail 25–45 cm (10–18 in) long
- **HABITAT** Streams and lakes bordered by trees
- **LOCATION** North America and northern Asia
- **DIET** Bark, twigs, leaves, and roots of trees; aquatic plants

DAMMING THE FLOW

Beavers build a dam to create a pond of deep, quiet water, where they can feed and make their lodge. First they make a foundation of stones and mud, on which they pile branches and small tree trunks. Then they strengthen it by plastering more mud and water plants on top. A family of beavers will look after their dam for many generations.

Dam

Water level between dam and lodge

Water level on stream side of dam is lower than in pond

CHEEKY CHISELLER

The beaver is one of the biggest rodents and is strong enough to carry large logs. It has powerful cheek muscles for cutting through timber, and its long orange front teeth are hard and sharp for chiselling wood. The ridged cheek teeth provide a good grinding surface for chewing tough plants.

Pond forms behind the dam, slowing the flow of the river and making it easier for the beavers to build a lodge

SAFE HAVEN

The lodge provides shelter from the elements and protection from predators. Inside it the cosy living chamber is raised above the water level and carpeted with dry plant material. The chamber is reached by one or more entrances, which can only be accessed underwater.

"Beavers can rebuild a broken dam overnight"

Outer branches are plastered with more mud in autumn to provide insulation against the cold

Underwater entrance to lodge

Small living chamber – sometimes there is a separate area where the beavers dry off before entering the main den

STATS AND FACTS

50 YEARS LIFESPAN IN CAPTIVITY

There is a beaver dam in Canada that is so big it can be seen from space. It is twice as long as the Hoover Dam in the USA.

DIAMETER

12 m (lodge)

| ft | 10 | 20 | 30 | 40 |
| m | 3 | 6 | 9 | 12 | 15 |

WIDTH

2 m (internal chamber)

| ft | 3 | 6 | 9 |
| m | 1 | 2 | 3 |

LONGEST DAM **850 METRES**

FASTEST DIGGER
AARDVARK

The word aardvark means "earth pig" and this animal deserves its name – no creature can dig into the ground faster. An aardvark digs to find food, escape predators, and to make burrows to live in. It can break through the hardest sun-baked ground, and when the earth is soft, its muscular body gives it the strength to tunnel away within minutes and stay hidden below ground.

AT A GLANCE

- **SIZE** Head and body 1–1.58 m (3¼–5 ft) long, plus tail 44–71 cm (17½–28 in) long
- **HABITAT** Grassland and open woodland
- **LOCATION** Africa, south of the Sahara Desert
- **DIET** Ants and termites

STATS AND FACTS

100 KG
MAXIMUM WEIGHT

An aardvark digs with its front legs and shifts the loose soil backwards with its hind legs. Young aardvarks become diggers at around 6 months old.

DIGS UP PREY IN

BURROW LENGTH

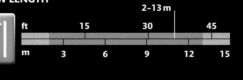

			2–13 m	
ft		15	30	45
m	3	6	9	12	15

HOME RANGE

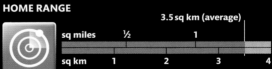

			3.5 sq km (average)	
sq miles	½	1		
sq km	1	2	3	4

TONGUE LENGTH

			25–30 cm	
in		5	10	15
cm	10	20	30	40

BURIED TREASURE

Aardvarks eat mostly ants and termites. Because of their large size, they need to eat a lot of the tiny insects. They dig to open the hardest ant nests with their

LAZIEST ANIMAL
SLOTH

It can take a whole day for a sloth to cross from one tree to the next – while another may scarcely ever move from a favourite tree. Sloths have little need to speed up as they are surrounded by their leafy food and well camouflaged from predators. Hanging upside down with their long claws hooked over the branches, their shaggy bodies blend in perfectly with the tree tops.

AT A GLANCE

Colour helps camouflage sloth

SIZE Head and body 41–74 cm (16–29 in) long; tail – in three-toed sloths only – 2–9 cm (¾–3½ in)

HABITAT Rainforest

LOCATION Central and South America

DIET Leaves and shoots of rainforest trees

Strongly curved claws

LEAFY DIET

Sloths are vegetarian and have large complicated stomachs to help them digest their food. Two-toed sloths travel from tree to tree in search of food, but three-toed sloths are usually fussier and stick to one tree.

Long, shaggy fur hangs down from the belly towards the back

STATS AND FACTS

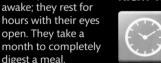

48 YEARS
LIFESPAN IN CAPTIVITY

Sloths spend little time awake; they rest for hours with their eyes open. They take a month to completely digest a meal.

TOP SPEED

0.6 km/h (in trees)

mph	⅛	¼	⅜	½
km/h	0.2	0.4	0.6	0.8

0.25 km/h (on ground)

NIGHT-TIME BEHAVIOUR

3 (active)	4 (resting)	6 (sleeping)
hours		

1.6 KM/H
TOP CLIMBING SPEED

"Sloth muscles work very slowly"

Slowly does it

A sloth wouldn't win any races, but it is an expert climber. Its hands and feet have fleshy pads for gripping branches – and the long, curved claws act like hooks. Some species are two-toed, others are three-toed, but all can climb a vertical tree trunk.

SLOTH MOTH

The fur of a sloth often appears greenish. The colour is due to the growth of algae, which thrives in the humidity of the rainforest. The coat is also home to the sloth moth – which lives nowhere else.

CRAWLING ON LAND

Sloths rarely come down to the ground, because they are vulnerable there and can only move by crawling awkwardly. Sometimes they descend to change trees, but otherwise they only do so to urinate and defecate – something that happens just once or twice a week.

ANIMAL ATHLETES

EXPERT GLIDER
COLUGO

Gliding through the air is an excellent way to get around the forest. As well as being quick, it saves energy because it doesn't use much muscle power. There are a few kinds of mammal that can air glide, such as flying squirrels and gliding possums – but the colugo is the best glider of all. The flaps of skin that stretch along the body of this unusual mammal act like a parachute. When it jumps from tree to tree, it can easily cross a forest clearing without losing much height.

AT A GLANCE

- **SIZE** Head and body 34–42 cm (13½–16½ in) long, plus tail 18–27 cm (7–11 in) long; weight 1¾ kg (4 lb)
- **HABITAT** Rainforest
- **LOCATION** Southeast Asia
- **DIET** Young leaves and buds

STATS AND FACTS

18 YEARS
LIFESPAN IN CAPTIVITY

When not gliding, colugos keep their parachute folded out of the way. Though graceful in the air, they climb slowly and are virtually helpless on the ground.

GLIDES PER NIGHT
4-29

LENGTH OF GLIDE

up to 150 m

ft	200	400	600
m	50	100	150	200

31 m (average)

DURATION OF GLIDE

1–15

sec	5	10	15	20

SPEED

4 m/sec (landing)　　10 m/sec (gliding)

ft/sec	10	20	30	40
m/sec		5	10	15

ANIMAL ATHLETES

FLYING HIGH

A large and brilliantly efficient "parachute" gives the colugo the edge. In other gliders, the flap of skin only connects the limbs, but the colugo's is huge, reaching to the ends of its toes, and right along its tail.

CHAMPION CHATTERBOX
AFRICAN GREY PARROT

The best talking parrots speak hundreds of words, and the African grey parrot is the chattiest of all. Many birds copy sounds in the wild – starlings and mynahs mimic other birds, and can even do a great impersonation of a car alarm. Although wild parrots are not great mimics, domestic parrots have particularly clear talking voices, which make them popular – though often noisy – pets.

AT A GLANCE

SIZE Body 28–39 cm (11 –15½ in) long; adult weight 402–490 g (14–17 oz)

HABITAT Rainforest and open woodland

LOCATION Central Africa

DIET Fruits, seeds, and grains

Red tail feathers

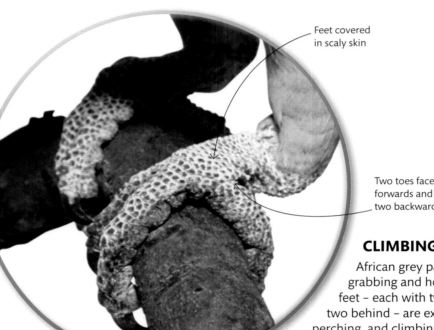

Feet covered in scaly skin

Two toes face forwards and two backwards

CLIMBING CLAWS

African grey parrots are great at grabbing and holding things. The feet – each with two toes in front and two behind – are excellent for grasping, perching, and climbing. They also use them to hold food up to their bills while feeding.

Long, narrow wings for acrobatic flying

STATS AND FACTS

60 YEARS

RECORD LIFESPAN

Some parrots have become well known for their talking skills. "Alex" was particularly famous because his amazing talents were studied by scientists.

VOCABULARY OF FAMOUS PARROTS

	100 (Alex)		800 (Prudle)		950 (N'kisi)
words	200	400	600	800	1,000
		300 (Bidi)			

LEVELS OF UNDERSTANDING (ALEX)

counted up to 6

recognized 7 colours

recognized 50 objects

LARGEST VOCABULARY

950 WORDS

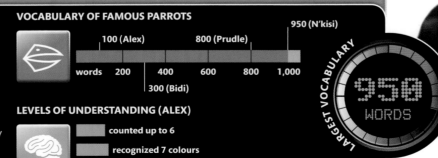

Adult birds have pale yellow eyes

Nostrils at top of bill

Moveable upper bill

Short, rounded chest feathers

WHO'S A PRETTY BOY?

Pet parrots are valued companions with friendly personalities. They can be taught to speak full sentences and may become closely attached to their owners.

"This parrot is as **clever** as a five-year-old **child**"

Feathered friends

Most parrot species have bright green feathers, but the African grey parrot is less colourful. Some are darker grey than others, but they all have a bright red tail and a white patch around the eyes.

NOT A BIRD BRAIN

Parrots are smart birds, and many people think they may have the intelligence of a human toddler. It used to be thought that they copied the sounds of words without understanding what they were saying, but scientists now suspect that they do. Some birds understand shapes, colours, and numbers – and can even solve simple problems for rewards of food. They are also good at manipulating objects, using their hinged bill like an extra foot to help them grasp and hook on to things.

BIRDS OF A FEATHER

Penguin feathers are short, but dense and well oiled. This traps a layer of air close to the skin, which locks in heat and helps to keep the penguins warm when swimming in icy seas. The trapped air also keeps the bird buoyant in water.

"Gentoos can stay underwater for **7 minutes** when diving"

SPEEDY SWIMMER
GENTOO PENGUIN

Penguins look comical on land but become speedy torpedoes at sea, and the gentoo penguin is the fastest of the lot. Its streamlined body is perfect for cutting through the water, and paddle-like wings – useless for flying – give it strong swimming power. Speed can be a matter of life or death in an Antarctic Ocean filled with predators, but gentoos swim so fast that they can launch out of the water like a missile to land on pack ice.

AT A GLANCE

- **SIZE** 76–81 cm (30–32 in) body length
- **HABITAT** Rocky coastlines and adjoining seas
- **LOCATION** Islands around Antarctica
- **DIET** Krill, fishes, worms, and squid

STATS AND FACTS

15 YEARS
MAXIMUM LIFESPAN

Gentoo penguins make short, shallow dives to search for prey and deeper, longer ones to catch it. When diving, their heart rate drops as they use up oxygen stored in their muscles.

TOP SWIMMING SPEED
36 KM/H

TEMPERATURE

-15°–10°C (surroundings)
39°C (body)

°F	0	25	50	75	100
°C	-15	0	15	30	45

DIVE

6 m deep (average search dive)
1–166 m deep (diving range)

ft	200	400	600
m	40	80	120	160	200

90 m (average food dive)

sec	25	50	100	150	200

50–170 (duration)

HEARTBEATS

bpm	30–50 (during dive)	1 min

bpm	86 (resting)	1 min

HIGHEST FLYER
RÜPPELL'S VULTURE

You don't expect to see a bird flying alongside a jet aeroplane, but then none can climb as high as a Rüppell's vulture. Several kilometres up, the air is very thin and it's hard to breathe, but a high vantage point is perfect for spotting carcasses. Its exceptional eyesight means that it can quickly pinpoint a meal – and be the first on the scene to gorge its fill.

Thick feathers keep bird warm at high altitudes

CRUISING FOR CARCASSES
Rüppell's vulture is a bird that really hits the heights – one reportedly collided with an aircraft at more than 11,000 m (36,000 ft). They regularly soar at 6,000 m (20,000 ft), riding rising columns of warm air to gain height. When a vulture spots a carcass it starts circling, alerting other members of the flock to its find.

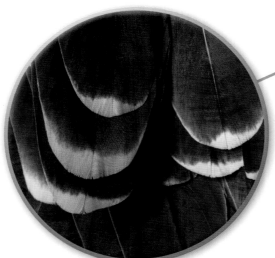

MOTTLED BROWN PLUMAGE
Vultures' wing feathers are broad – excellent for soaring and gliding. In the Rüppell's vulture they are distinctly patterned – dark brown with white tips – which gives the bird a white-spotted appearance from a distance.

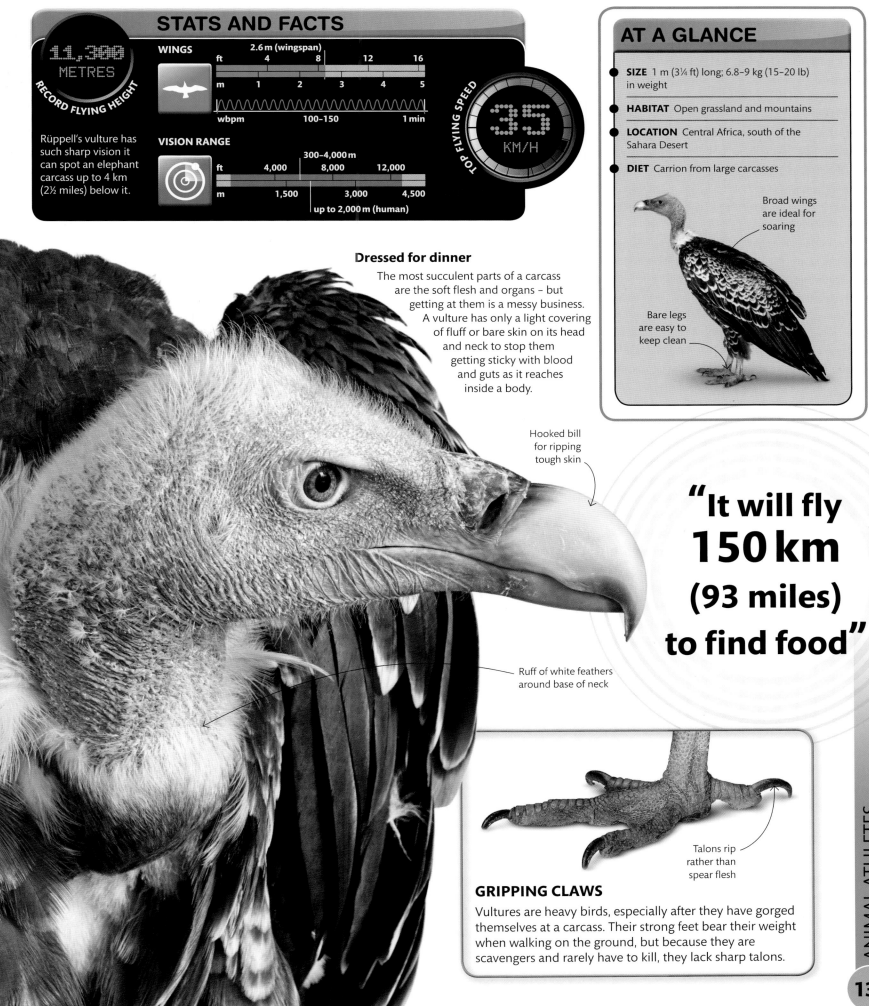

STATS AND FACTS

11,300 METRES
RECORD FLYING HEIGHT

Rüppell's vulture has such sharp vision it can spot an elephant carcass up to 4 km (2½ miles) below it.

WINGS

2.6 m (wingspan)

ft	4	8	12	16
m	1	2	3	4	5

wbpm   100–150   1 min

VISION RANGE

300–4,000 m

ft	4,000	8,000	12,000
m	1,500	3,000	4,500

up to 2,000 m (human)

TOP FLYING SPEED

35 KM/H

AT A GLANCE

- **SIZE** 1 m (3¼ ft) long; 6.8–9 kg (15–20 lb) in weight
- **HABITAT** Open grassland and mountains
- **LOCATION** Central Africa, south of the Sahara Desert
- **DIET** Carrion from large carcasses

Broad wings are ideal for soaring

Bare legs are easy to keep clean

Dressed for dinner

The most succulent parts of a carcass are the soft flesh and organs – but getting at them is a messy business. A vulture has only a light covering of fluff or bare skin on its head and neck to stop them getting sticky with blood and guts as it reaches inside a body.

Hooked bill for ripping tough skin

Ruff of white feathers around base of neck

"It will fly 150 km (93 miles) to find food"

Talons rip rather than spear flesh

GRIPPING CLAWS

Vultures are heavy birds, especially after they have gorged themselves at a carcass. Their strong feet bear their weight when walking on the ground, but because they are scavengers and rarely have to kill, they lack sharp talons.

ANIMAL ATHLETES

137

FASTEST ANIMAL

PEREGRINE FALCON

Diving downwards at over 300 km/h, a peregrine falcon moves faster than any other animal. It spots its victim from a high vantage point, then gives chase, closing in with a final drop, and grabbing its prey with its feet. The force of impact alone is usually enough to kill or stun the target.

Oxygen boost

The high-speed lifestyle of the peregrine demands lots of oxygen. Although its lungs are not that big, its breathing system has nine large air sacs that act like bellows. These flush air through the lungs so that more oxygen can enter the blood.

Talons sharply curved for tearing flesh

Tail acts as a rudder during flight

Flight feathers are long and rigid, reducing drag

BEAK AND CLAWS

Falcons need good weaponry to catch their prey. The tip of the bill is notched, which helps the bird grip its prey and kill it quickly. The legs are short and stout and armed with fearsome talons – they can hit prey in midair with great force.

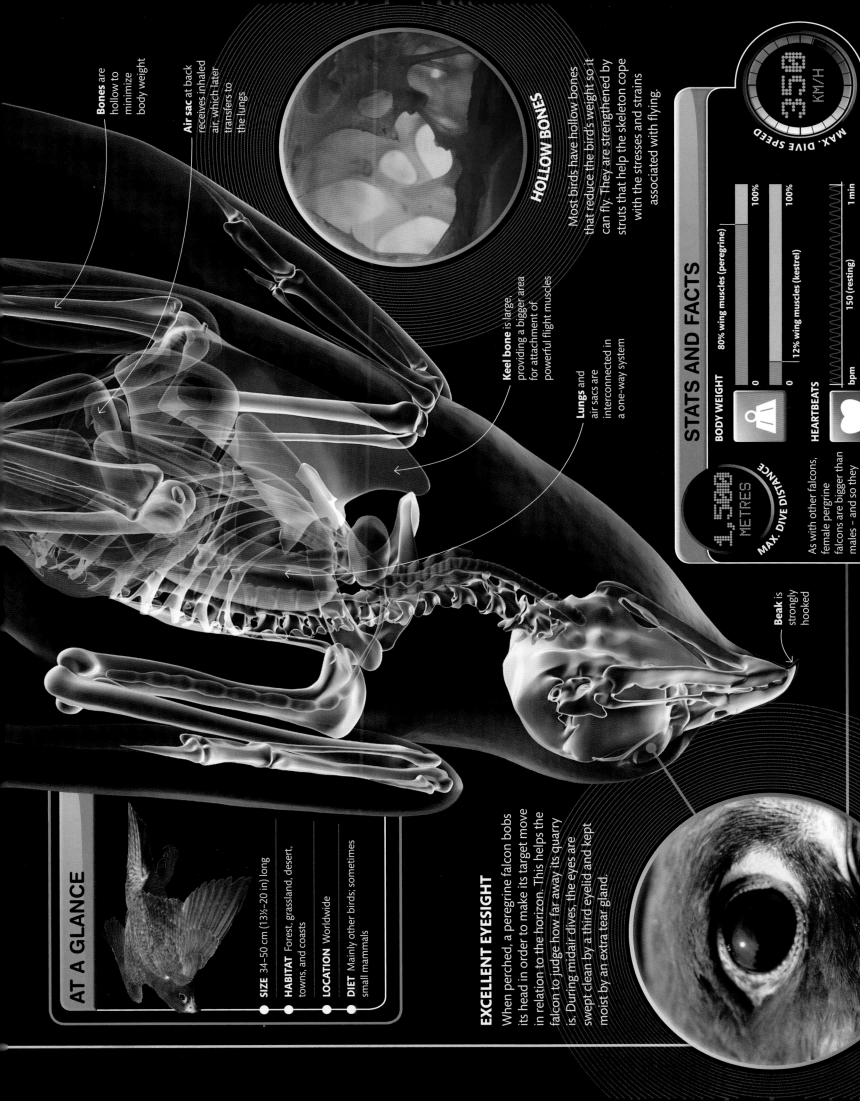

HOLLOW BONES

Bones are hollow to minimize body weight

Air sac at back receives inhaled air, which later transfers to the lungs

Most birds have hollow bones that reduce the bird's weight so it can fly. They are strengthened by struts that help the skeleton cope with the stresses and strains associated with flying.

Keel bone is large, providing a bigger area for attachment of powerful flight muscles

Lungs and air sacs are interconnected in a one-way system

Beak is strongly hooked

STATS AND FACTS

MAX. DIVE SPEED

389 KM/H

MAX. DIVE DISTANCE

1,500 METRES

As with other falcons, female peregrine falcons are bigger than males – and so they take the biggest prey.

BODY WEIGHT

80% wing muscles (peregrine)

0 ──────────────── 100%

12% wing muscles (kestrel)

0 ──────────────── 100%

HEARTBEATS

150 (resting)

bpm ──────────────── 1 min

350 (in flight)

bpm ──────────────── 1 min

AT A GLANCE

SIZE 34–50 cm (13½–20 in) long

HABITAT Forest, grassland, desert, towns, and coasts

LOCATION Worldwide

DIET Mainly other birds; sometimes small mammals

EXCELLENT EYESIGHT

When perched, a peregrine falcon bobs its head in order to make its target move in relation to the horizon. This helps the falcon to judge how far away its quarry is. During midair dives, the eyes are swept clean by a third eyelid and kept moist by an extra tear gland.

AERIAL ARCHITECT
BALD EAGLE

This large sea eagle likes the high life. It is a champion nest builder, choosing the tallest tree or cliff to raise its chicks in safety. Pairs mate for life and use the same nest – a tangle of branches and sticks – from year to year. That doesn't mean the nest is finished: every year they add new material, so the nests get wider, heavier, and deeper as time goes by.

SPACE TO GROW

Chicks hatch after 35 days of incubation, and at first are dwarfed by their giant nest. There are usually between one and three chicks in the nest but not all will survive. One parent tends the chicks while the other hunts for food. The chicks spend up to three months in the nest before flying. They will be ready to breed themselves after about four years, returning to the area they were born in.

"Its grip is **ten times stronger** than that of **a human**"

STATS AND FACTS

1 TONNE
WEIGHT OF NEST

The same taloned feet that bald eagles use for grabbing slippery fish are put to good use in lifting branches for the nest. This eagle is so strong, it can even lift a small deer.

NEST DIAMETER

2.5 m (average)

ft	3	6	9	12
m	1	2	3	4

GRIP STRENGTH

400 (human)　　3,500–4,000

N	2,000	4,000	6,000
lb	5	10	15
kg	2	4	6	8

6.8 kg (max. weight lifted)

LENGTH OF CLAWS

6 cm

in	1	2	3	
cm	2	4	6	8	10

FLYING SPEED
48 KM/H

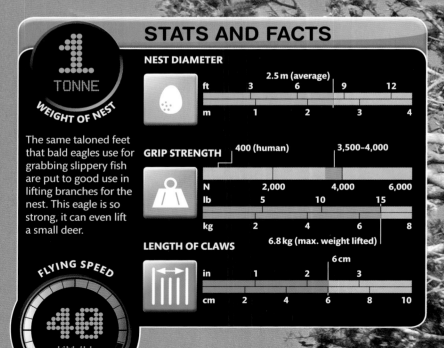

LETHAL WEAPONS

The bald eagle has a massive hooked bill that is used to tear prey apart. However, the kill is usually carried out with the feet – its sharply-hooked talons grip the victim and may pierce its vital organs.

Fish supper

Bald eagles take a variety of prey, but have a particular preference for fish – especially salmon, which they snatch from the rivers of their native North America. The youngsters grow fast on their protein-rich diet.

BIGGEST
TREE NEST
BUILT BY A BIRD

Adult birds will tear food into strips for feeding to the young

AT A GLANCE

SIZE Head to tail 71–96 cm (28–38 in) long, weight 3–6.3 kg (6½–14 lb)

HABITAT Tundra and open land near water

LOCATION North America

DIET Fish, mammals, other birds, and carrion

White feathers on the head and tail

Young birds are mainly brown in colour

Nests are built in large trees or on rocky outcrops near rivers or coasts

GREATEST ARTIST
SATIN BOWERBIRD

A supreme show-off, the male satin bowerbird woos females with his artistic skills. He builds a bower of sticks or straw in a specially cleared arena and decorates it with anything in the forest that takes his fancy. Flowers, berries – even brightly coloured bottle tops – may be added to complete the effect. Females that approve of his efforts mate with him, then leave to raise their families alone.

AT A GLANCE

- **SIZE** 23–27 cm (9–10½ in) long

- **HABITAT** Rainforest and the edges of drier eucalyptus forest

- **LOCATION** Coastal and adjacent inland areas of Eastern Australia

- **DIET** Fruits, seeds, leaves, nectar, and small animals

STATS AND FACTS

36

NUMBER OF DECORATIONS

The arch of the satin bowerbird's bower runs north-south, forming an avenue with a decorated area at each end.

TIME TO MAKE BOWER

2 DAYS

BOWER

35 cm (height of bower)
30 cm (length of central avenue)

in		5	10		15	
cm	10	20		30		40

BOWER COLOURS PREFERRED

5% (purple and yellow)
35% (white)   20% (blue)

0	25% (purple)		15% (yellow)	100%

DISTANCE

100 m (distance between competing bowers)

ft	100	200	300	400	
m		50		100	150

"Males **often steal** decorations from **rivals**"

TOUGH-SKINNED TURTLE

Unlike other turtles, the leatherback has thick, ridged skin on its back instead of a hard bony shell. Its body is countershaded – darker above than below – so it is less likely to be seen by predators searching for a big dinner. Its pale belly looks like sunlight to anything looking up, while from above a predator sees only a dim shadow in the dark ocean.

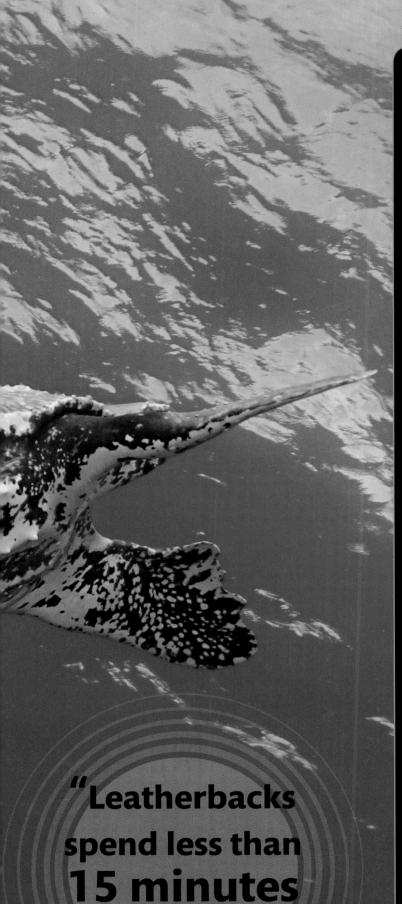

POWER SWIMMER
LEATHERBACK TURTLE

Speeding through the water, the leatherback is the largest turtle and the fastest reptile. Enormous front flippers and a slimline body help make it a champion swimmer, even in very cold waters. Unlike most reptiles, the leatherback can generate a lot of body heat, and this keeps its muscles at peak performance. It makes the most of this central heating by spending almost all its waking hours swimming. This frantic lifestyle is fuelled by a diet made up almost entirely of jellyfish.

AT A GLANCE

- **SIZE** Usually up to 2 m (6½ ft) long, but record-breaking individuals are around 3 m (10 ft) long
- **HABITAT** Open ocean waters
- **LOCATION** Worldwide, even reaching into the Arctic Circle
- **DIET** Almost entirely jellyfish, but sometimes squid and other soft prey

*"*Leatherbacks spend less than **15 minutes** a day resting*"*

STATS AND FACTS

1,200 METRES
RECORD DIVE DEPTH

A leatherback turtle's blood flows around its body in a way that traps heat close to its vital organs. This enables it to swim in colder waters than other marine reptiles.

RECORD SPEED
35.3
KM/H

DISTANCE SWUM DAILY

				30–65 km	
miles	10	20	30		40
km	10	20	30	40	50	60	70

DIVE

	12–15 (duration)			
		85 (record duration)		
min	20	40	60	80	100
ft	250	500	750	
m	100	200	300

200 m (dive depth)

BODY TEMPERATURE

			25°C
°F	50	70	
°C	10	20	30

SPLASHY SPRINTER
BASILISK LIZARD

In the flooded forest habitat of a basilisk lizard, predators lurk in the trees, as well as in the water. Sometimes, the fastest escape route is a quick dash on two legs across the surface of a stream. Basilisks are also called "Jesus Christ" lizards after the Bible story of Jesus walking on water, but in fact they run rather than walk.

Powerful hind legs for running

MIRACLE FEET

Basilisk lizards have specially adapted feet to help them make their water crossings. Their back feet are unusually large, and each toe is edged with flaps of skin. These are kept folded when the lizard runs on land, but are unfolded when it runs on water to create a greater surface area and help it to stay afloat.

Long fingers

Tail helps lizard to balance

STATS AND FACTS

13 YEARS
LIFESPAN IN CAPTIVITY

Younger, more lightweight basilisks are the best water runners. As they get older they eventually become too heavy to do it at all.

RUNNING ON WATER   2–7 (duration)

	sec	2	4	6	8
	ft	30	60	90	

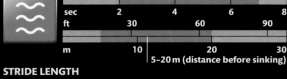

	m	10	20	30

5–20 m (distance before sinking)

STRIDE LENGTH

15 cm (when standing on 2 legs)

	in	2	4	6	
	cm	5	10	15	20

18 KM/H
RUNNING SPEED ON WATER

CLIMBING CLAWS

As well as their extraordinary ability to run on water, basilisk lizards are expert swimmers and climbers, too. Long, sharp claws help the lizard to grip as it climbs forest trees to escape predators.

IN MOTION

Each stride the basilisk lizard takes over the water has three phases. During the first phase, the lizard's foot goes straight down, moving water aside and making a bubble of air around the foot. In the second phase, the upward force created by the first phase is enough to keep the lizard's body above water. In the final phase, the lizard kicks its leg back, pushing itself forward. Each foot only makes brief contact with the water surface, and the lizard has to keep moving quickly to avoid sinking.

Green colouring camouflages lizard in forest

"Bubbles under its feet keep the lizard afloat"

The need for speed

Many tiny insects can stand on still water because their weight is supported by the tightness of the water surface, which acts like an elastic film. But a basilisk is too heavy for this and can only be supported when it runs. It leaves a trail of water droplets as it races across the surface.

Arms held out as it runs

Strong back legs

HEAVIEST WATER-WALKING ANIMAL

FASTEST SWIMMER
SAILFISH

Nothing can out-swim a sailfish. Its sleek body is built for speed. The body muscles are flushed blood-red because they contain a pigment that can store oxygen to provide an energy boost when needed. A sailfish chases down its prey of smaller fishes and squid by flashing its sail to herd shoals together into a bait ball and thrashing the water with its bill to stun as many as possible.

AT A GLANCE

- **SIZE** Length 2.4–3.5 m (7¾–11 ft); maximum recorded weight 100 kg (220 lb)
- **HABITAT** Warm surface waters of the open ocean
- **LOCATION** Worldwide
- **DIET** Smaller fishes and squid

STATS AND FACTS

13 YEARS
MAXIMUM LIFESPAN

In addition to oxygen-storing muscle, a sailfish also has a heat generator in its head to keep its brain and eyes warm, maximizing their performance.

MAXIMUM SPEED
110 KM/H

DISTANCE SWUM

35,000 km (in a lifetime)

miles	6,000	12,000	18,000	24,000
km	10,000	20,000	30,000	40,000

SWIMMING DEPTH

0–200 m

ft	200	400	600	800
m	50	100	150	200	250

TEMPERATURE

20°–30°C (surroundings) 34°–35°C (brain)

°F	50	70	90	110
°C	10	20	30	40	50

"**A sailfish can swim faster than a sprinting cheetah**"

COLOUR CHANGE
During high-speed chases, the sailfish's sail is folded and so not clearly visible, but when excited – or when closing in on a kill – the sail can be raised. Like a chameleon, the sailfish can rapidly change its skin colour, depending on its mood.

COCOONED CORAL CRUNCHER
PARROTFISH

Many of Earth's white-sand beaches have been created by fish. In warm, shallow tropical seas, parrotfishes are responsible for dumping tonnes of sand each year – and in calm coastal waters this can build up to form a beach. Parrotfishes get their name from their teeth, which are fused together to form a hard beak – used for rasping at hard coral. The algae living in the coral are nutritious, but the hard rocky skeleton is not. It crumbles inside the fish, but then passes straight through the digestive system and emerges at the other end as white coral sand.

AT A GLANCE

- **SIZE** 0.3–1.3 m (1–4¼ ft) long, depending on the species
- **HABITAT** Shallow ocean waters and coral reefs
- **LOCATION** Worldwide, but especially in the tropics
- **DIET** Coral and algae

STATS AND FACTS

15 YEARS
MAXIMUM LIFESPAN

Around three-quarters of a parrotfish's diet is hard rock.

FOOD CONSUMPTION

5% (other organisms and detritus)
50% (chalky rock)
0   25% (sand)   20% (algae)   100%

WEIGHT OF SAND PRODUCED

90 kg/year by one parrotfish

1,000 kg/year by parrotfishes on one acre of reef

DEPTH AT WHICH FOUND
200 METRES

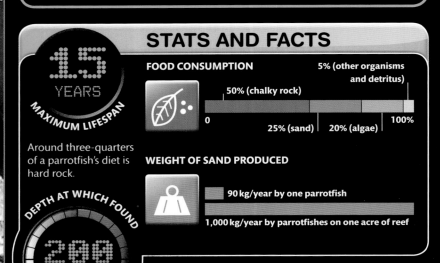

SWEET DREAMS
During the day, the queen parrotfish is busy rasping at coral, but at night it sleeps in a bubble-like cocoon, made from its own mucus. The function of the cocoon is uncertain, but it may help to disguise the scent of the parrotfish from predators.

BEST
BEACH BUILDER

HITTING THE TARGET

When the archerfish fixes its tongue against a groove running along the roof of the mouth it forms a narrow tube. By squeezing its gills, it can shoot a jet of water through the tube. Young archerfishes get better at shooting down insects with practice.

"Archerfishes jump **30 cm** (12 in) out of the water to grab **prey**"

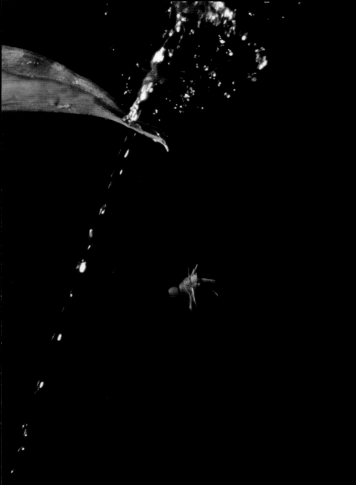

BEST SHOT
ARCHERFISH

Rarely missing a target, the archerfish produces a jet of water from its mouth to knock prey into the water. It can shoot the waterjet more than two metres (6½ ft) into the air to catch an unwary insect or a spider resting on an overhanging leaf. Not only does the archerfish have excellent eyesight, it can even adjust its aim to make up for the fact that from below the water, the target's position looks different to what it really is. The power of its shot depends upon the size of its prey.

AT A GLANCE

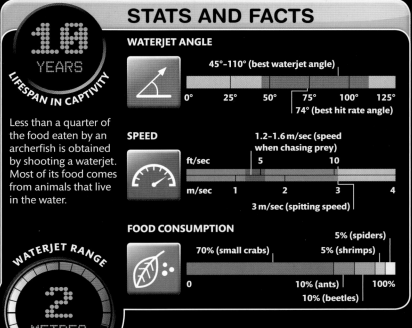

- **SIZE** 10–40 cm (4–16 in), depending on the species
- **HABITAT** Typically in brackish water of estuaries and mangroves
- **LOCATION** From India to the west Pacific islands, New Guinea, and North Australia
- **DIET** Insects, spiders, small fishes, and crustaceans

STATS AND FACTS

18 YEARS
LIFESPAN IN CAPTIVITY

Less than a quarter of the food eaten by an archerfish is obtained by shooting a waterjet. Most of its food comes from animals that live in the water.

WATERJET RANGE
2 METRES

WATERJET ANGLE

45°–110° (best waterjet angle)

| 0° | 25° | 50° | 75° | 100° | 125° |

74° (best hit rate angle)

SPEED

1.2–1.6 m/sec (speed when chasing prey)

| ft/sec | | 5 | | 10 | |
| m/sec | 1 | 2 | | 3 | 4 |

3 m/sec (spitting speed)

FOOD CONSUMPTION

5% (spiders)
70% (small crabs)   5% (shrimps)

| 0 | | 10% (ants) | 100% |

10% (beetles)

ANIMAL ATHLETES

153

SLOW MOVER
SEAHORSE

Seahorses are built for hanging on – not for speed. Even if a seahorse was in a hurry, it could still take half an hour to swim the length of a human arm. Most fish have a thrashing tail that they use to propel themselves forwards. A seahorse has a long, thin tail with a coil at the end that it uses to clutch onto seaweed and other underwater objects, but not for swimming. Instead, a seahorse swims slowly forwards by flickering a fin on its back – but it prefers to cover short distances, staying close to the protection of seaweed.

Strange fish

Seahorses are unusual fish in many ways. A seahorse swims upright, it has a flexible neck, and it holds its head at right angles to the rest of its body. It has no scales, instead bony rings of armour lie under the skin. A seahorse also has a very small mouth. This means it can only eat tiny animals that live around underwater weeds.

Small mouth at end of tubular snout

DORSAL FIN

The fluttering dorsal (back) fin of a seahorse provides all the propulsion for swimming – but it doesn't generate much speed. This fin flutters from side to side around 40 times per second. In comparison, most other fishes have a dorsal fin that hardly moves at all. The seahorse uses another a pair of fins located just behind its head to steer itself through the water.

Fin controls movement

Tail grabs hold of weeds

SLOWEST-SWIMMING FISH

CARING FATHERS

Male seahorses do all the parental caring. After an elaborate courtship, the female lays her eggs in the belly pouch of a male, and he fertilizes them. The eggs hatch in this pouch and when the seahorses are big enough to be released, their father actually gives birth.

Father's belly swollen with fertilized eggs

Eggs hatch in the father's pouch

STATS AND FACTS

SPEED PER HOUR OF SLOWEST

15 METRES

HOME RANGE

1–400 sq m

| sq ft | 1,000 | 2,000 | 3,000 | 4,000 | 5,000 |
| sq m | 100 | 200 | 300 | 400 | 500 |

MAXIMUM DEPTH

100 METRES

PREY SIZE

0.25–3 mm

| in | 1/16 | 1/8 | 3/16 |
| mm | 1 | 2 | 3 | 4 | 5 |

A seahorse may move slowly, but it's possible that its fluttering fin confuses predators and helps camouflage the fish in the weeds.

Prehensile tail can wrap around coral or seaweed

"The dwarf seahorse from the Bahamas is the slowest of all"

AT A GLANCE

● **SIZE** 3–35 cm (1¼–14 in) long

● **HABITAT** Shallow coastal ocean waters

● **LOCATION** Worldwide

● **DIET** Tiny swimming animals, such as crustaceans

SLIMIEST ANIMAL
HAGFISH

When threatened, a hagfish squirts slime from up to 200 pores along the sides of its body in order to distract its attacker. Predatory fish learn to leave hagfishes well alone, since an encounter could leave them with clogged gills and unable to breathe. The hagfish is a deep-sea scavenger, often burrowing into whale corpses to get at the flesh.

Short sensory tentacles are used to detect food

Hagfish have three pairs of sensory tentacles around the mouth

*"The **hagfish** is also known as the **snot eel**"*

Slime is produced from two rows of tiny pores on both sides of the body

FILING ITS FOOD
Instead of jaws, the hagfish has a circular mouth with a hard plate made of cartilage that it can push in and out. On the plate are two rows of triangular teeth that are used for clasping and rasping at dead flesh, like a file.

Backward-pointing teeth direct food towards the throat

CONTORTIONIST
The body of a hagfish is so flexible that it can tie itself into a knot. The lack of a backbone and a higher than average amount of body fluid allow it to do this. A hagfish deliberately knots itself so that more of its body can push against the wall of a carcass. This gives it the power to tear off large chunks of flesh.

Body twisted into a knot

AT A GLANCE

- **SIZE** Length 20–130 cm (8–51 in) long, depending on the species
- **HABITAT** Cool ocean waters and the deep sea
- **LOCATION** Worldwide
- **DIET** Carcasses of larger animals and living worms

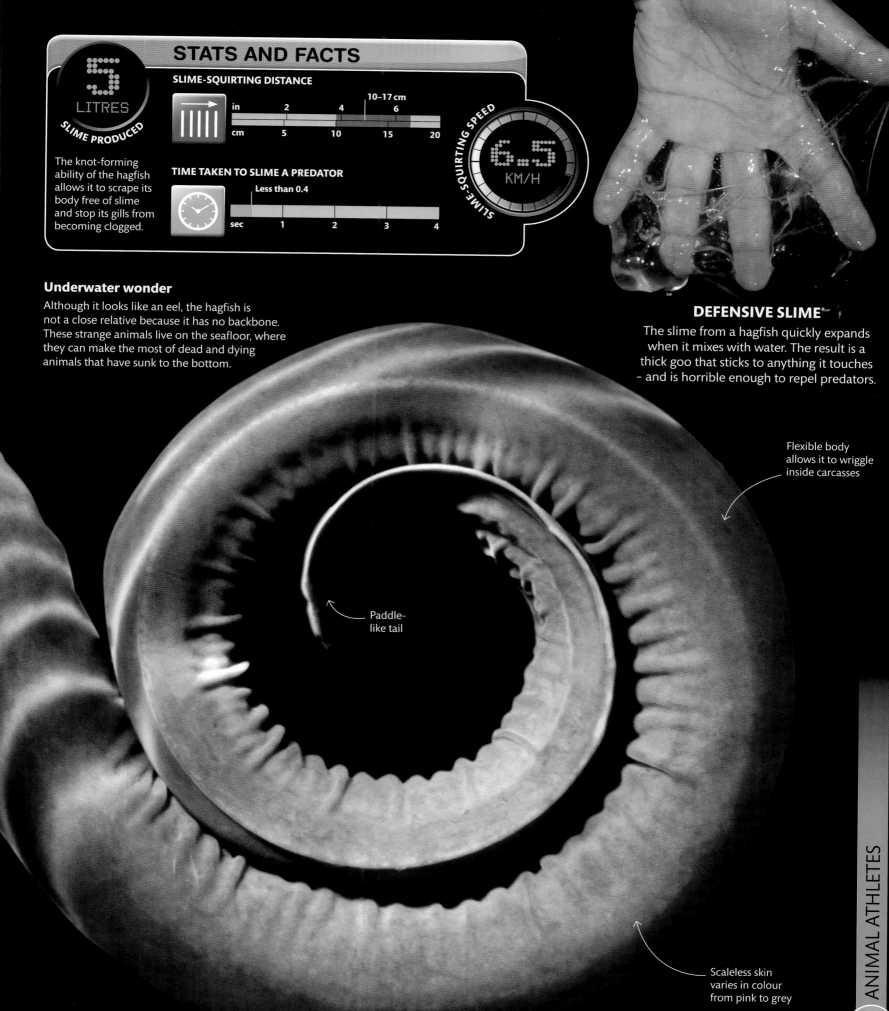

STATS AND FACTS

5 LITRES
SLIME PRODUCED

The knot-forming ability of the hagfish allows it to scrape its body free of slime and stop its gills from becoming clogged.

SLIME-SQUIRTING DISTANCE

10–17 cm

| in | | 2 | | 4 | | 6 | |
| cm | 5 | | 10 | | 15 | | 20 |

TIME TAKEN TO SLIME A PREDATOR

Less than 0.4

| sec | 1 | 2 | 3 | 4 |

SLIME-SQUIRTING SPEED
6.5 KM/H

Underwater wonder

Although it looks like an eel, the hagfish is not a close relative because it has no backbone. These strange animals live on the seafloor, where they can make the most of dead and dying animals that have sunk to the bottom.

DEFENSIVE SLIME

The slime from a hagfish quickly expands when it mixes with water. The result is a thick goo that sticks to anything it touches – and is horrible enough to repel predators.

Flexible body allows it to wriggle inside carcasses

Paddle-like tail

Scaleless skin varies in colour from pink to grey

DEADLIEST ANIMAL
ANOPHELES MOSQUITO

It only takes one bite from a very small insect to pass on a potentially fatal disease. Malaria is an illness caused by a microscopic parasite that infects the blood. It is carried by the *Anopheles* mosquito, which lives in tropical areas around the globe. Males drink nectar but the females also need blood to make their eggs. When a female bites and sucks blood, she passes on the malaria parasite too.

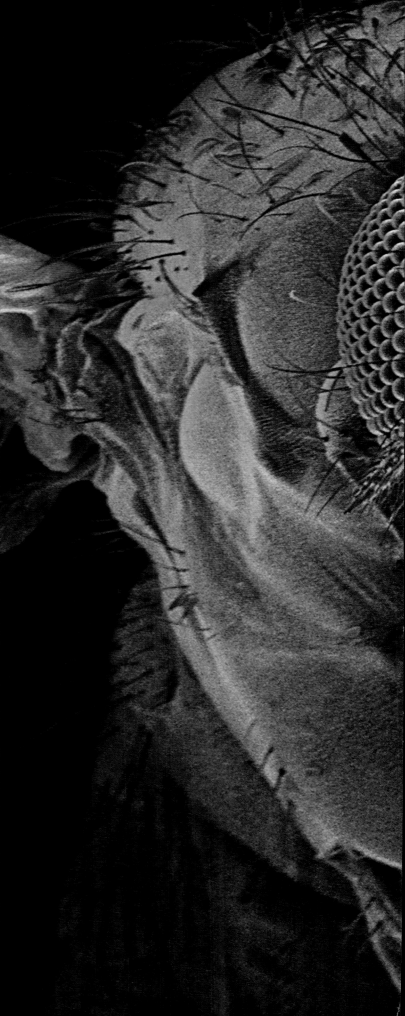

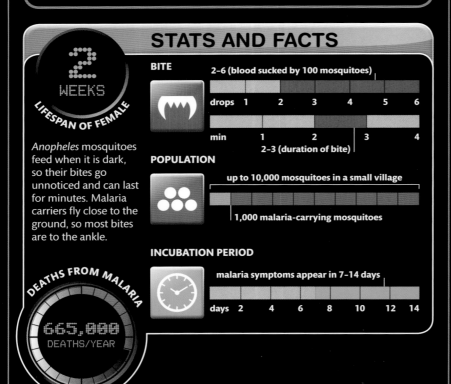

AT A GLANCE

- **SIZE** Body length 3–6 mm (⅛–¼ in)
- **HABITAT** Any warm habitat close to water, where the eggs are laid and larval and pupal stages mature
- **LOCATION** Tropical zone and other warm regions
- **DIET** Females drink nectar and feed on blood to make eggs; males drink nectar

STATS AND FACTS

2 WEEKS
LIFESPAN OF FEMALE

Anopheles mosquitoes feed when it is dark, so their bites go unnoticed and can last for minutes. Malaria carriers fly close to the ground, so most bites are to the ankle.

DEATHS FROM MALARIA
665,000
DEATHS/YEAR

BITE

2–6 (blood sucked by 100 mosquitoes)

drops	1	2	3	4	5	6

min	1	2	3	4

2–3 (duration of bite)

POPULATION

up to 10,000 mosquitoes in a small village

1,000 malaria-carrying mosquitoes

INCUBATION PERIOD

malaria symptoms appear in 7–14 days

days	2	4	6	8	10	12	14

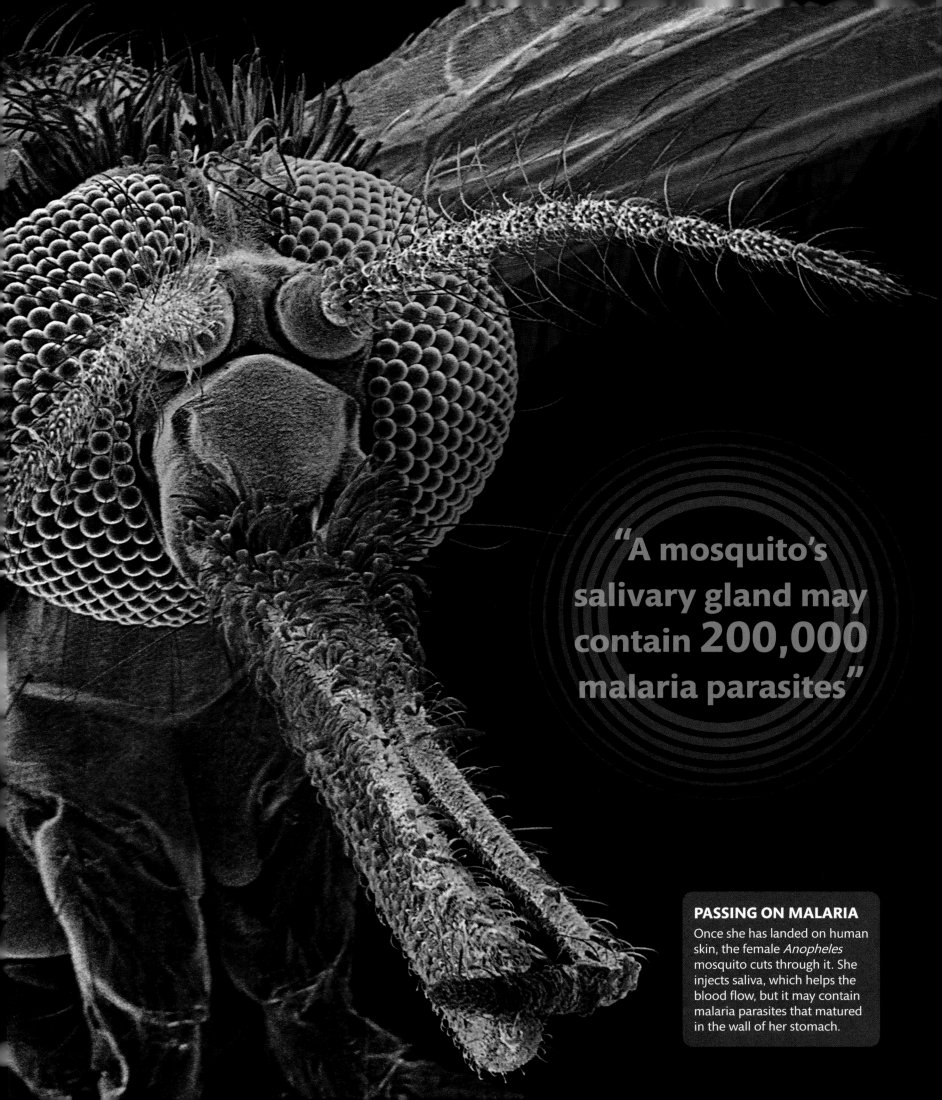

"A mosquito's salivary gland may contain **200,000** malaria parasites"

PASSING ON MALARIA
Once she has landed on human skin, the female *Anopheles* mosquito cuts through it. She injects saliva, which helps the blood flow, but it may contain malaria parasites that matured in the wall of her stomach.

HOT SHOT
BOMBARDIER BEETLE

When a bombardier beetle senses that it is under attack, it takes drastic action to defend itself – it blasts its assailant with a jet of boiling fluid from its rear end. As well as being extremely hot, this liquid also stings the attacker. The beetle can aim its spray with extreme accuracy, hitting its target – such as marauding ants with dangerous bites and stings – square on.

AT A GLANCE

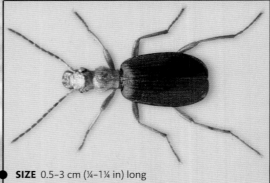

SIZE 0.5–3 cm (¼–1¼ in) long

HABITAT Forest and grassland

LOCATION Worldwide

DIET Other insects

TAKING AIM

Ants will attack from any angle, so the bombardier's spray has to be able to reach its front legs (1), back legs (2), and behind itself (3). Its abdomen can curl up or down and there are tiny shield-like deflectors in the nozzle exit that help angle the spray. The mystery behind this amazing weapon is how the beetle remains unharmed by its effects:

MOST EXPLOSIVE ANIMAL

STATS AND FACTS

100 °C
TEMPERATURE OF SPRAY

SPEED OF EMERGING SPRAY

2.5–20 m/sec

ft/sec		20	40	60	80
m/sec	5	10	15	20	25

The bombardier beetle's strike is not only fast and accurate, but it can spray an attacker some distance away.

SPRAYING DISTANCE

20–30 cm for a 2 cm-long beetle

in	4	8	12	16
cm	10	20	30	40

20–29
SPRAYS PER CHAMBER OF FLUID

Spray nozzle

Abdomen raised to spray over its head

Chemical stores

Mixing chamber

Ejection nozzle

CHEMICAL COCKTAIL

The explosion is created by mixing two chemicals that are stored in separate chambers in the beetle's abdomen. The reaction is so fast it generates a huge amount of heat. The spray is fired out from a revolving nozzle at the tip of the beetle's abdomen with a loud pop.

"They can squirt 20 times before running out of fluid"

Keep off!

Although the beetles have hard wing covers, these may not give them enough protection when under attack. Squirting their scalding spray gives them more time to unfurl their wings and get away.

ANIMAL ATHLETES

SMALL, BUT MIGHTY
COPEPOD

Copepods are tiny creatures that live in the world's ponds and oceans. They look simple but they hold more records than almost any other animal. Firstly, they are the most numerous animal, with trillions of times more living now than the number of humans who have ever lived. They also contend for the titles of fastest and strongest animals for their size.

STATS AND FACTS

1 BILLION TRILLION COPEPODS IN OCEANS

Copepods do not tire easily. They use some legs for swimming, and others for jumping to escape predators.

JUMP

50 cm (distance)

in	5	10	15	20
cm	20	40		60

50–140 (while jumping)

leg beats/sec 50 100 150

SPEED 0.6 M/SEC

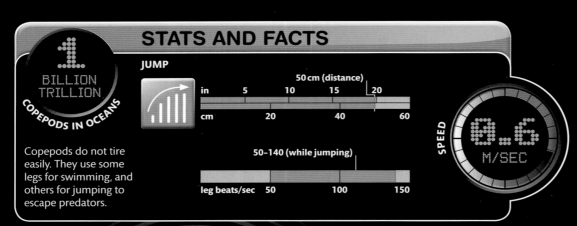

"There are 13,000 species of copepod"

Antennae for sensing predators and prey

Tear-shaped body is almost clear

Females have two egg sacs at rear of body

Tail

Speed and strength

A copepod's leg muscles allow it to thrust through water at record speed, pushing forward with a jerky, jumping motion. Moving through water for a copepod is like swimming through syrup for a human, so it is also ten times stronger than any animal for its size.

WALK THIS WAY
MILLIPEDE

Millipede means "a thousand legs", and this creature tries hard to live up to its name. Despite their impressive number of legs, millipedes cannot run fast but are excellent burrowers, using their leg power to push into the earth.

Millipedes coil to expose a thick, protective armour

Pair of short antennae on head

MOST LEGS

Body armour

Millipedes are not very speedy so to escape predators they coil up and rely on their armour, or release poisonous oils to warn off attackers. When a millipede walks, its legs work together and a wave of movement ripples down its body.

"Millipedes hatch with only 6 legs"

STATS AND FACTS

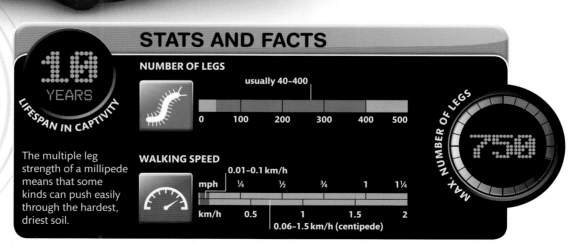

18 YEARS LIFESPAN IN CAPTIVITY

NUMBER OF LEGS

usually 40–400

| 0 | 100 | 200 | 300 | 400 | 500 |

The multiple leg strength of a millipede means that some kinds can push easily through the hardest, driest soil.

WALKING SPEED

0.01–0.1 km/h

| mph | ¼ | ½ | ¾ | 1 | 1¼ |
| km/h | 0.5 | 1 | 1.5 | 2 |

0.06–1.5 km/h (centipede)

MAX. NUMBER OF LEGS **750**

ANIMAL ATHLETES

163

STUNNING SNAPPER
PISTOL SHRIMP

Meet the shrimp with a sonic weapon. The snapping claws of pistol shrimps make so much noise in the ocean that they are said to interfere with ships' sonar and whale songs. The shrimp's enlarged claw snaps shut so fast it creates a shock wave, which can be used to kill prey.

Hard carapace is produced by the skin

TOUGH SHELL SUIT

Unlike a human, a shrimp wears its skeleton on the outside – in the form of hard armour called a carapace. Its skin produces this coating using a tough substance called chitin. A few parts stay thin and flexible – such as around the moveable leg joints – but the whole lot has to be shed at intervals so the body inside can grow.

Cells will form new carapace when shrimp moults

Heart pumps blood into body cavity via a few blood vessels

Stomach

Fleshy inner skin

LOUDEST ANIMAL OF ALL

Tail fan

Swimming legs (five pairs)

AT A GLANCE

SIZE Up to 5 cm (2 in) long

HABITAT Coastal waters, mostly on coral reefs and in tidal pools

LOCATION Worldwide

DIET Other shrimps, crabs, and small fishes

Feeling the pinch

Like other crustaceans, pistol shrimps have two front claws. One claw is used as a pincer to manipulate food, the other is much larger. The moveable part of this claw acts like a miniature hammer that snaps down to create a sudden pulse of sound energy that can knock out its prey.

Walking legs (three pairs)

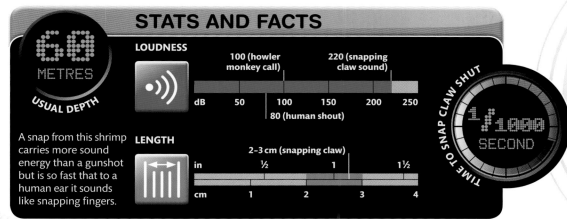

60 METRES
USUAL DEPTH

LOUDNESS

100 (howler monkey call) · 220 (snapping claw sound)

dB	50	100	150	200	250

80 (human shout)

A snap from this shrimp carries more sound energy than a gunshot but is so fast that to a human ear it sounds like snapping fingers.

LENGTH

2–3 cm (snapping claw)

in	½	1	1½

cm	1	2	3	4

TIME TO SNAP CLAW SHUT

1/1000 SECOND

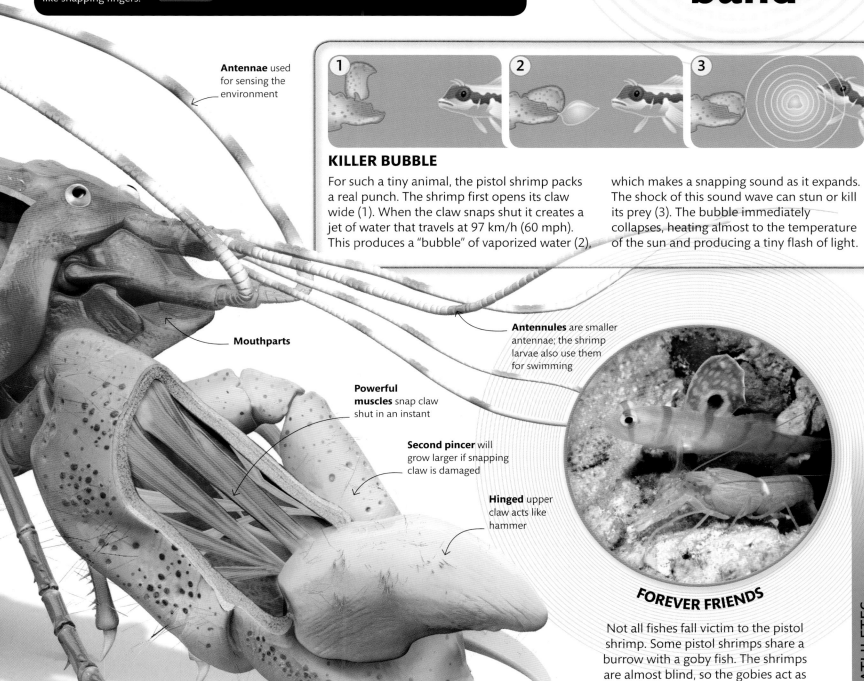

Antennae used for sensing the environment

KILLER BUBBLE

For such a tiny animal, the pistol shrimp packs a real punch. The shrimp first opens its claw wide (1). When the claw snaps shut it creates a jet of water that travels at 97 km/h (60 mph). This produces a "bubble" of vaporized water (2), which makes a snapping sound as it expands. The shock of this sound wave can stun or kill its prey (3). The bubble immediately collapses, heating almost to the temperature of the sun and producing a tiny flash of light.

Antennules are smaller antennae; the shrimp larvae also use them for swimming

Mouthparts

Powerful muscles snap claw shut in an instant

Second pincer will grow larger if snapping claw is damaged

Hinged upper claw acts like hammer

Lower claw acts as anvil

FOREVER FRIENDS

Not all fishes fall victim to the pistol shrimp. Some pistol shrimps share a burrow with a goby fish. The shrimps are almost blind, so the gobies act as "minders" and watch out for large predators. In return, the goby gets a place to shelter.

ANIMAL ATHLETES

MASTER OF DISGUISE
MIMIC OCTOPUS

In shallow Asian seas lives perhaps the best impersonator in the natural world. Discovered in 1998, the mimic octopus is a superb imitator of other sea creatures, switching from one to another in an instant. It uses its patterned arms and ability to change colour to full effect, turning into a drifting jellyfish one minute and wriggling like a brittle star the next. Its antics are good enough to repel attackers and are its only defence in waters that are full of predators.

FOR MY NEXT IMPRESSION...

The mimic octopus's favourite impersonation is of a flounder – a type of flatfish. The flat shape is perfect for swimming quickly through water. When threatened, however, it can change into more dangerous characters – such as a deadly sea snake or a scorpion fish – in less than 10 seconds.

BRITTLE STAR

Partially buries its body and six arms and waves the other two to look like a snake

SEA SNAKE

FLOUNDER

Folds all its arms behind its body to look like a flatfish

STATS AND FACTS

13
SPECIES IMPERSONATED

The mimic octopus controls the pigment in its skin with its nervous system, and so can change colour very quickly.

DEPTH

ft	10	20	2–12 m 30	40

| m | 2 | 4 | 6 | 8 | 10 | 12 | 14 |

DAILY ACTIVITIES

3 hours (sitting)
1.5 hours (crawling)
1.5 hours (swimming)
6 hours out of den
18 hours in den

TOP SWIMMING SPEED

1
KM/H

"It changes shape to fool its predators"

Brown and white patterning can quickly change to brown all over

SIZE 60 cm (2 ft) armspan

HABITAT Muddy-bottomed shallow waters, usually at the mouths of rivers

LOCATION Tropical Southeast Asia

DIET Small animals, such as fishes and crabs

That sinking feeling

The mimic octopus is also thought to impersonate a jellyfish. When swimming in the upper levels of the ocean, it sometimes puts its arms above its head to look like the bell of a jellyfish, then lets itself sink slowly to the bottom. This impersonation may deter predators that fear a jellyfish's sting.

ANIMAL ATHLETES

167

RECORD-BREAKERS

Animals move around to search for food, patrol their territories, find mates, and escape from attack. Many have developed startling athletic prowess due to their strength, speed, and stamina. Bigger muscles make animals stronger, and some animals have muscles that can work faster too. Animals also show amazing agility and skill when they catch their food, defend themselves, or build their homes. Some even make and use tools.

*"Bolas spiders catch their **prey** by **swinging** a sticky blob of **silk** on a line"*

FASTEST WINGBEATS

● Honey bee	230 beats per second
● Club-winged manakin (displaying)	100 beats per second
● Horned sungem	90 beats per second
● Skipper butterfly	20 beats per second

HONEY BEE

TINIEST NEST

The vervain hummingbird builds the smallest nest, just 2 cm (¾ in) in diameter – about the size of half a walnut.

WALNUT

FASTEST FLAPPER

True flight occurs in bats, and most insects and birds. They all need wings to fly and the fastest flapper of all is the midge, a small fly that beats its wings a staggering 1,046 times every second. The rapid wingbeat also allows the midge to hover.

1,046 TIMES

200 METRES

LONGEST GLIDES

● Colugo	150 m (490 ft)
● Paradise tree snake	100 m (330 ft)
● Flying squirrel	90 m (295 ft)
● Flying dragon	60 m (200 ft)
● Gliding treefrog	30 m (98 ft)

SURPRISE TACTICS

When under attack, a horned lizard squirts a jet of blood from its eyes to scare away its enemy. The gory jet can be shot as far as 1.2 m (4 ft).

HORNED LIZARD

EASY GLIDER

Riding on updrafts of air as they jump out of the water, flying fish can glide for 200 m (655 ft) or farther. They can reach speeds of 60 km/h (37 mph) and rise as high as 1.2 m (4 ft) above the ocean.

PARADISE TREE SNAKE

CHEETAH

FASTEST ANIMALS

●	Peregrine falcon	350 km/h (220 mph)
●	Cheetah	114 km/h (70 mph)
●	Atlantic sailfish	100 km/h (62 mph)
●	Pronghorn	98 km/h (60 mph)
●	Ostrich	70 km/h (44 mph)
●	Sei whale	60 km/h (37 mph)
●	Spiny-tailed iguana	35 km/h (22 mph)
●	Camel spider	16 km/h (10 mph)

PATIENT EATER

The Lahore sheep tick – a bloodsucking parasite – has phenomenal stamina. It can survive for 18 years between meals.

CHIMPANZEE

SWIFTEST FLYERS

A peregrine falcon may move more rapidly when diving in pursuit of prey, but the fastest bird in flapping flight is the spine-tail swift, which can reach speeds of 160 km/h (100 mph).

160 KM/H

"Some wild chimps make spears from sharpened sticks to skewer small prey"

PEREGRINE FALCON

HIGH JUMPER

Many fish leap out of the water, but the highest jumper is the mackerel shark. It leaps as high as 6 m (20 ft).

12 METRES

LONGEST JUMPS

●	Snow leopard	17 m (56 ft)
●	American bullfrog	2 m (6½ ft)
●	Kangaroo rat	2 m (6½ ft)
●	Jumping spider	0.8 m (2½ ft)

BIG BOUNDER

Bouncing over the Australian outback, the red kangaroo is the champion long jumper of the marsupials. Its powerful, springy back legs allow it to hop in bounds of up to 12 m (39 ft) for long periods without tiring.

AMERICAN BULLFROG

KANGAROO

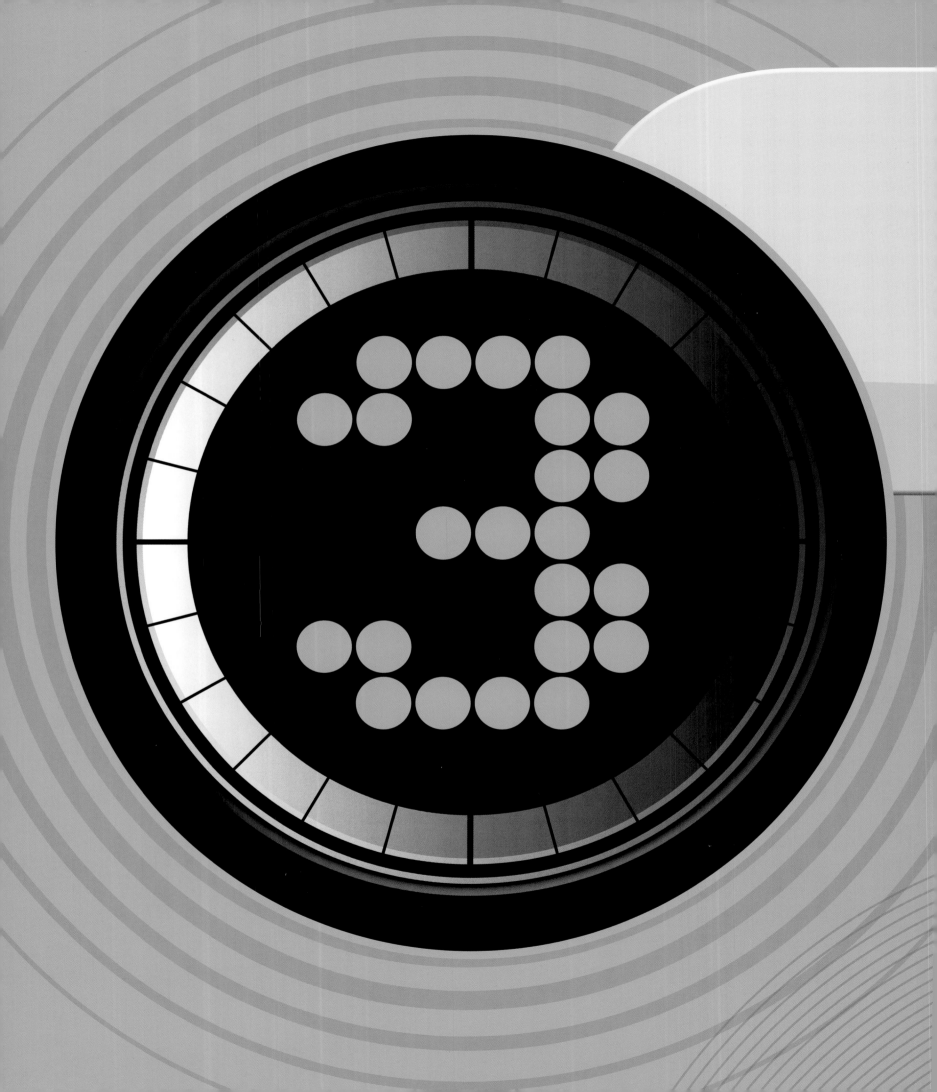

LIFE STORIES

Life on planet Earth can be tough. Conditions may be difficult – too hot, too cold, not enough food – so animals have had to adapt their lifestyles to cope. Some animals go to extreme lengths to ensure that they and their offspring survive.

BEAN-SIZED BABY
RED KANGAROO

Baby kangaroos are born very small. They are no bigger than a bean and so underdeveloped that their hind legs are just stumps. Like other marsupials, a kangaroo baby, or joey, spends little time in the womb – instead, most growth is fuelled by milk and happens in the pouch after birth.

RAISING A FAMILY

A kangaroo can have a joey that is old enough to leave the pouch, another developing on a teat, and a third waiting to be born. Because each of the mother's teats has entirely separate plumbing, different milk can be produced from each to cater for the specific needs of each joey. After a year they start to eat grass.

STATS AND FACTS

27 YEARS
LIFESPAN

Joeys continue to suckle even after leaving the pouch.

NEWBORN WEIGHS
1 GRAM

TIME

235 (permanently leaves the pouch)

33 (gestation period)

| days | 100 | 200 | 300 |

190 (first leaves the pouch)

GROWTH RATE

| 1 g | 238 g | 2,250 g | 6,230 g |

| days | 100 | 200 | 300 |

Muscular tail acts as support when standing upright

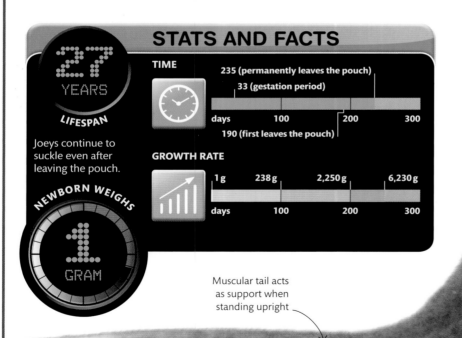

Waiting for a space
Female kangaroos usually mate again soon after giving birth. However, the embryo does not develop immediately and will not be born until the existing joey is old enough to leave the pouch.

"Adults are 90,000 times heavier than newborns"

Large, mobile ears

Large eyes are very sensitive to movement

Kangaroos lick forearms to aid cooling

Joey riding in mother's pouch

Large hind feet are good for jumping

AT A GLANCE

- **SIZE** Head and body 0.8–1.6 m (2½–5¼ ft) long, plus tail 0.7–1.2 m (2¼–4 ft) long
- **HABITAT** Grassland and semi-desert
- **LOCATION** Most of Australia
- **DIET** Mostly grass and other low vegetation

NOURISHED BY MILK

Tiny grasping forelimbs pull the newborn kangaroo up into its mother's pouch where it attaches to one of the teats. The teat swells in the joey's mouth so it remains firmly attached.

SMALLEST BABY IN PROPORTION TO PARENT

KEEPING SAFE

At 130 days old, a joey is still hidden away in its mother's pouch, but is no longer attached to a teat. It will remain there for a further 60 days, gaining strength and growing fur before leaving the pouch for the first time.

LONGEST PREGNANCY
AFRICAN ELEPHANT

The world's heaviest land mammal also has the longest pregnancy. Elephants do things over long periods of time: it takes nearly two years before a baby is ready to be born and youngsters need to reach their teens before they become fully independent from their mothers.

TEMPERATURE CONTROL

An animal the size of an elephant generates a lot of heat. To avoid overheating, the blood is cooled as it travels through a network of blood vessels that lie just below the skin in the ears.

Enamel ridges grind down food

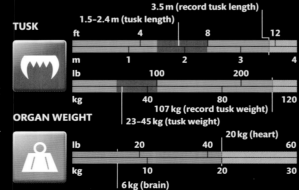

TOOTH REPLACEMENT

In most mammals replacement teeth push up from below, but in elephants worn teeth are replaced from behind. The elephant's mouth is so short that usually only one large cheek tooth is ever in use on each side, above and below.

AT A GLANCE

SIZE Shoulder height 1.6–4 m (5¼–13 ft). Males are bigger than females; forest elephants are smaller than savanna elephants.

HABITAT Grassland, semi-desert, forest, and marshes

LOCATION Africa

DIET Grass and other vegetation

Womb, inside which calf develops (dotted line shows how the womb expands when a baby is in it)

Birth canal

Neck is short and broad to support large head and tusks

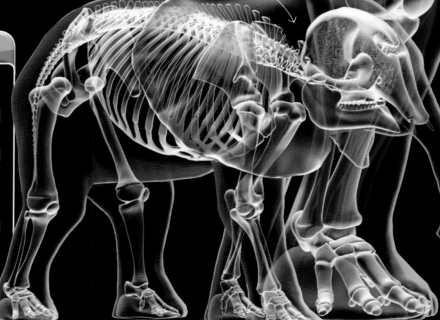

STATS AND FACTS

22 MONTHS
PREGNANCY LASTS

Continuously growing tusks are giant teeth made of a bone-like substance called ivory.

MAXIMUM WEIGHT

7,500 KG

TUSK
3.5 m (record tusk length)
1.5–2.4 m (tusk length)

ft		4		8		12
m	1		2		3	4
lb		100		200		
kg		40		80		120

ORGAN WEIGHT
107 kg (record tusk weight)
23–45 kg (tusk weight)

20 kg (heart)

lb		20		40		60
kg		10		20		30

6 kg (brain)

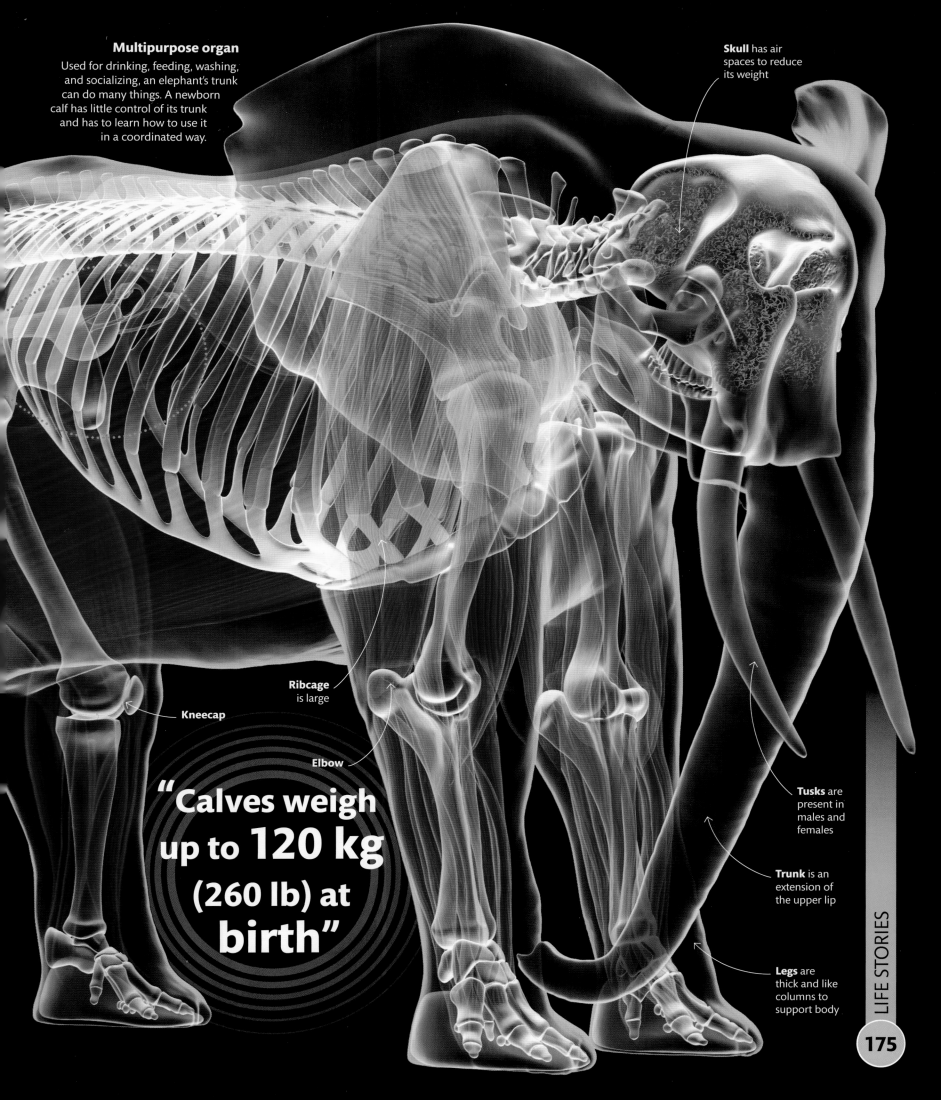

Multipurpose organ
Used for drinking, feeding, washing, and socializing, an elephant's trunk can do many things. A newborn calf has little control of its trunk and has to learn how to use it in a coordinated way.

Skull has air spaces to reduce its weight

Ribcage is large

Kneecap

Elbow

"**Calves weigh up to 120 kg (260 lb) at birth**"

Tusks are present in males and females

Trunk is an extension of the upper lip

Legs are thick and like columns to support body

SENSITIVE BLOODSUCKER

VAMPIRE BAT

Vampire bats have a scary reputation, but they're not as bad as they're made out to be. They fly out each night from their caves to feast on the blood of warm-blooded animals – but not all of them find what they want. Back in the cave, hungry bats are kept going by their full-bellied neighbours who share what they have eaten – the hungry ones beg, and the well-fed regurgitate some blood.

AT A GLANCE

- **SIZE** Head and body 7–9 cm (2¾–3½ in) long
- **HABITAT** Forest and pasture
- **LOCATION** Central and South America
- **DIET** Blood of mammals and sometimes large birds

STATS AND FACTS

28 GRAMS BLOOD DRUNK IN ONE FEED

FLYING SPEED 14 KM/H

Vampire bats have razor-sharp teeth that are first used to shave off some fur before biting away a skin flap to lap up blood. Their saliva stops the blood from clotting.

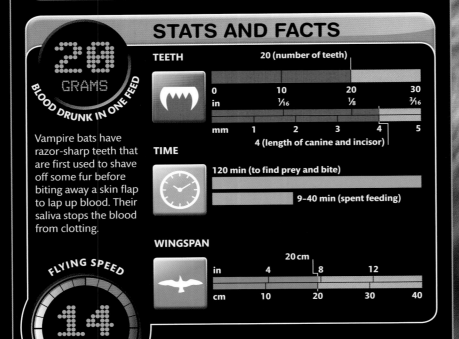

TEETH

	20 (number of teeth)		
0	10	20	30
in	¹⁄₁₆	⅛	³⁄₁₆
mm	1 2 3 4		5

4 (length of canine and incisor)

TIME

120 min (to find prey and bite)

9–40 min (spent feeding)

WINGSPAN

		20 cm		
in	4	8	12	
cm	10	20	30	40

"In one year a colony can drink the blood equivalent of a small herd of cows"

A NOSE FOR BLOOD
Vampire bats have special sensors in their noses that help them detect the heat of blood vessels close to the skin of their prey. Vampire bats are also good at detecting the breathing sounds of the sleeping animals that they feed on.

LONGEST CHILDHOOD
ORANG-UTAN

Orang-utans have already lived up to a third of their life by the time they leave home. There is a lot for young orang-utans to learn about living in the rainforest – and they must learn it all from their mother. Even when they are grown up, some offspring stay so close that they end up helping their mother to raise their younger brothers and sisters.

AT A GLANCE

SIZE Head and body 1.25–1.5 m (4–5 ft) long

HABITAT Rainforest

LOCATION Sumatra and Borneo

DIET Mainly fruit; sometimes leaves and small animals

Adults have darker fur than babies

Single life
Apart from mothers and babies, orang-utans choose to live alone in the forest. Even if feeding from the same tree, they ignore each other. Every evening, they bend branches together to make a solitary nest to sleep in.

"Orang-utan means man of the forest"

STATS AND FACTS

48 YEARS
MAXIMUM LIFESPAN

Young females have the longest childhood of all. They may stay with their mother into their teens to learn how to be mothers themselves.

TIME

227–275 (gestation period)

| days | 73 | 146 | 219 | 292 | 365 |

243–298 (human)

BABIES

4–5 (produced in a lifetime)

| 0 | 2 | 4 | 6 |

15 YEARS
LENGTH OF CHILDHOOD

LOVING BOND

The bond between mother and infant is strong in orang-utans. The baby spends a year clinging to its mother's belly, and continues to drink its mother's milk until it is almost four years old. At least the same amount of time is then spent learning how to survive in the rainforest.

Long, strong fingers for grasping

LONG ARMS

Of all the great apes, the orang-utan is least comfortable on the ground. Its arms are long and strong for climbing and swinging among the branches, but its legs are short and weak. It spends most of its life in the trees.

LONG-DISTANCE TRAVELLER

AMERICAN CARIBOU

Travelling in enormous herds, American caribou cover up to 50 km (30 miles) a day for three months to reach their summer and winter ranges. They start to move northward in April to spend the summer on the Arctic tundra, where they give birth to their calves. During the autumn, the caribou start to move southward again to winter on more sheltered, wooded land.

AT A GLANCE

- **SIZE** 1.2–2.2 m (4–7¼ ft) head and body length, plus 7–21 cm (2¾–8½ in) tail length
- **HABITAT** Tundra and coniferous forest
- **LOCATION** Arctic region, travelling south into USA
- **DIET** Shoots and leaves of birch and willow, grass, and other ground-dwelling plants, lichen

STATS AND FACTS

5,000 KM/YEAR
DISTANCE TRAVELLED

Caribou burn up a great deal of energy because they live in a cold climate and need to keep warm. Females use most energy when they calve in summer.

TOP SPEED
88
KM/H

HERD SIZE

50,000–500,000 individuals

| 0 | 200,000 | 400,000 | 600,000 |

DAILY FOOD CONSUMPTION

60 cal/kg of body (winter and migration)

100 cal/kg of body (when calving)

TEMPERATURE

13°C (legs)   40°C (body)
°F   50   70   90   110
°C   10   20   30   40   50
37°C (human body)

"**Caribou can live in temperatures of −50°C (−58°F)**"

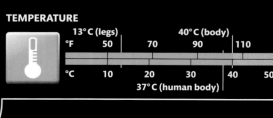

LONGEST OVERLAND MIGRATION

STRONG SWIMMERS

During migrations, caribou swim across any river or lake that blocks their path. Their large feet, which act as snowshoes on land in winter, make excellent paddles. In most deer only males grow antlers, but in caribou females have them too.

BIG-EARED BURROWER
FENNEC FOX

The tiny fennec fox thrives in one of the hottest and driest places on Earth – the Sahara Desert. It is so used to desert life that if temperatures drop below 20°C (68°F) it starts to shiver. Its ears – the biggest in proportion to the head of any carnivore – funnel the sound of the smallest prey, but also radiate the blood's heat for cooling. Fennecs get all the water they need in the food they eat and may even go through their entire life without touching a single drop.

THE FOX'S LAIR

A burrow protects the fennec from bigger predators, but also keeps it cool. Fennecs dig large dens that are often close to or connect with those of other families. They are more sociable than other types of foxes, with the previous year's litter staying in the family den to help raise the new cubs. This fox also uses its digging skills to hunt prey, such as rodents and insects – and is so fast that it can quickly vanish beneath the sand.

AT A GLANCE

- **SIZE** Head and body 36–41 cm (14–16 in) long, plus tail 18–31 cm (7–12 in) long
- **HABITAT** Desert
- **LOCATION** Northern Africa and Middle East
- **DIET** Small animals, such as rodents, birds, and insects

Fur coat keeps it warm during cold nights

Furry soles protect paws from hot sand

Black-tipped tail

"Fennecs are the smallest of all foxes"

Large ears help it lose heat

RAPID PANTING

A fennec is in danger of overheating after chasing prey, so it pants to cool down: it loses heat when water evaporates from its mouth and tongue. It can pant hundreds of times a minute – the fastest rate known for any animal.

Dark stripe runs from eye to muzzle

Beating the heat

In the desert landscape, the pale colour of the fennec's coat serves not only as camouflage, but also helps reflect the fierce heat of the sun. A thick coat protects the fennec from the cold desert night, which is when it does most of its hunting. Even the soles of its feet are hairy to stop them getting burnt.

STATS AND FACTS

15 YEARS
LIFESPAN IN CAPTIVITY

Fennec foxes tolerate drought even better than heat because their kidneys are adapted to release only small amounts of water in their urine.

TEMPERATURE

				38°C	
			37°C (human)		
°F	50	70	90	110	
°C	10	20	30	40	50

10–40°C (surroundings)

SOUND DETECTION

1.5 km (hears a mouse)

miles	½	1
km	0.5 1 1.5	2

<0.1 km (human detects sound)

JUMP

69–70 cm (height)

in	10	20	30	40	
cm	25	50	75	100	125

120 cm (length)

PANTS PER MINUTE

690

SOLE SURVIVOR
PRZEWALSKI'S HORSE

The only surviving wild horse, Przewalski's horse lives on the plains of Central Asia at the extreme north of the area it used to live in. It can survive in this harsh environment because its digestive system can extract nourishment from the tough, stringy grass that is worthless to other grazers.

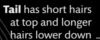

Powerful hind quarters generate speed

Spine is relatively rigid compared to that of a carnivore

Tail has short hairs at top and longer hairs lower down

Large pouch in hind gut contains microbes that help break down grass

Knee

FLICKING TAILS

During hot summer weather, insects can be a nuisance. Przewalski's horses will often stand head to tail, making use of each other's tails as fly whisks. This behaviour has another advantage – with eyes looking out for predators in all directions, it is much easier to relax.

WILDEST HORSE

Fibula (one of the lower leg bones) is short and thin

AT A GLANCE

- **SIZE** Shoulder height 1.2–1.5 m (4–5 ft)
- **HABITAT** Grassland
- **LOCATION** Central Asia
- **DIET** Mainly grass, some other low vegetation

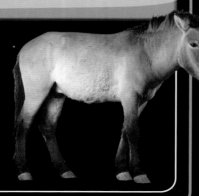

Hoof encloses a single toe

Supreme grazer

Grazing animals have microbes in their gut to help them digest plant matter. Horses graze all day, pushing grass through their intestines where microbes have plenty of time to break it down.

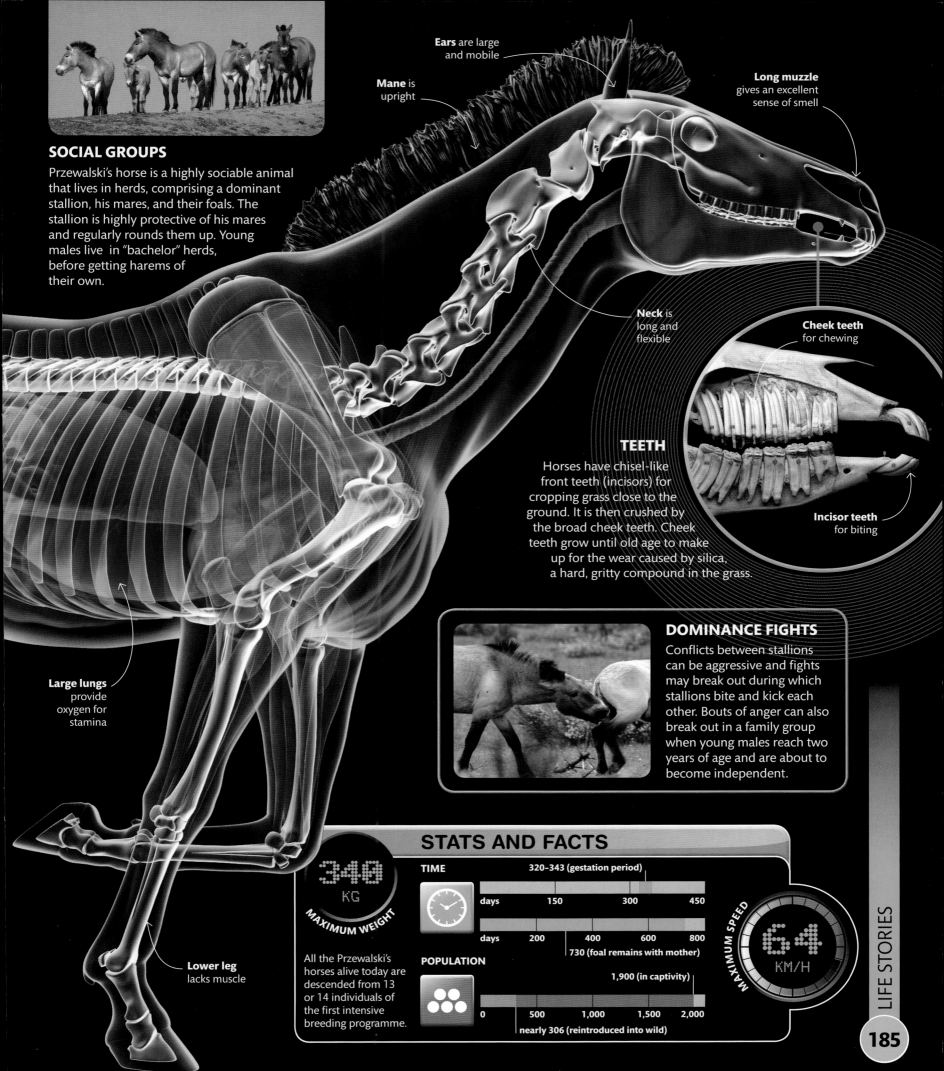

SOCIAL GROUPS

Przewalski's horse is a highly sociable animal that lives in herds, comprising a dominant stallion, his mares, and their foals. The stallion is highly protective of his mares and regularly rounds them up. Young males live in "bachelor" herds, before getting harems of their own.

Ears are large and mobile

Mane is upright

Long muzzle gives an excellent sense of smell

Neck is long and flexible

Cheek teeth for chewing

TEETH

Horses have chisel-like front teeth (incisors) for cropping grass close to the ground. It is then crushed by the broad cheek teeth. Cheek teeth grow until old age to make up for the wear caused by silica, a hard, gritty compound in the grass.

Incisor teeth for biting

Large lungs provide oxygen for stamina

DOMINANCE FIGHTS

Conflicts between stallions can be aggressive and fights may break out during which stallions bite and kick each other. Bouts of anger can also break out in a family group when young males reach two years of age and are about to become independent.

Lower leg lacks muscle

STATS AND FACTS

340 KG
MAXIMUM WEIGHT

All the Przewalski's horses alive today are descended from 13 or 14 individuals of the first intensive breeding programme.

TIME

320–343 (gestation period)

| days | 150 | 300 | 450 |

| days | 200 | 400 | 600 | 800 |

730 (foal remains with mother)

POPULATION

1,900 (in captivity)

| 0 | 500 | 1,000 | 1,500 | 2,000 |

nearly 306 (reintroduced into wild)

MAXIMUM SPEED
64 KM/H

SLEEPIEST SQUIRRELS
ALPINE MARMOT

Imagine spending more than half the year asleep. That is exactly what the Alpine marmot – a type of ground-living squirrel – does. For a vegetarian that relies on tender shoots, this is the best thing to do when a long, cold, winter stops plants from growing. After a frantic summer of raising families and building up their body fat, Alpine marmots retreat to their burrows as early as October and don't emerge again until the following spring.

LONGEST HIBERNATION

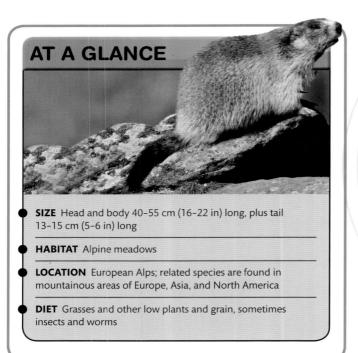

AT A GLANCE

SIZE Head and body 40–55 cm (16–22 in) long, plus tail 13–15 cm (5–6 in) long

HABITAT Alpine meadows

LOCATION European Alps; related species are found in mountainous areas of Europe, Asia, and North America

DIET Grasses and other low plants and grain, sometimes insects and worms

One marmot is always on lookout duty

"**Adult marmots need to weigh 7 kg (15 lb) to survive hibernation**"

SOCIAL SKILLS
Marmot families are occasionally the focus of squabbles, even at playtime. Youngsters stand upright and box one another or wrestle with each other on the ground.

STATS AND FACTS

3,200 METRES
HIGHEST ALTITUDE

The Alpine marmot lives off its body fat during its long hibernation, and slows its body functions to save energy. Only those animals with enough stored fat will last the winter.

LONGEST HIBERNATION
9 MONTHS

BODY TEMPERATURE

37°C (human)

10–35°C

°F	50	70	90	110
°C	10	20	30	40	50

BREATHS/MIN

1–3 breaths (hibernation)

100–150 breaths (awake and resting)

HEARTBEATS

bpm	5 (hibernating)	1 min

bpm	130–160 (awake)	1 min

CUDDLING UP

Alpine marmots produce up to seven babies. The mother suckles them for just over a month before they emerge from the nest to start eating plants. It is especially important that small youngsters build up enough fat to survive the long hibernation. The colony hibernates as a group – huddling together gives the young marmots a better chance of surviving through the winter.

Defending the territory

Alpine marmots live in colonies consisting of a number of females and offspring, and a dominant male. He jealously defends his patch from intruding males.

Young marmots live with their family until they are two years old

Thick fur protects against chilly winds

DADDY COOL

EMPEROR PENGUIN

The world's biggest penguin goes through a lot to raise a family. Emperor penguin pairs walk to their breeding stations on the Antarctic continent just before winter sets in – and travel up to 200 km (125 miles) to get there. As the temperatures drop to their lowest, the males huddle together in colonies, each incubating a single egg. Meanwhile, the females have returned to feed out at sea, leaving the males alone to mind the babies.

- **SIZE** 112–115 cm (44–45 in) long
- **HABITAT** Icy coastlines and adjoining seas; breeds inland
- **LOCATION** Antarctica
- **DIET** Mainly fishes and squid

Long wait for dinner

An Antarctic winter is harsh, with temperatures up to 60°C (76°F) below freezing and constant darkness. The male emperor penguin will not eat until his mate returns with some regurgitated fish for him and the newly hatched chick. If she is late he can feed the chick with an emergency meal using a special curd produced in food pipe.

Bright yellow ear patches

Pinky orange lower bill

MOST DEVOTED FATHER

GROUP HUG

Male emperors spend several months enduring the howling gales of an Antarctic winter. To keep warm they huddle close together with their heads down, slowly shuffling from the outside of the group to the centre. That way, everyone gets a turn at being in the middle.

STATS AND FACTS

TIME

		9 (incubation period)					
weeks	5	10	15	20	25		
		20 (fledging period)					
weeks	5	10	15	20	25		

WEIGHT OF EGG

			450–500g		
oz	5	10	15	20	
	40–70g (chicken egg)				
g	200	400	600		

LOWEST TEMPERATURE ENDURED

-40 ˚C

MAXIMUM LIFESPAN

50 YEARS

The emperor penguin is the only animal that breeds on the Antarctic continent in the middle of winter.

Chick is kept warm through contact with the male's skin under the flap

Chicks are held above the ice on the male penguin's feet

KEEPING WARM

Penguins have a special way of preventing heat loss through their feet. Blood vessels going from the lower leg into the foot transfer some of their heat across to vessels returning from the foot, warming it up. Because the blood in the foot is already cooler, the foot loses heat less quickly.

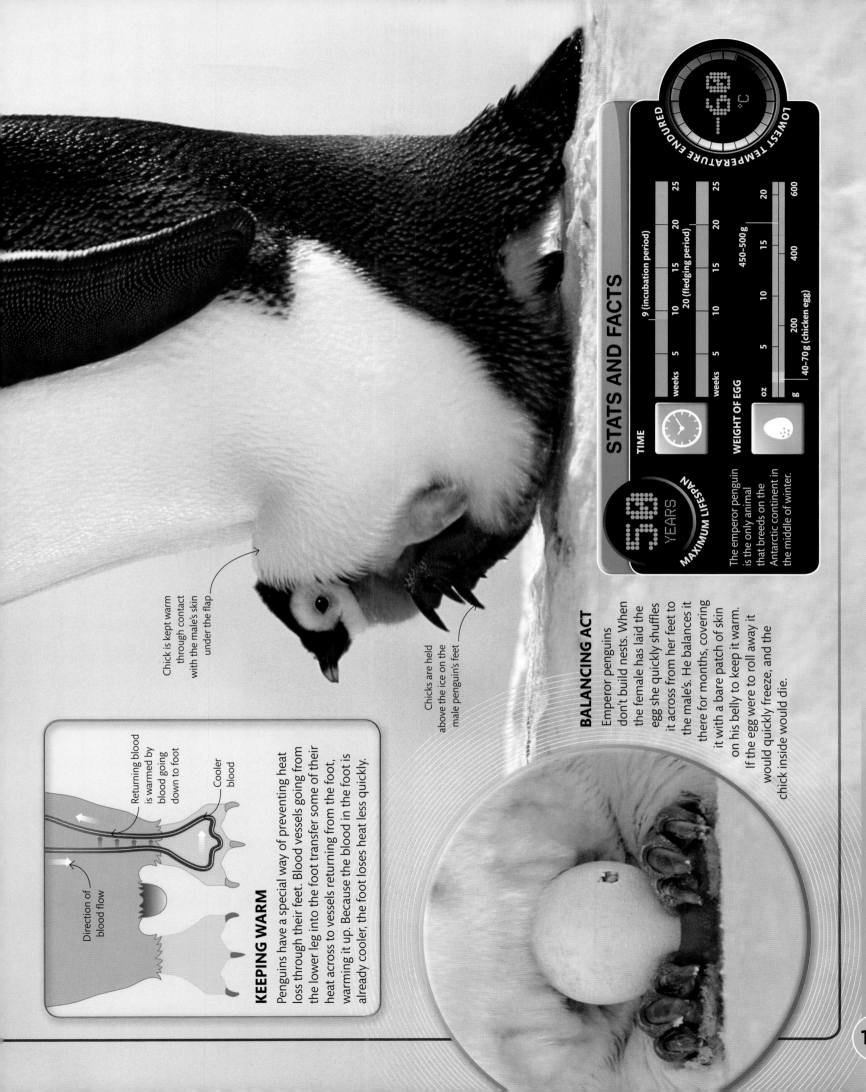

Direction of blood flow

Returning blood is warmed by blood going down to foot

Cooler blood

BALANCING ACT

Emperor penguins don't build nests. When the female has laid the egg she quickly shuffles it across from her feet to the male's. He balances it there for months, covering it with a bare patch of skin on his belly to keep it warm. If the egg were to roll away it would quickly freeze, and the chick inside would die.

AERIAL ATTACKER

The Arctic tern is a graceful sea-going acrobat, with long wings and a forked tail. It hovers in the air while searching for food, before plunge-diving to snatch small fish. Occasionally terns will harass other seabirds to steal their catch.

INCREDIBLE JOURNEY
ARCTIC TERN

No other animal travels as far as an Arctic tern – from the Arctic to the Antarctic and back again every year. Over the course of its lifetime it may cover more than 2.4 million km (1.5 million miles). The Arctic tern breeds in the north and rests in the south, synchronizing its visits with the northern and southern summers to feast on plentiful food supplies.

AT A GLANCE

- **SIZE** Body length 33–36 cm (13–14 in)
- **HABITAT** Coastal regions, nesting on tundra, beaches, and grassland; on open sea when not breeding
- **LOCATION** Mostly breeds north of the Arctic Circle; migrates to Antarctica when not breeding
- **DIET** Mainly small fishes and invertebrates

STATS AND FACTS

34 YEARS
MAXIMUM LIFESPAN

Arctic terns feed at sea, which enables them to make such an epic migration. They also follow wind currents when moving north for a speedier return journey.

DISTANCE COVERED
70,900 KM/YEAR

DURATION OF MIGRATION

93 days (N–S)	
	40 days (S–N)

WINGS

76–85 cm (wingspan)

in	10	20	30
cm	25	50	75	100

wbpm	250 (hovering)	1 min

DAILY FOOD CONSUMPTION

0.48–1.36 cal/g of body

0.026 cal/g of body (human)

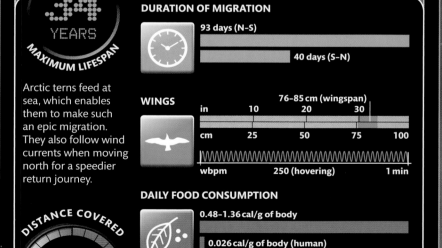

"This bird sees more **daylight** than any other animal"

SAFETY IN NUMBERS

Each pair of flamingos lays a single egg. A few days after hatching, the chick is strong enough to leave the nest and joins other chicks in a huge flamingo crèche. Chicks return to their parents at feeding time.

"The largest recorded flock of flamingos had over 2 million birds"

BIGGEST NURSERY
LESSER FLAMINGO

Lesser flamingos breed in huge numbers in the shallows of alkaline soda lakes. In places the soda is so strong that it burns the skin, but this keeps predators at bay. When the chicks hatch they must be taken to fresher drinking water. A few adults herd all the flightless babies together into a huge crèche and lead the way on foot across many kilometres of sun-baked land.

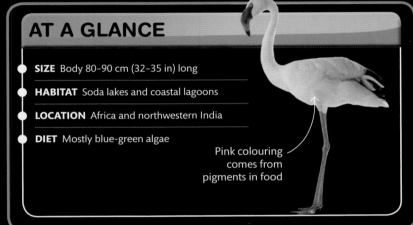

AT A GLANCE

- **SIZE** Body 80–90 cm (32–35 in) long
- **HABITAT** Soda lakes and coastal lagoons
- **LOCATION** Africa and northwestern India
- **DIET** Mostly blue-green algae

Pink colouring comes from pigments in food

STATS AND FACTS

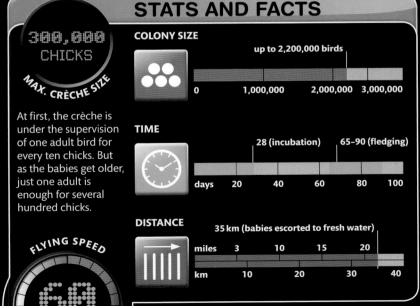

300,000 CHICKS
MAX. CRÈCHE SIZE

At first, the crèche is under the supervision of one adult bird for every ten chicks. But as the babies get older, just one adult is enough for several hundred chicks.

FLYING SPEED
60 KM/H

COLONY SIZE
up to 2,200,000 birds

| 0 | 1,000,000 | 2,000,000 | 3,000,000 |

TIME
28 (incubation)   65–90 (fledging)

| days | 20 | 40 | 60 | 80 | 100 |

DISTANCE
35 km (babies escorted to fresh water)

| miles | 3 | 10 | 15 | 20 |
| km | 10 | 20 | 30 | 40 |

"This bird's gut can **shrink** to make way for extra **muscle**"

MARATHON FLYER
BAR-TAILED GODWIT

Many birds migrate long distances, but the bar-tailed godwit makes the most epic journey of all. Godwits that breed in Europe and Asia migrate overland and along the coastlines to Africa and Southern Asia. Those that breed in Alaska fly non-stop across across the Pacific Ocean to Australia and New Zealand in a journey that takes over a week. No other animal travels so far without resting.

AT A GLANCE

- **SIZE** Body 37–41 cm (14½–16 in) long
- **HABITAT** Tundra, wetlands, coastlines, and meadows
- **LOCATION** Europe, Asia, Africa, Australasia, and Alaska; breeds near the Arctic
- **DIET** Insects, worms, molluscs, seeds, and berries

STATS AND FACTS

11,680 KM

LONGEST NON-STOP FLIGHT

Taking the non-stop route across the Pacific may be hard, but there are advantages: the distance is shorter than following the coastlines, and there are fewer predators.

AVERAGE SPEED

56 KM/H

MIGRATION DISTANCE   11,680 km (in 8 days)

7,008 km (in 5 days)

miles	3,000	6,000	9,000
km	4,000	8,000	12,000 16,000

WEIGHT

450–515 g (start of migration)

180–245 g (end of migration)

WINGSPAN   70–80 cm

in	10	20	30
cm	20 40	60	80 100

IN GOOD SHAPE

The bar-tailed godwit's huge journey needs stamina and plenty of fuel. These birds build up muscle and body fat on coastal mudflats in Alaska to ensure they are in peak condition before setting off.

LONGEST-LIVING ANIMAL
ALDABRA TORTOISE

Tortoises live life in the slow lane – and do it for a very long time. Island giants, such as those from Aldabra in the Indian Ocean, are lumbering plant eaters that survive up to 200 years or more. One male who lived in a zoo since 1875 was at least 130 when he died in 2006, and may have hatched from an egg as early as 1750.

Horny plates cover the bony shell

Head is small and rounded

BEAKY BROWSER

An Aldabra tortoise has no teeth, and instead uses a sharp-edged horny beak to browse on vegetation. The tapering shape enables it to crop grass and other low-growing plants close to the ground, and the tortoise is the biggest and most important grazer on Aldabra.

Strong jaws for chewing tough plants

Flexible neck can pull head back into shell

Reaching out

Aldabra tortoises have long necks to help them reach up to more succulent leaves. On some individuals, the shell curves up at the front so they can reach into low trees. This tortoise can drink water from the shallowest puddles through its nostrils.

AT A GLANCE

- **SIZE** Males up to 1.2 m (4 ft) long; females up to 0.9 m (3 ft) long
- **HABITAT** Grazes on open grassland but prefers to stay under shady vegetation
- **LOCATION** Aldabra Island, Seychelles
- **DIET** Grass, leaves, plant stems, and occasionally carrion

"They knock over small trees to reach juicy leaves"

Lungs are moved in and out by contractions of muscles in the body; the ribcage is part of the shell so it cannot move

Intestines complete the digestive process

STATS AND FACTS

360 KG
RECORD WEIGHT

Of the four species of giant tortoise from the Seychelles, only the Aldabra is not extinct in the wild.

GROWTH RATE

		100 kg	200–250 kg (max. size)
years		25	50

EGGS

		4–25 (per clutch)				
0	5	10	15	20	25	30

255 YEARS
ESTIMATED MAX. LIFESPAN

Kidney removes waste from the blood and turns it into urine

GROWTH RINGS

The outer surface of the shell is covered with a mosaic of horny plates that forms a hard, protective shell. These plates grow wider as the animal gets bigger, producing rings. The rings can indicate seasons of fast and slow growth.

Short tail

Stomach is where tough plant material is stored while digestive juices get to work

Bladder is used to store water when it rains – useful on a dry island like Aldabra

Skin is scaly and armoured

Clawed toes on each foot

PRODUCES
MOST EGGS

"A female produces
almost as many
eggs as there
are **people** in
the USA"

MOTHER OF MILLIONS
OCEAN SUNFISH

At first sight, a sunfish, or mola, looks strangely incomplete – just a massive head with no obvious body or tail. Instead of a proper tail fin, its upper and lower body fins meet around its rear end to form a frilly rudder. Despite its huge size, the sunfish has very few bones in its spine, giving it a unique, dumpy shape. Although it's the heaviest bony fish, its skeleton is made of lightweight cartilage, like that of a shark. Female sunfish produce a vast number of tiny eggs – more than any other backboned animal – although few survive to adulthood.

AT A GLANCE

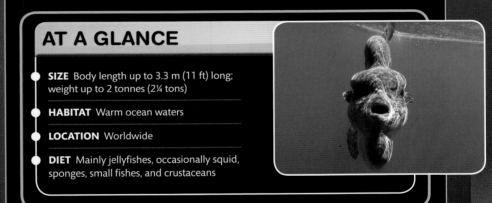

- **SIZE** Body length up to 3.3 m (11 ft) long; weight up to 2 tonnes (2¼ tons)
- **HABITAT** Warm ocean waters
- **LOCATION** Worldwide
- **DIET** Mainly jellyfishes, occasionally squid, sponges, small fishes, and crustaceans

STATS AND FACTS

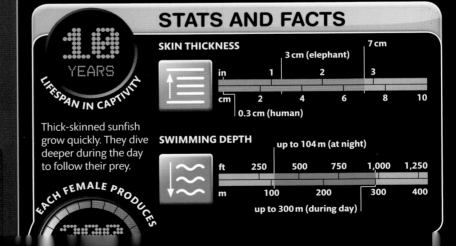

19 YEARS
LIFESPAN IN CAPTIVITY

Thick-skinned sunfish grow quickly. They dive deeper during the day to follow their prey.

EACH FEMALE PRODUCES

SKIN THICKNESS

	in	1	2	3	7 cm

3 cm (elephant)

cm	2	4	6	8	10

0.3 cm (human)

SWIMMING DEPTH

up to 104 m (at night)

ft	250	500	750	1,000	1,250
m	100	200	300	400	

up to 300 m (during day)

SHORT-SPINED SUNBATHER

The ocean sunfish has an appropriate name: it is often seen basking in warm sunshine just below the ocean surface. Considering its size, it has a small brain

HOTTEST HOME
POMPEII WORM

Colonies of this deep-sea worm live on hot volcanic chimneys on the ocean floor. Here, water heated inside Earth's crust pours out and animals living near these vents have to survive or die. Named after an ancient Roman city destroyed by a volcanic eruption, the Pompeii worm can take the heat. Each worm builds a mineral-encrusted tube to live in, with its tail end near the hot rock and its head sticking out to breathe and feed in the cooler surrounding water.

AT A GLANCE

- **SIZE** 10 cm (4 in) long and less than 1 cm (½ in) in diameter
- **HABITAT** On volcanic chimney vents of the ocean floor
- **LOCATION** Eastern Pacific Ocean
- **DIET** Bacteria that live on its body hairs

STATS AND FACTS

2.3 KM — DEPTH BELOW SURFACE

The Pompeii worm makes its mineral-encrusted tubes from keratin, the same tough material that strengthens human skin, but its version is far more heat resistant.

TIME TO FORM COLONY — **2 MONTHS**

TEMPERATURE OF WATER AROUND WORM TUBE

6–45°C

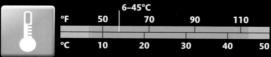

°F	50	70	90	110
°C	10	20	30	40	50

TEMPERATURE INSIDE WORM TUBE

14°C (head end)

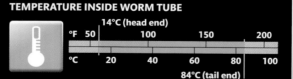

°F	50	100	150	200
°C	20	40	60	80	100

84°C (tail end)

TEMPERATURE OF ROCK UNDER WORM TUBE

40–175°C

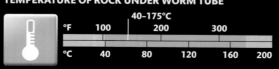

°F	100	200	300
°C	40	80	120	160	200

"Its tail almost reaches **boiling** point"

FLEECY FRIENDS
A Pompeii worm has red feathery gills on its head and a slimy fleece along its back that is home to billions of bacteria. The worm helps the bacteria grow and in turn they provide the worm with nutrients.

SPACE TRAVELLER
TARDIGRADE

The biggest tardigrades are hardly longer than a millimetre but these tiny invertebrates can survive some extreme conditions. In 2007, the European Space Agency sent some into space to see if they could survive the sub-zero temperatures and solar winds in space – remarkably, they did.

AT A GLANCE

- **SIZE** 0.05–1.2 mm (less than ⅟₃₂ in) long
- **HABITAT** Films of moisture on mosses, mud, and aquatic weeds
- **LOCATION** Worldwide
- **DIET** Microbes, plants, and other tiny animals

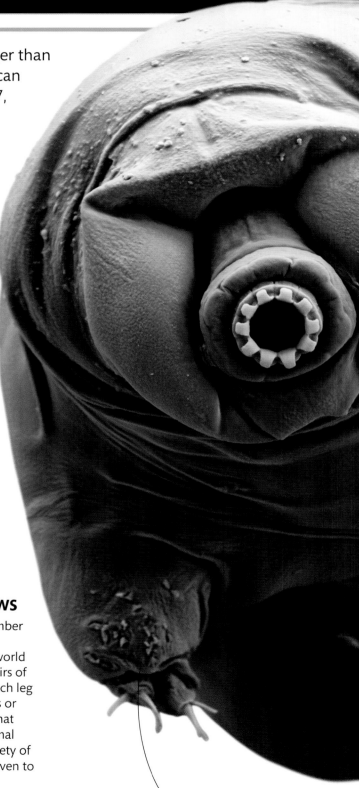

LEG AND CLAWS
Tardigrades clamber through their microscopic world using four pairs of short legs. Each leg ends in claws or sticky discs that help the animal cling to a variety of surfaces and even to walk on ice.

Short, stumpy legs

DORMANT TUN

A tardigrade can survive extreme conditions for many years by turning into a dehydrated bundle called a tun. Its head and bottom contract inwards, the legs disappear, and its life processes only just keep going.

ULTIMATE SURVIVOR

STATS AND FACTS

100 YEARS
LIFESPAN AS A TUN

When it enters its inactive state as a tun, a tardigrade can lose more than 90% of its water, and its body processes slow down to just one 10,000th of their active level.

SURVIVAL IN SPACE
10 DAYS

TEMPERATURE

-272–151°C (survival as a tun)

°F	-300°		0°	300°
°C	-150°		0°	150°	300°

RADIATION

570,000 (kills a tardigrade)
500 (kills a human)

units of radiation	200,000	400,000	600,000

WATER CONTENT OF BODY

3% (as a tun)

85% (when active)

STAR-LIKE EGG

The eggs of tardigrades have finely sculpted hard casings that protect them from drying out. This way, the eggs can still hatch out after months with no moisture. Female tardigrades lay up to 30 eggs at a time.

"It can survive at 200°C (392°F) below freezing"

Lumbering water bear

These animals live in thin films of moisture and are sometimes called water bears, on account of their appearance. Their body is protected by a tough skin, which they moult to grow. If active, they live for a few months. But if their habitat dries up, they do too, and survive until revived by water.

"This tiny spider lives on the slopes of Mt Everest"

EYE ON THE PRIZE

Jumping spiders have the best vision of all spiders – vital when you live where prey is scarce and a successful catch can be the difference between life and death. Two big forward-facing eyes help them judge distance.

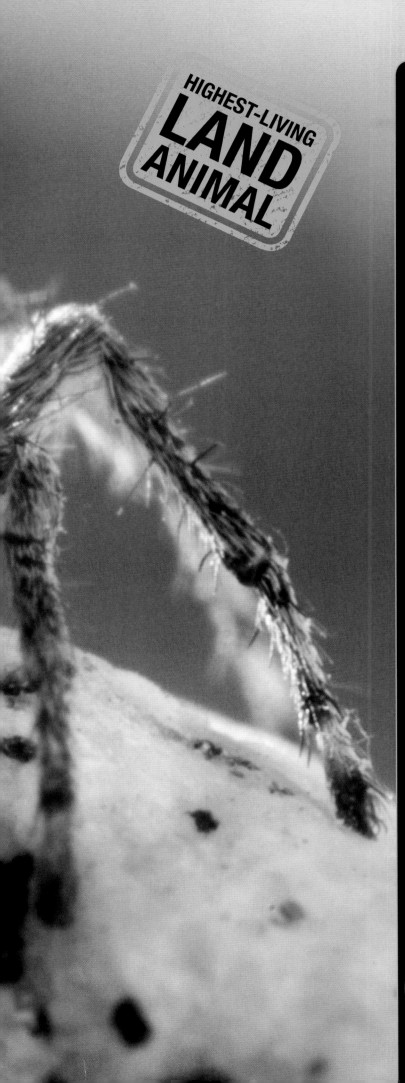

ON TOP OF THE WORLD

HIMALAYAN JUMPING SPIDER

Surviving at the top of a mountain is tough. Some animals just visit the cold, snowy peaks, but the tiny Himalayan jumping spider lives there all the time. It shelters between rocks and hunts insects that graze on bits of vegetation blown up by mountain winds.

AT A GLANCE

- **SIZE** Body 3–4 mm (⅛ in) long
- **HABITAT** Hidden among rocks on mountains at 6,700 m (22,100 ft)
- **LOCATION** Himalayas
- **DIET** Small insects

STATS AND FACTS

6,700 METRES
ALTITUDE

Himalayan jumping spiders are small but mighty. They survive on little food in freezing temperatures, and can jump up to a whopping 25 times their own body length.

JUMPING SPEED
0.7 M/SEC

SURROUNDING TEMPERATURE

-15–0°C

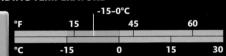

°F	15	45	60
°C	-15	0	15	30

EXTENT OF ONE LEAP

5–10 cm

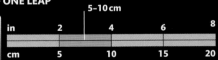

in	2	4	6	8
cm	5	10	15	20

FOOD CONSUMPTION

50% (small flies)   50% (springtails)

0   100%

"Spends
17 years in
the soil –
4 weeks
above it"

**GREATEST
SYNCHRONIZED
EMERGENCE**

MASS BREAKOUT
PERIODICAL CICADA

On a warm spring morning in North America, the air may suddenly be filled with swarms of large insects called periodical cicadas erupting from the ground. It happens when the temperatures start to rise and occurs just once every 13 or 17 years. The wingless juveniles have spent all this time underground, feeding on the roots of plants. When they finally see the light, they moult, unfold their wings, and the males sing to attract a mate. Within just weeks, they have mated, laid eggs, and died.

AT A GLANCE

- **SIZE** Adults 2.5–3.5 cm (1–1½ in) long, depending on the species
- **HABITAT** Woodland, towns, and gardens; juvenile nymphs live underground
- **LOCATION** Eastern North America
- **DIET** Plant sap

STATS AND FACTS

15,000
PER SQ KM
NUMBER EMERGING

The deafening songs of male cicadas – sometimes sounding like a lawnmower starting up – are precisely tuned to attract females of the correct species.

TEMPERATURE

17°C (nymphs emerge underground)

°F	40	50	60	70	80
°C	5	10	15	20	25	30

5–25°C (spring soil in eastern USA)

LOUDNESS

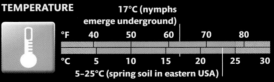

100 (singing cicada males)

dB	20	40	60	80	100	120

80 (human shout)

EGGS

20 in each batch

600 laid in total

TIME UNDERGROUND

SAFETY IN NUMBERS

Emerging together has its advantages: thousands of cicadas can overwhelm potential predators. Even though the insect eaters gorge their fill, there are always plenty of cicadas left over to

HIGH-RISE BUILDER

AFRICAN TERMITE

Termites are the supreme architects of the insect world. Each mound houses a super-colony – a giant family born to a single queen and her mate. The mound is staffed by their blind offspring. Some are large-jawed soldiers that fight off intruders. Others are workers that build the mound from clay, collect food, and look after the queen and the young.

AT A GLANCE

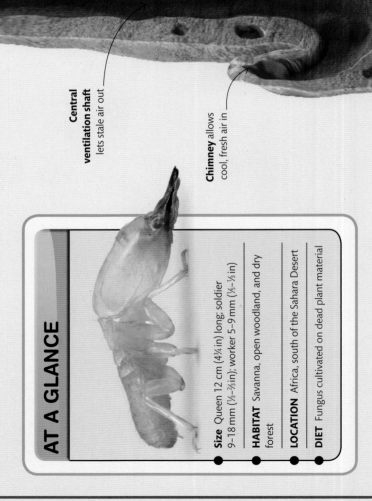

Size Queen 12 cm (4¾in) long; soldier 9–18 mm (⅓–⅔in); worker 5–9 mm (⅕–⅓in)

HABITAT Savanna, open woodland, and dry forest

LOCATION Africa, south of the Sahara Desert

DIET Fungus cultivated on dead plant material

STATS AND FACTS

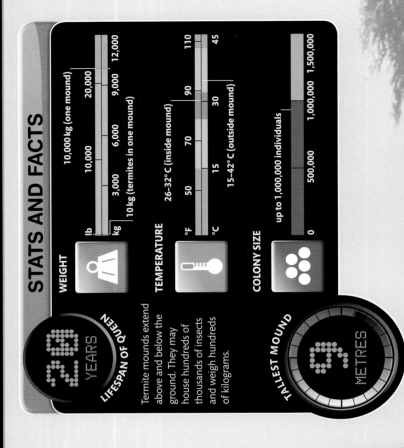

WEIGHT

10,000kg (one mound)

lb	3,000	6,000	9,000	12,000
kg	10,000	20,000		

10kg (termites in one mound)

TEMPERATURE

26–32°C (inside mound)

°F	50	70	90	110
°C	15	30	45	

15–42°C (outside mound)

COLONY SIZE

up to 1,000,000 individuals

0	500,000	1,000,000	1,500,000

28 YEARS
LIFESPAN OF QUEEN

Termite mounds extend above and below the ground. They may house hundreds of thousands of insects and weigh hundreds of kilograms.

TALLEST MOUND
9 METRES

FUNGUS GARDEN

Termites eat wood but are unable to digest it. Instead, they grow fungus on the wood pulp in their faeces. This fungus absorbs the nutrients in the pulp and is then eaten by the termites as food.

Central ventilation shaft lets stale air out

Chimney allows cool, fresh air in

Clay wall is built by worker termites

Air conditioning

A complex system of channels ventilate the mound, keeping its internal temperature stable. The temperature will vary by only a few degrees over the course of a day. Air is drawn in to freshen and cool the colony.

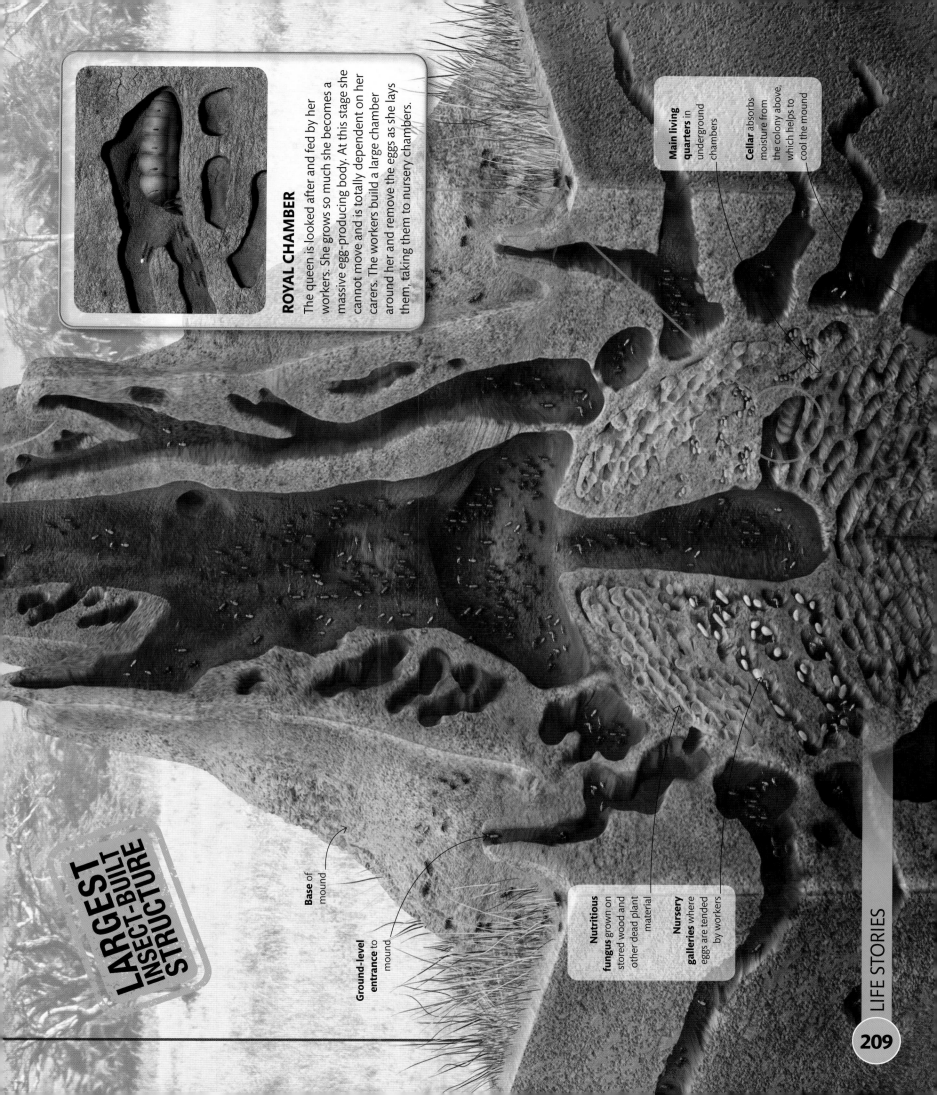

LARGEST INSECT-BUILT STRUCTURE

ROYAL CHAMBER

The queen is looked after and fed by her workers. She grows so much she becomes a massive egg-producing body. At this stage she cannot move and is totally dependent on her carers. The workers build a large chamber around her and remove the eggs as she lays them, taking them to nursery chambers.

Base of mound

Ground-level entrance to mound

Nutritious fungus grown on stored wood and other dead plant material

Nursery galleries where eggs are tended by workers

Main living quarters in underground chambers

Cellar absorbs moisture from the colony above, which helps to cool the mound

"Despite being **chewed**, the larvae suffer **no real harm**"

BLOODSUCKING BABYSITTERS

DRACULA ANT

Life as a baby dracula ant is a mixture of good and bad. Like other ants, these larvae hatch out in a protective nest that is tended by a colony of workers. The worker ants keep the nest clean and feed the larvae and the main queen, who is the mother of all of them. But when the workers get peckish, the tables are turned – they chew into the thin skin of the larvae and drink their blood.

AT A GLANCE

- **SIZE** Workers average 3 mm (⅛ in) long
- **HABITAT** Rotting logs in tropical rainforest and dry forest
- **LOCATION** Madagascar
- **DIET** Larvae eat insect prey captured and stung by workers; workers drink the blood of the larvae

STATS AND FACTS

95 PER CENT

LARVAE WITH SCARS

Worker ants have stingers for killing insect prey. They bring them back to the underground colony to nourish the larvae, so the larvae can make more blood.

EATS A CENTIPEDE IN 24 HOURS

COLONY SIZE

1,000–5,000 workers (female)

| 0 | 2,000 | 4,000 | 6,000 |

1,000–5,000 drones (male)

| 0 | 2,000 | 4,000 | 6,000 |

1,000–3,000 larvae

| 0 | 2,000 | 4,000 | 6,000 |

5–10 queens

| 0 | 2,000 | 4,000 | 6,000 |

FOOD CONSUMPTION

10% (small insects and their larvae)

| 0 | 90% (centipedes) | 100% |

GROWING UP FAST
WATER FLEA

Water flea populations can multiply rapidly. Females can reproduce very quickly because they don't have to wait for fertilization from a male. Within days, a quiet summer pond could be teeming with thousands of these little crustaceans.

STATS AND FACTS

2 MONTHS
LIFESPAN IN CAPTIVITY

Water fleas reproduce so quickly that there can be ten times as many of them within the space of a month.

TIME

days			
1 (eggs hatch)	5	5–10 (young produce eggs)	15
	3 (young leave brood chamber)	10	

POPULATION GROWTH

days			1,000 (day 30)
100 (day 1)	150 (day 10)	300 (day 20)	
	10	20	30

BIGGEST CLUTCH OF EGGS
100

Large eye

Oar-like antennae are used for swimming

AT A GLANCE

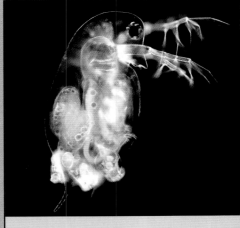

- **SIZE** 0.2–18 mm (less than ¾ in) long
- **HABITAT** Mostly fresh water; sometimes the ocean
- **LOCATION** Worldwide
- **DIET** Microbes, detritus, and sometimes other small animals

"**Females carry eggs in a pouch**"

Eggs in brood pouch

Winter survivor
The water flea's outer shell is transparent, so you can see the algae-filled gut (green), as well as the female's brood of eggs. At the end of the season, she mates with males and produces hard-shelled "winter" eggs that can survive cold, dry conditions.

GIRL POWER
PLANKTONIC ROTIFER

Mothers rule among rotifers. Many populations of these tiny aquatic animals don't have any males at all, so the females reproduce by making eggs that can develop into babies without being fertilized. In the few types of rotifer that have two sexes, the males are small, cannot feed, and only live long enough to fertilize eggs.

AT A GLANCE

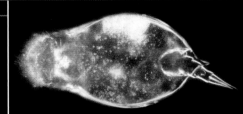

SIZE 0.05–2 mm (up to 1/16 in) long

HABITAT Mostly fresh water; some in soil or the ocean

LOCATION Worldwide

DIET Microbes and debris

Wheel-like fringe of hair

Foot is sometimes used for attaching to surfaces

What's in a name?
Rotifers live in nearly all watery habitats and get their name from a unique fringe of beating hairs that looks like a rotating wheel. This "wheel organ" is used for collecting food or in some species, for swimming.

STATS AND FACTS

10x MALE SIZE OF FEMALE

A single female rotifer and her descendants can produce thousands of babies – without a male.

SIZE

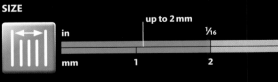

up to 2 mm

in		1/16	
mm	1	2	3

POPULATION

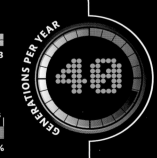

up to 50% males   up to 100% females

| 0 | 25% | 50% | 75% | 100% |

GENERATIONS PER YEAR **48**

MOST FEMALE-DOMINATED POPULATION

SELFLESS SUPERMUM
OCTOPUS

A female octopus goes to enormous lengths to protect her babies before they hatch. Male octopuses die soon after mating, so it's up to the female to raise her brood alone. After laying up to 500,000 eggs, she gives up hunting for food to take care of her offspring. When they hatch a month later, she will be so weak that she will probably be killed by predators.

"A hungry mother may eat her own tentacle"

GUARDING THE EGGS

After laying her eggs in an underwater cavern, the female octopus starves while she defends her brood from predators. She keeps the eggs clean and supplied with oxygen by blowing sea water over them with her tube-like funnel.

Bag-like body, or mantle

Cluster of eggs

SUCKERS

Each of the octopus's eight arms has two rows of circular suction cups underneath. The octopus uses the suckers to grip rocks on the seabed and grasp prey – it can even smell and taste with them.

AT A GLANCE

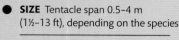

- **SIZE** Tentacle span 0.5–4 m (1½–13 ft), depending on the species
- **HABITAT** Oceans
- **LOCATION** Worldwide
- **DIET** Crabs, molluscs, and fishes

Eight long tentacles

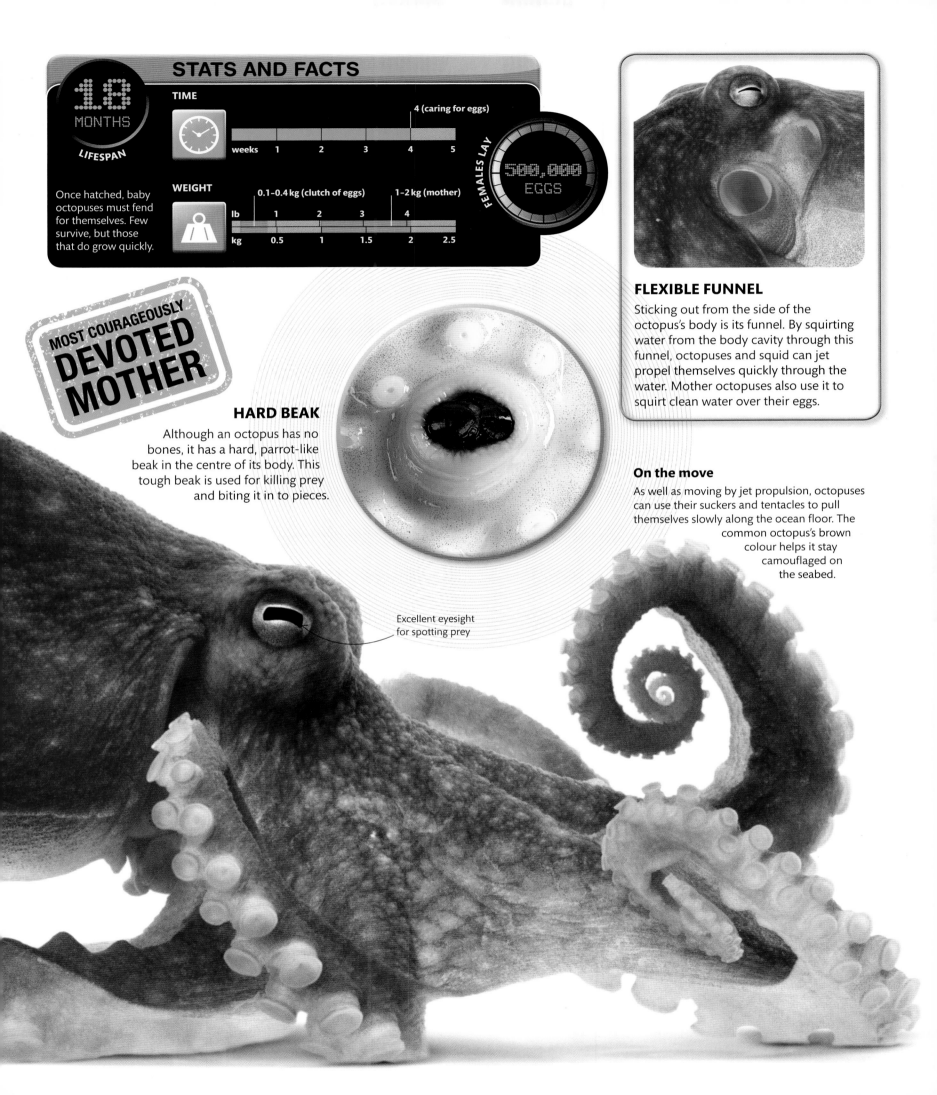

STATS AND FACTS

18 MONTHS LIFESPAN

Once hatched, baby octopuses must fend for themselves. Few survive, but those that do grow quickly.

TIME

weeks	1	2	3	4	5

4 (caring for eggs)

WEIGHT

0.1–0.4 kg (clutch of eggs)　　1–2 kg (mother)

lb	1	2	3	4
kg	0.5	1	1.5	2	2.5

500,000 EGGS FEMALES LAY

FLEXIBLE FUNNEL

Sticking out from the side of the octopus's body is its funnel. By squirting water from the body cavity through this funnel, octopuses and squid can jet propel themselves quickly through the water. Mother octopuses also use it to squirt clean water over their eggs.

MOST COURAGEOUSLY DEVOTED MOTHER

HARD BEAK

Although an octopus has no bones, it has a hard, parrot-like beak in the centre of its body. This tough beak is used for killing prey and biting it in to pieces.

On the move

As well as moving by jet propulsion, octopuses can use their suckers and tentacles to pull themselves slowly along the ocean floor. The common octopus's brown colour helps it stay camouflaged on the seabed.

Excellent eyesight for spotting prey

RECORD-BREAKERS

Animals have many different ways of producing young. Insects and most fish lay hundreds or thousands of eggs in the hope that some will live survive into adulthood. Birds and mammals, on the other hand, have a few young and take care of them once they are born or hatch, to increase their chances of survival. During their lives, animals do whatever it takes to survive, and raise their families successfully. This may even involve travelling long distances to look for food, attract a mate, or find somewhere warm to spend the winter.

"Some cichlid fish keep their eggs in their mouths until they hatch to protect them"

MBUNA CICHLID

MOST EGGS OR YOUNG

- Ocean sunfish — 300 million eggs
- African driver ant — 3–4 million eggs
- Australian ghost moth — 29,100 eggs
- Hawksbill turtle — 264 eggs
- Tenrec — 32 young
- Grey partridge — 24 eggs
- Blue tit — 19 eggs

BLUE TIT NEST

SHORTEST LIFESPAN

The gastrotrich is a tiny animal that lives in water between grains of sand. Its average lifespan – from hatching to dying – is just three days.

BEST BREEDERS

Like ants and bees, naked mole rats live in colonies controlled by a single queen. She is the only female in the colony that has babies. One queen is known to have given birth to 33 pups, the largest recorded litter of any mammal.

33 BABIES

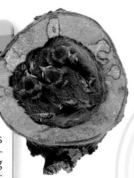

MONARCH BUTTERFLY

LONGEST MIGRATION (ONE WAY)

- Arctic tern — 34,600 km (21,500 miles)
- Leatherback turtle — 20,560 km (12,775 miles)
- Bluefin tuna — 10,000 km (6,200 miles)
- Humpback whale — 8,400 km (5,220 miles)
- Eel — 5,000 km (3,100 miles)
- Monarch butterfly — 4,635 km (2,880 miles)
- Caribou — 2,500 km (1,550 miles)

NAKED MOLE RAT

BUBBLE BLOWER

SIAMESE FIGHTING FISH

The male Siamese fighting fish makes an unusual nest. He blows a mass of saliva bubbles and places the eggs in it. He then guards his nest for several days until the eggs hatch.

MARATHON MILEAGE

Every year, globe skimmer dragonflies migrate from southern India to Africa. They stop off in the Maldive Islands to rest, but have to keep going because there's very little fresh water there for them to lay their eggs. This trip is the farthest-known insect migration.

9,000 KM

LONGEST LIVES

●	Giant barrel sponge	2,300 years
●	*Arctica islandica* mollusc	400 years
●	Aldabra giant tortoise	255 years
●	Bowhead whale	211 years
●	Rougheye rockfish	140 years
●	Tuatara	111 years
●	Olm	100 years
●	Asian elephant	86 years
●	Macaw	80 years
●	Spiny dogfish	70 years

ASIAN ELEPHANT

"In some animals, males and females look completely different"

PARADOXICAL FROG

MALE AND FEMALE ECLECTUS PARROTS

OCEAN OLDIES

Corals are colonies made up of tiny living animals, called polyps, and their stony skeletons. Scientists have discovered that some of the black corals that grow as deep as 3 km (1.9 miles) below the sea are truly ancient. One black coral was found to have started life 4,265 years ago.

4,265 YEARS

LARGEST TADPOLE

The tadpoles of the paradoxical frog grow to 25 cm (10 in) long, but shrink to about a fifth of that length when they become adult frogs.

DEEPEST DWELLER

A type of roundworm, dubbed the "devil worm" and just 0.5 mm (1/64 in) long, has been found living 3.5 km (2¼ miles) underground by South African gold miners.

KIWI

DEEPEST SWIMMERS

●	Snailfish	7.7 km (4¾ miles)
●	Dumbo octopus	7 km (4½ miles)
●	Supergiant amphipod	7 km (4½ miles)
●	Leatherback turtles	1.28 km (¾ miles)
●	Emperor penguin	0.275 km (⅙ mile)

"Kiwis lay the biggest eggs in relation to their body size"

EMPEROR PENGUIN

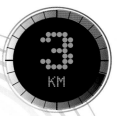
3 KM

DIVING CHAMPIONS

Sperm whales are one of the deepest diving mammals and can reach depths of 3 km (1.9 miles) in search of their favourite food – giant squid. Other challengers for the diving title are elephant seals and Cuvier's beaked whales.

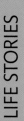

LIFE STORIES

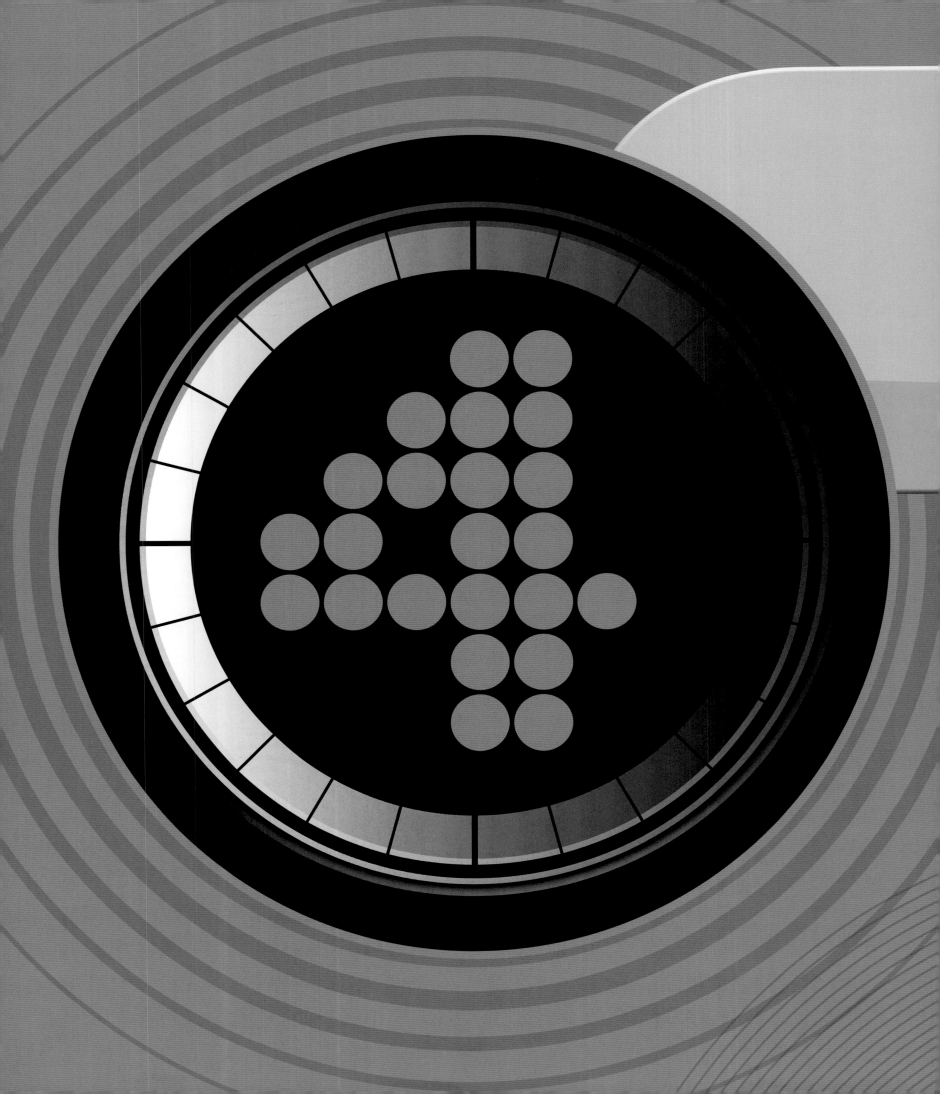

SUPERNATURAL SENSES

Many animals have extraordinary powers of sight, hearing, touch, and smell, which they use for sensing the world around them. These outstanding abilities help them avoid danger, find food, or communicate with others of their kind – sometimes to spectacular effect.

MIXED-UP MAMMAL
PLATYPUS

The platypus looks like it's made from parts of different animals – when scientists first saw one, they thought somebody was playing a joke. But the platypus is well adapted to river life. Its beaver-like tail and webbed feet are perfect for swimming, and its sensitive bill helps it find prey in murky waters.

Thick coat of fur keeps the platypus warm

Strong, webbed feet are excellent for swimming

AT A GLANCE

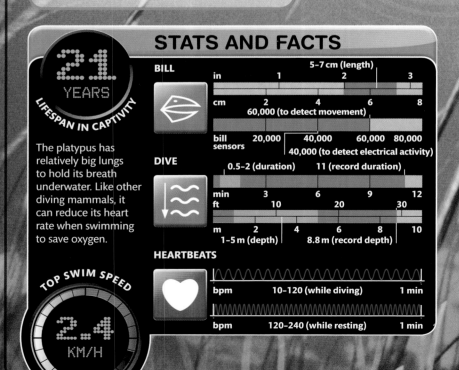

SIZE Head and body 30–45 cm (12–18 in) long, plus tail 10–15 cm (4–6 in) long

HABITAT Streams, rivers, and lakes

LOCATION Eastern Australia and Tasmania

DIET Crayfish, shrimp, insect larvae, worms, snails, and small fishes

"The platypus is a mammal that lays eggs"

STATS AND FACTS

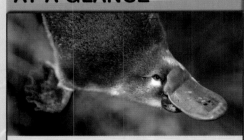

21 YEARS
LIFESPAN IN CAPTIVITY

The platypus has relatively big lungs to hold its breath underwater. Like other diving mammals, it can reduce its heart rate when swimming to save oxygen.

TOP SWIM SPEED
24 KM/H

BILL

		5–7 cm (length)	
in	1	2	3

cm	2	4	6	8

60,000 (to detect movement)

bill sensors	20,000	40,000	60,000	80,000

40,000 (to detect electrical activity)

DIVE

0.5–2 (duration)		11 (record duration)	

min	3	6	9	12
ft	10	20	30	

m	2	4	6	8	10

1–5 m (depth)   8.8 m (record depth)

HEARTBEATS

bpm	10–120 (while diving)	1 min

bpm	120–240 (while resting)	1 min

Life by the river

The platypus is a brilliant swimmer and can stay underwater for up to five minutes to search for food. When on land, it digs burrows in river banks for shelter. The tunnel leading from the water to its nest is so narrow that it squeezes the water from the animal's coat, helping it to dry out.

POISONOUS SPUR

All platypuses are born with spiky ankle spurs, but only males keep them as adults. The spurs develop poison glands, and are used for jabbing other males as well as for fighting off predators. The effect of the venom is very painful, so territorial males keep their distance.

MOST
SENSITIVE
BILL

WEBBED FEET

The platypus's unique webbed feet pull it through the water as it swims. Each foot is also equipped with five strong, clawed toes, which help the platypus to dig burrows on the river bank.

SENSITIVE SNOUT

The platypus's rubbery bill is extra sensitive, and helps it to find food in the muddy water. The bill is able to sense the movement of tiny animals, and can even pick up electrical signals from their muscles. As the platypus sweeps its head from side to side, it collects all these signals from the space around the bill to form a kind of map. From this, it can instantly work out the direction and distance of a meal.

The bill senses signals in the water to map the location of prey

SUPERNATURAL SENSES

221

SMELLIEST MAMMAL
SKUNK

A squirt from a skunk's bottom is the very worst kind of stink bomb, smelling like a mixture of burnt rubber, rotten onions, and bad eggs. Predators soon learn to link the skunk's striking black-and-white markings with a pong that is strong enough to make their eyes water. A direct hit in the face can cause temporary blindness, and even the biggest enemies steer well clear.

AT A GLANCE

- **SIZE** Head and body 12–49 cm (4¾–19½ in) long, plus tail 7–43 cm (2¾–17 in) long
- **HABITAT** Woodland, grassland, and desert
- **LOCATION** North, Central, and South America
- **DIET** Small animals, vegetation, grain, and fruit

NEWBORN BABIES

Skunks usually have four or five babies in underground dens, though they may have up to ten. Born during summer, by autumn the youngsters are fully independent.

The skunk's own sense of smell is very sensitive

"You can smell a skunk from 1 km (½ mile) away"

EASY PICKINGS

Skunks make the most of anything nutritious they can find, including birds' eggs. Their eating habits may keep pests such as rodents and insects down, although they sometimes make themselves unpopular with humans by raiding poultry farms.

Spray is squirted from scent glands either side of the skunk's bottom

STINKY SPRAY

When its tail is raised and its bottom is facing your way, stand well back. To be sure its enemy has got the message, an angry skunk arches its back and stamps its feet. It then looks back to be sure it hits its target.

Back off

The striped skunk's black-and-white coat is a warning to keep away. During a spraying attack, the long hairs on the back and tail are fanned out to make the skunk look scarier.

STATS AND FACTS

13 YEARS
LIFESPAN IN CAPTIVITY

A skunk can spray quite a distance, but is only accurate up to about 3 m (10 ft).

VOLUME

15–18 ml (fluid in scent glands)

fl oz		¼		½	
ml	5	10	15	20

DISTANCE

2–6 m (distance scent sprayed)

ft		10		20	
m	2	4	6	8

16 KM/H
RUNNING SPEED

DAWN CHORUS

Howler monkeys make most of their calls at dawn and dusk. Their large lower jaws and wide throats help to make the call sound louder. They are expert climbers and spend most of their time in the trees.

NOISY NEIGHBOUR
HOWLER MONKEY

The jungle can be a noisy place, and the thundering calls of the South American howler monkey can be heard echoing through the thickest of forests. Male howlers roar like lions, and a troop of 20 animals can be heard up to 5 km (3 miles) away across open space, and 3 km (2 miles) through forest. By calling out, howlers prevent dangerous conflicts with their rivals over territory or food. They usually live in groups of up to 11, but may form troops with as many as 65 animals.

AT A GLANCE

- **SIZE** Head to tail 95–135 cm (37–53 in) long; weight 4–11.5 kg (8¾–25 lb); males are larger than females
- **HABITAT** Rainforest, dry forest, mangroves
- **LOCATION** Tropical South America, from southern Mexico to northern Argentina
- **DIET** Prefers fruit (even unripe) if available; otherwise young leaves, flowers, and seeds

STATS AND FACTS

28 YEARS
MAXIMUM LIFESPAN

Howlers are the largest monkeys in South America. When not calling, much of their day is spent snoozing in the tree canopy, digesting leaves.

HOME RANGE

32,000–75,000 sq m

| sq ft | 400,000 | 800,000 |
| sq m | 30,000 | 60,000 | 90,000 |

CALL

100
20 (human whisper)

| dB | 30 | 60 | 90 | 120 |
70 (human shout)

DAYTIME ACTIVITY

1% (social activity)
80% (resting)   2% (movement and travel)

| 0 | 17% (feeding) | 100% |

TROOP SIZE

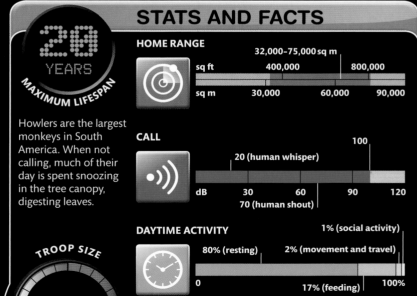

BIG BUG EYES

Tarsiers have the biggest eyes for their size of any mammal. Although the eyes are fixed in their sockets, tarsiers can twist their head almost full circle to give them an all-round view. Once their prey is spotted, they can leap great distances to grab it with their grasping hands.

"A tarsier can leap **70 times** its own **body length**"

SILENT SQUEAKER
TARSIER

Tarsiers are tiny tree-living primates that come out at night to hunt in the rainforest. Unlike their noisy monkey cousins, tarsiers call at such a high pitch that humans cannot hear them. Using this ultrasound frequency could be a way of avoiding danger, since it lets them communicate with one another without attracting the attentions of large predators.

AT A GLANCE

- **SIZE** Head and body 9–16 cm (3½–6½ in) long, plus tail 14–28 cm (5½–11 in) long
- **HABITAT** Rainforest
- **LOCATION** Sumatra, Borneo, Philippines, and Sulawesi (Southeast Asia)
- **DIET** Insects, small lizards, sometimes birds and snakes

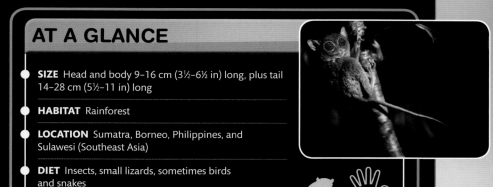

STATS AND FACTS

13 YEARS
MAXIMUM LIFESPAN

With each eye as big as its brain and its constantly moving ears, the tarsier's senses of sight and hearing are vital in judging how far to jump to catch prey.

MAX. LEAPING DISTANCE

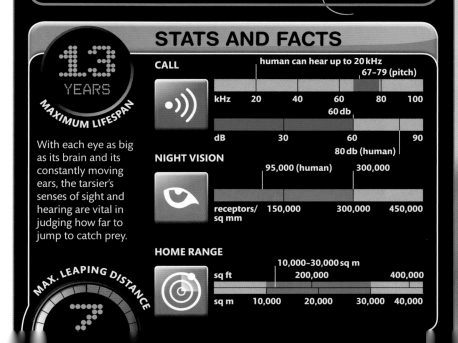

CALL

human can hear up to 20 kHz

67–79 (pitch)

kHz	20	40	60	80	100

60 db

dB	30	60	90

80 db (human)

NIGHT VISION

95,000 (human)   300,000

receptors/ sq mm	150,000	300,000	450,000

HOME RANGE

10,000–30,000 sq m

sq ft	200,000	400,000

sq m	10,000	20,000	30,000	40,000

BEST TEAMWORK
ORCA

The arrival of a group of orcas causes panic among other ocean animals. The largest members of the dolphin family, orcas travel in fearsome groups called pods. No other sea predator is so calculated when attacking prey, and none hunts so well in groups.

AT A GLANCE

SIZE 8.5–9.8 m (28–32 ft) long (males are bigger than females)

HABITAT Oceans; mainly coastal and cooler waters

LOCATION Worldwide

DIET Mammals, fishes, and seabirds

STATS AND FACTS

98 YEARS
MAXIMUM LIFESPAN

Orcas usually live together in pods of 40 or so animals, but may sometimes form even larger groups. Clans may be formed by several pods with similar habits or family links.

SWIMMING SPEED
45 KM/H

POD SIZE

	2–40		
0	20	40	60

DIVE

1,000 m (record depth)
50–250 m (depth)

ft	1,000	2,000	3,000	4,000
m	250	500	750	1,000 1,250

1–4 (duration)

min	5	10	15	20	25

21 (record duration)

PREY WEIGHT

1–100 kg

lb	100	200	
kg	25	50	75	100	125

POINTY TEETH

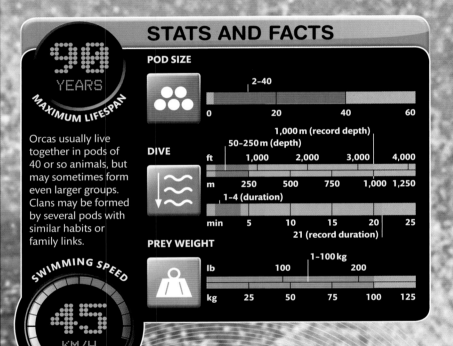

Orcas have large, sharp teeth. The teeth are very strong and curve backwards to help this dolphin hold on to large, struggling prey, such as sharks, seals, and sea lions.

BEACH ATTACK

Although some types of orca only eat fish, others eat seals and even prey on other whales. These determined hunters will sometimes nearly strand themselves on a beach in a risky move to catch a seal.

HUNTING IN TEAMS

Orcas are excellent at working together to catch seals on icebergs. First, they lift their heads to spot their prey. Then they swim under the ice, making a huge wave that washes over it and knocks the seal off. If that fails, they nudge the ice to make sure the seal falls in to the water.

Orca is poised to nudge the ice

Seal resting on block of ice

Orcas surface to spy for prey

Orcas swim together to make a big wave

Wave begins to form

Seal is pushed into the orca's waiting mouth

Wave washes over ice

Water acrobat

When swimming at speed orcas will jump out of the water, which helps them move even faster. They slap their tails and flippers on the water to establish dominance and communicate with each other by using a series of screams and whistles.

"Orcas can eat a small seal whole"

MOST COMPLEX SONG
HUMPBACK WHALE

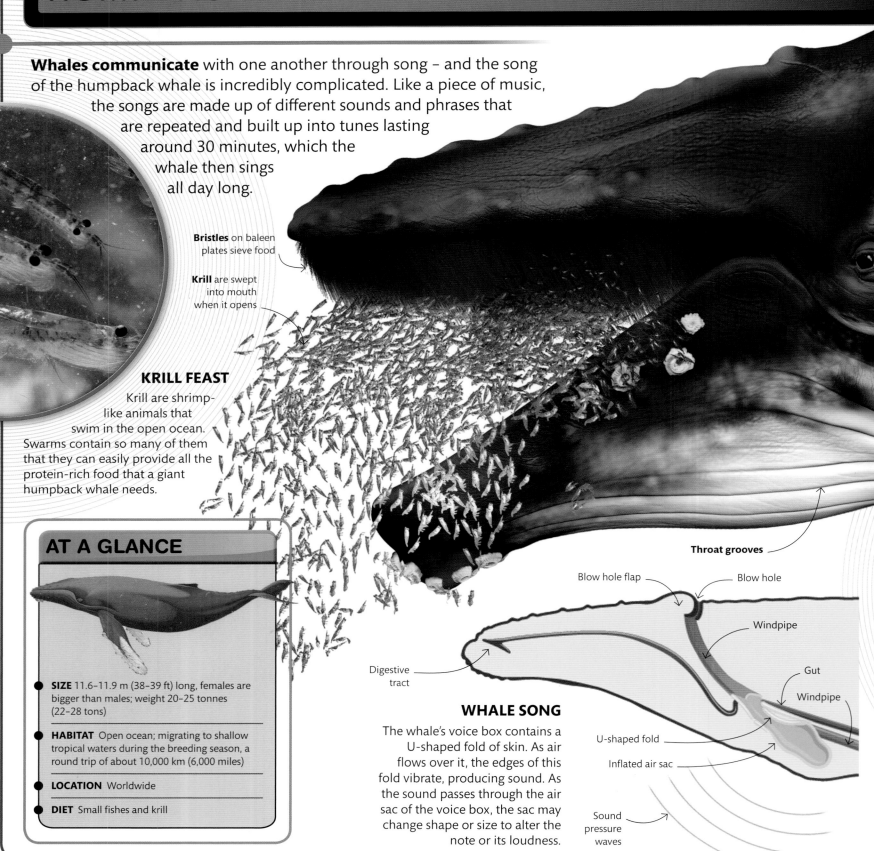

Whales communicate with one another through song – and the song of the humpback whale is incredibly complicated. Like a piece of music, the songs are made up of different sounds and phrases that are repeated and built up into tunes lasting around 30 minutes, which the whale then sings all day long.

Bristles on baleen plates sieve food

Krill are swept into mouth when it opens

KRILL FEAST
Krill are shrimp-like animals that swim in the open ocean. Swarms contain so many of them that they can easily provide all the protein-rich food that a giant humpback whale needs.

Throat grooves

Blow hole flap

Blow hole

Windpipe

Digestive tract

Gut

Windpipe

U-shaped fold

Inflated air sac

Sound pressure waves

AT A GLANCE

- **SIZE** 11.6–11.9 m (38–39 ft) long, females are bigger than males; weight 20–25 tonnes (22–28 tons)

- **HABITAT** Open ocean; migrating to shallow tropical waters during the breeding season, a round trip of about 10,000 km (6,000 miles)

- **LOCATION** Worldwide

- **DIET** Small fishes and krill

WHALE SONG
The whale's voice box contains a U-shaped fold of skin. As air flows over it, the edges of this fold vibrate, producing sound. As the sound passes through the air sac of the voice box, the sac may change shape or size to alter the note or its loudness.

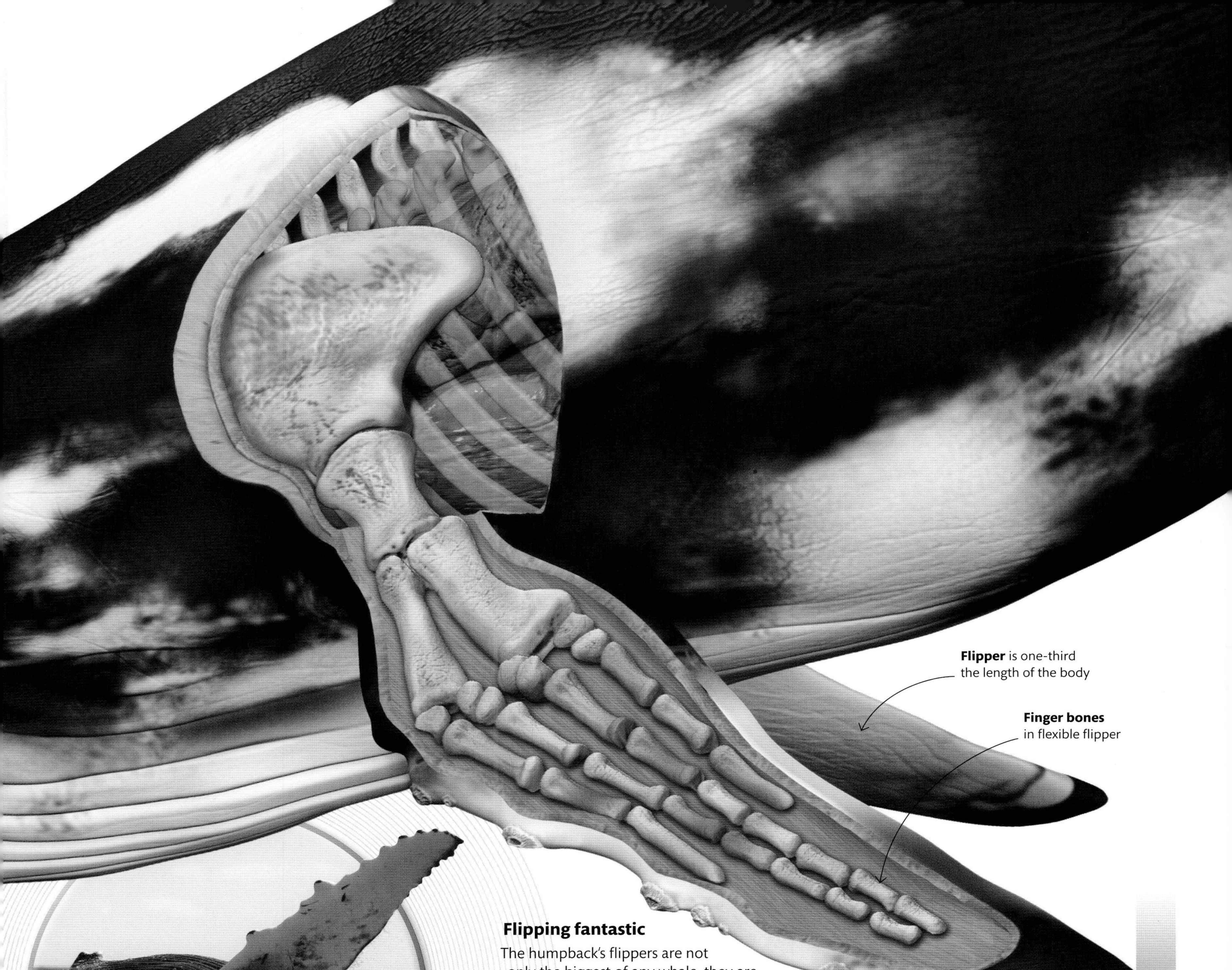

Flipper is one-third the length of the body

Finger bones in flexible flipper

Flipping fantastic

The humpback's flippers are not only the biggest of any whale, they are the biggest of any animal. Flippers have the same kind of bones as human arms, but are adapted for swimming.

MAKING A SPLASH

The humpback is one of the most acrobatic whales. Its streamlined, torpedo-like body makes it great for swimming, but it can also leap out of the water with belly-up somersaults.

STATS AND FACTS

24 HOURS
TIME SPENT SINGING

Males from a single population sing very similar songs and scientists are able to tell groups apart by listening to their songs.

LOUDNESS OF SONG

160-190

| dB | 50 | 100 | 150 | 200 |

80 (human shout)

BREATHING RATE

90 surfacings per hour (max.)

20 surfacings per hour (resting)

35 MIN
LENGTH OF A SINGLE SONG

TOUCHIEST SNOUT

STAR-NOSED MOLE

Looking like an alien from another world, the star-nosed mole has a unique face. Its nose has 22 short tentacles that wiggle around to sense the surroundings more by touch than smell, alerting it to small animal prey practically all the time. The mole has a frantic lifecycle – always moving, always hunting – and has a lightning-speed reaction time that some scientists believe makes it the natural world's fastest eater. It also searches for food underwater by blowing air bubbles towards its prey then breathing them back in to capture its scent.

AT A GLANCE

- **SIZE** Head and body 10–13 cm (4–5 in) long, plus tail 6–8 cm (2¼–3 in) long
- **HABITAT** Burrows in wet ground, swims and dives in ponds and streams
- **LOCATION** North America
- **DIET** Aquatic insects, earthworms, crustaceans, and small fish

STATS AND FACTS

25,000 TOUCH SENSORS ON NOSE

The mole's rapid responses help it make the most of its fiddly invertebrate prey.

SPOTS AND EATS PREY IN

PREY SIZE

0.001–30 mm

in	½	1	1½
mm	10	20	30	40

FOOD CONSUMPTION RATE

1–3 invertebrates/sec

0	1	2	3	4	5

INSECT DETECTOR

The nose tentacles of a star-nosed mole are packed with microscopic touch sensors. With its tiny eyes and poor vision, feeling around is the best way to explore a dark burrow. Other moles have these sensors too, but the star-nosed mole has five times as many.

SILENT HUNTER
BARN OWL

Not only can the barn owl find a mouse in total darkness, but it can swoop down and catch it without making a sound. Flying so quietly helps it listen for prey, so that it can even home in on a mouse hidden beneath a layer of grass or snow, judging its position with deadly accuracy.

Upswept wings provide a strong downstroke for takeoff

Hooked beak for tearing prey

Silent flight
When the owl locates its prey, it takes to the air. Its broad wings are so good at creating lift that the owl doesn't need to flap them very often. The feathers are softly fringed around the edge to muffle any wingbeat sound.

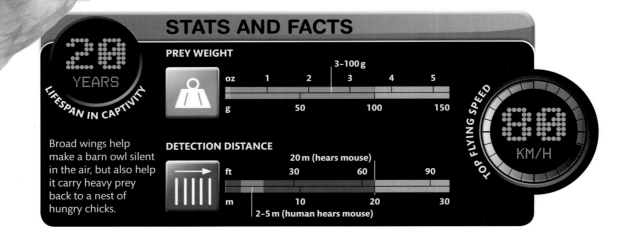

STATS AND FACTS

20 YEARS
LIFESPAN IN CAPTIVITY

Broad wings help make a barn owl silent in the air, but also help it carry heavy prey back to a nest of hungry chicks.

PREY WEIGHT

3–100 g

oz	1	2	3	4	5
g	50	100	150		

DETECTION DISTANCE

20 m (hears mouse)

ft	30	60	90
m	10	20	30

2–5 m (human hears mouse)

88 KM/H
TOP FLYING SPEED

"Barn owls don't **hoot**: they **screech**"

BIRD'S EYE VIEW

An owl's eyes are so big that they cannot move. Instead, the owl's flexible neck allows it to swivel its head in an almost complete circle to look behind it, or twist sideways to examine something in front.

Eyes are adapted for dim light

Sharp claws are ready to grab prey

Wings spread out like a parachute for landing

QUIETEST FLYING **PREDATOR**

PINPOINTING PREY

The owl's heart-shaped face reflects sound to amplify the quietest squeak. Having an ear on each side of the face and one higher than the other helps the brain calculate the direction and height of a target.

BUNDLES OF FLUFF

Female barn owls usually lay between four and seven eggs, but they may not all survive. At around five weeks, the owlets start to lose their downy fluff and begin to grow their adult flying feathers.

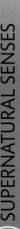

BEST DANCER
HONEY BEE

Female worker bees are great on the dancefloor. Whenever one finds a rich source of nectar she performs a dance that tells her fellow workers where it is. While the queen bee stays at home and lays eggs, surrounded by hundreds of male bees called drones, thousands of workers fly out to collect energy-rich nectar and protein-rich pollen to fuel the activities in the hive.

Forewing is larger than hindwing

Thorax, or chest section of the bee contains flight muscles

Antennae help the bee detect odours

The faster she dances, the nearer the food

DANCING WORKER

When a worker finds food she doesn't keep it to herself. She returns to the hive and performs a dance to her sisters to let them know where to find it. She does a round dance if it's nearby and a figure-of-eight or "waggle" dance if it's further away.

Compound eye made up of thousands of tiny cells

Nectar is collected through its tube-like mouthparts, or proboscis

Champion worker

Workers have many jobs: they keep the hive clean, defend it from intruders, and care for the young. They drink nectar and process it in their stomachs to make honey, and collect pollen in special "baskets" on their legs.

AT A GLANCE

- **SIZE** 1–2 cm (½–¾ in) long
- **HABITAT** Woodland and gardens
- **LOCATION** Europe, Africa, and Southern Asia; introduced elsewhere
- **DIET** Nectar and pollen

"**A honey bee can tell workers about food 10 km (6 miles) away**"

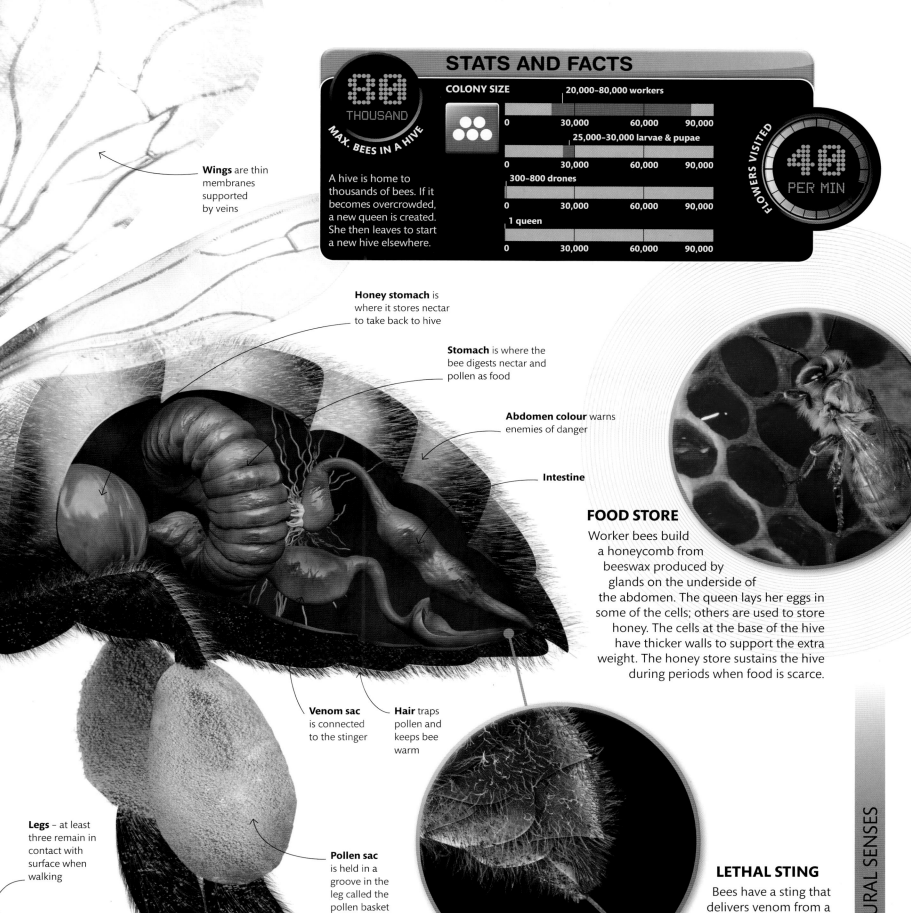

STATS AND FACTS

88 THOUSAND

MAX. BEES IN A HIVE

A hive is home to thousands of bees. If it becomes overcrowded, a new queen is created. She then leaves to start a new hive elsewhere.

COLONY SIZE

20,000–80,000 workers

| 0 | 30,000 | 60,000 | 90,000 |

25,000–30,000 larvae & pupae

| 0 | 30,000 | 60,000 | 90,000 |

300–800 drones

| 0 | 30,000 | 60,000 | 90,000 |

1 queen

| 0 | 30,000 | 60,000 | 90,000 |

FLOWERS VISITED

40 PER MIN

Wings are thin membranes supported by veins

Honey stomach is where it stores nectar to take back to hive

Stomach is where the bee digests nectar and pollen as food

Abdomen colour warns enemies of danger

Intestine

Venom sac is connected to the stinger

Hair traps pollen and keeps bee warm

Legs – at least three remain in contact with surface when walking

Pollen sac is held in a groove in the leg called the pollen basket

Lower legs have structures used for grooming and pollen removal

FOOD STORE

Worker bees build a honeycomb from beeswax produced by glands on the underside of the abdomen. The queen lays her eggs in some of the cells; others are used to store honey. The cells at the base of the hive have thicker walls to support the extra weight. The honey store sustains the hive during periods when food is scarce.

LETHAL STING

Bees have a sting that delivers venom from a poison gland. They are most likely to use it when defending the hive. A bee sting is jagged, so when the insect attacks a thick-skinned enemy the sting gets stuck. When the bee flies away, part of its abdomen is torn off and it dies.

HAWK-EYED PREDATOR
DRAGONFLY

With enormous eyes that have an all-round view of their surroundings, and two sets of independently moving wings, dragonflies are fearsome predators. Brilliant sight and acrobatic flying skills make them expert at catching moving insect targets.

Each eye is made of lots of tiny units

Eyes are large and powerful

Strong jaws to tear up prey

AT A GLANCE

- **SIZE** Body 1.5–12 cm (½–4¾ in) long
- **HABITAT** Most habitats near fresh water
- **LOCATION** Worldwide
- **DIET** Other flying insects

STATS AND FACTS

6 MONTHS
MAX. LIFESPAN (ADULT)

The eyes of a dragonfly are so big that they cover most of the insect's head.

TOP SPEED
68 KM/H

VISION

lenses per eye	25,000	30,000	50,000

BRAIN

20% (information from other senses)
80% (visual information)

0   100%

Eye on the prize

Like all insects, dragonflies have compound eyes. This means that each one is made up of thousands of tiny sight units called lenses. Each lens is too small and simple to see anything in detail, but all the units work together to help the dragonfly spot other insects moving around it.

BIGGEST COMPOUND EYES

HEAT-SEEKING INSECT
KISSING BUG

The kissing bug is attracted to the body heat of warm-blooded animals, including humans. Most victims are asleep, so hardly notice when it lands on their skin looking for a meal. The bite itself is harmless but the insect can carry a nasty illness called Chagas disease, which can be fatal to humans.

SIZE Body 1–2 cm (½–¾ in) long

HABITAT Grassland and human habitations

LOCATION South America

DIET Blood

STATS AND FACTS

18 MONTHS
MAXIMUM LIFESPAN

Once it bites, a kissing bug makes the most of its meal. It can swell up to four times its body weight with blood before it lets go.

BITE

80 (blood taken by one bug)

drops   20   40   60   80   100

TIME

94% (to drink blood)
6% (to probe for blood vessel)

0   100%

DURATION OF BITE
30 MIN

Pucker up
The name "kissing bug" comes from the insect's preference for parts of the body where skin is thin – like the lips.

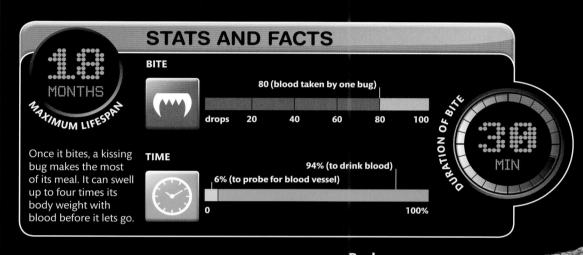

Long mouthparts drinking blo[od]

"A female moth can **attract** up to **100 males** with her scent"

TUNING IN

Emperor moths "smell" with their antennae – each is coated with sensors that pick up scent in the air. When one antenna detects a stronger scent than the other, the moth changes its course so that it is always following the most direct path to the source of the smell.

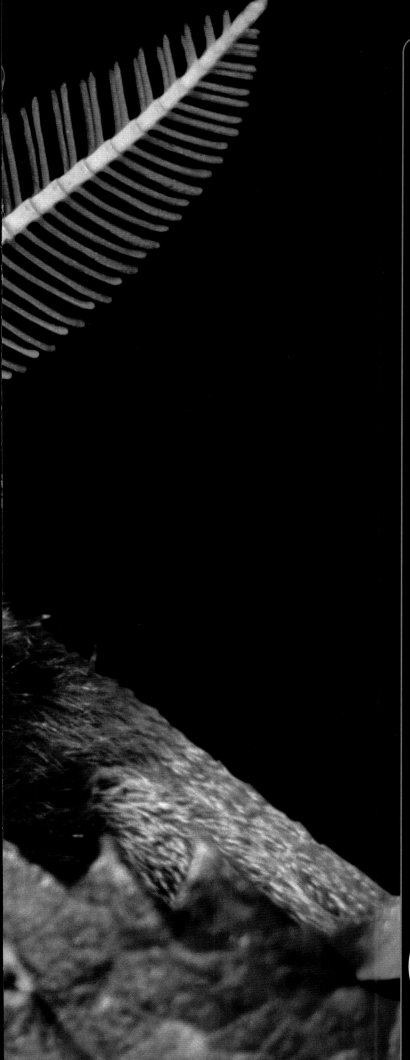

SUPER-SENSITIVE SNIFFER
EMPEROR MOTH

A moth's sense of smell is astonishing: a single molecule of scent can be sensed 10 kilometres (6 miles) away – that's even better than a person smelling someone else's perfume in another country. For an insect that flies by night, scent is the best way to let others know where you are. Female moths produce tiny quantities of a substance called pheromone, which males follow to find them.

AT A GLANCE

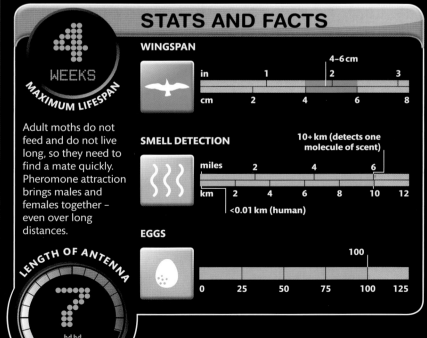

- **SIZE** Moth body length 2 cm (¾ in); caterpillar body length up to 6 cm (2¼ in)

- **HABITAT** Heathland and open country

- **LOCATION** Europe and northern Asia

- **DIET** Adults do not feed; caterpillars eat heather and bramble

STATS AND FACTS

4 WEEKS
MAXIMUM LIFESPAN

Adult moths do not feed and do not live long, so they need to find a mate quickly. Pheromone attraction brings males and females together – even over long distances.

7 MM
LENGTH OF ANTENNA

WINGSPAN

in		1		4–6 cm 2		3
cm		2	4		6	8

SMELL DETECTION

10+ km (detects one molecule of scent)

miles		2		4		6	
km	2	4	6	8	10	12

<0.01 km (human)

EGGS

				100	
0	25	50	75	100	125

STRONGEST PUNCH

MANTIS SHRIMP

Lightning-quick predators with a devastating punch, mantis shrimps can kill with one blow. They probably have the most complex eyes in the animal kingdom and are expert at detecting movement and judging distance. They even have better colour vision than humans. Seeing their surroundings in such detail means that few animals escape their notice.

AT A GLANCE

- **SIZE** Up to 35 cm (14 in) long, depending on the species
- **HABITAT** Muddy, sandy, and gravelly ocean floors and coral reefs, in shallow coastal waters
- **LOCATION** Worldwide, with more species in the tropics
- **DIET** Crabs, snails, and fishes

STATS AND FACTS

20 YEARS
MAXIMUM LIFESPAN

The claws of the mantis shrimp are lethal weapons that may be used as clubs or spears. Each of its eyes is a compound eye, made up of many different units.

STRIKE SPEED
23 M/SEC

VISION

12 different colour receptors

0	3	6	9	12	15

3 receptors (human)

10,000 units in one eye

0	5,000	10,000	15,000

STRIKE FORCE

400–1,500

N	500	1,000	1,500	2,000

DEPTH

up to 1,500 m

ft	1,500	3,000	4,500	6,000
m	500	1,000	1,500	2,000

SHARP EYESIGHT

Mantis shrimps have compound eyes. Upper and lower bands of each eye detect movement and can judge distance for striking prey. A central band concentrates on colour vision, allowing shrimps to see colours that humans cannot, such as ultraviolet.

MOST EYES
SCALLOP

Most shelled molluscs seem to be dull-witted, slow-moving animals, but scallops have rows of complex eyes to see the world, and can swim rapidly by clapping their shells together. The soft body of the scallop is enclosed by a pair of hinged shells that open so they can feed on plankton on muddy and sandy seabeds.

Rows of eyes

Scallops cannot see detail as humans can, but are able to detect shadows and movement – which is enough to spot predators. Scallop eyes also detect the size of plankton so they can open up their shells to get the most amount of food in.

Shells create movement by clapping together

Tiny eyes along edge of fleshy body

STATS AND FACTS

18 MONTHS
LIFESPAN

The scallop's eyes contain tiny mirrors that improve the amount of light they can gather, which helps in muddy waters.

EYE

40–100 (usual range)

number of eyes	50	100	150
in	½	1	

mm	10	20	30
1 mm (eyeball diameter)			

24 mm (human eyeball diameter)

SHELL OPENS

23% (around specks of food)

25–50% (around bigger particles)

MAX. NUMBER OF EYES

110

AT A GLANCE

SIZE Shell 2–30 cm (¾–12 in) long

HABITAT Mostly coastal ocean waters

LOCATION Worldwide

DIET Mostly plankton

BEST AMBUSHER
TRAPDOOR SPIDER

Invisible under a lid made of silk and soil that covers the entrance to its burrow, a trapdoor spider waits patiently for its prey. When a passing insect triggers one of the silk trip lines that fan out from the burrow entrance, the trapdoor spider pounces.

Multi-purpose fangs

A trapdoor spider's fangs inject venom into its prey. The fangs also have small barbs, which act like rakes to move soil around when the spider digs its burrow.

Thick, shiny black legs

STATS AND FACTS

20 YEARS
MAXIMUM LIFESPAN

A trapdoor spider has super-fast reactions to ambush prey walking across its trip lines.

FASTEST AMBUSH
0.03 SEC

BURROW

		10–40 cm (depth)		
in	5	10	15	
cm 10	20	30	40	50
in	½		1	
cm	1	2		3

0.5–2.5 cm (trapdoor diameter)

FOOD CONSUMPTION

90% (insects)	10% (other invertebrates)
0	100%

AT A GLANCE

- **SIZE** Head and body 0.5–3 cm (¼–1¼ in) long
- **HABITAT** Forest, grassland, and semi-desert
- **LOCATION** Worldwide, mostly in warm and tropical regions
- **DIET** Insects and other small animals

MONSTER EYES
COLOSSAL SQUID

This huge predator spends its entire life in the darkest depths of the ocean. It is an active, highly intelligent hunter with enormous eyes. This squid is also the world's biggest animal without a backbone. Its big eyes are forward-facing, allowing it to judge distance when hunting light-producing fishes.

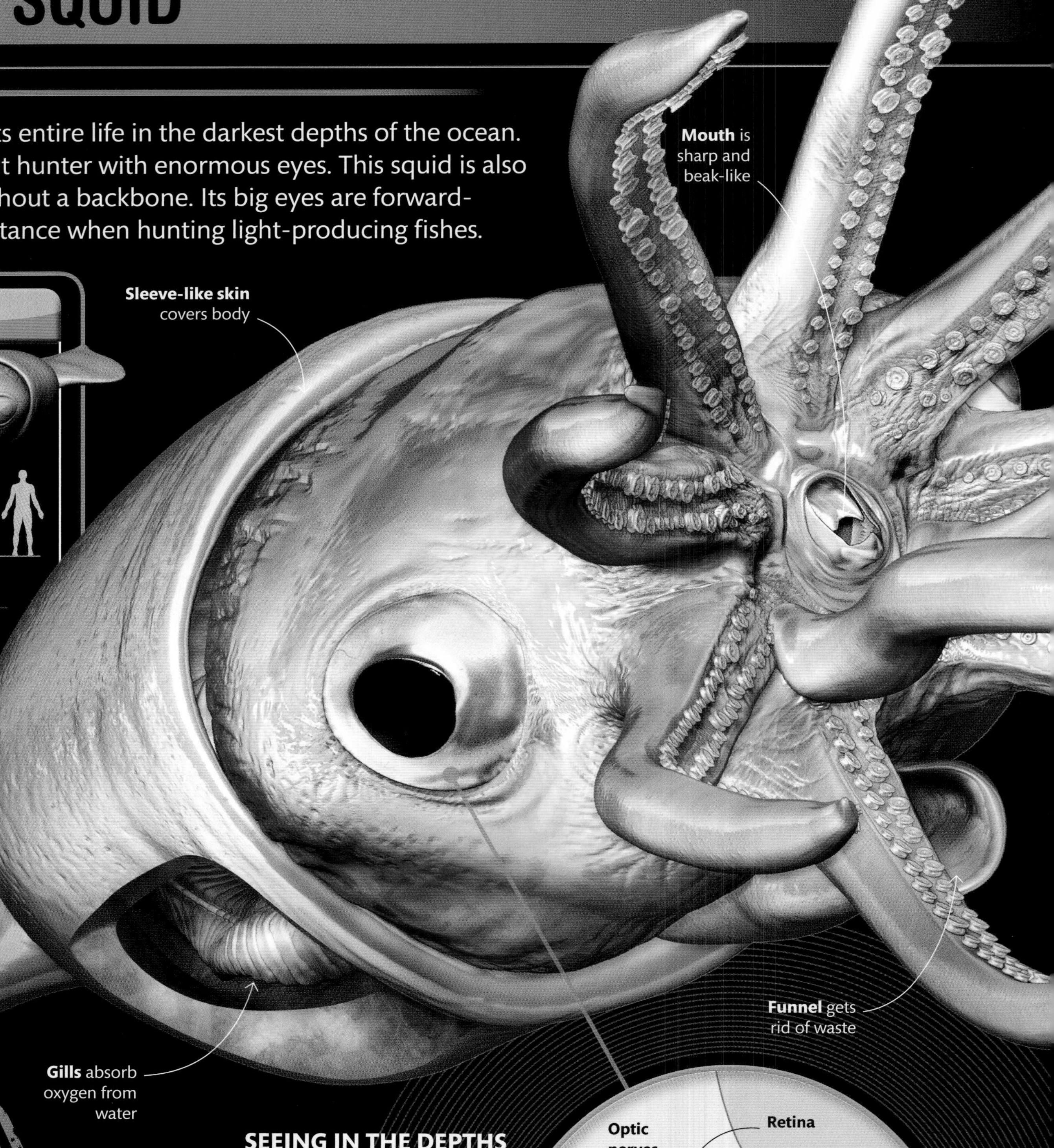

AT A GLANCE

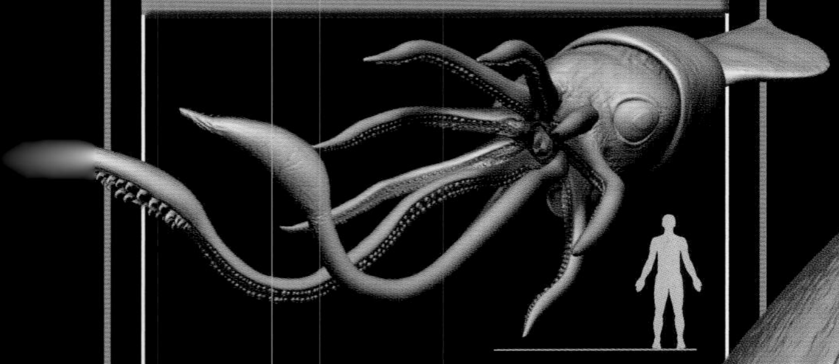

SIZE 12–14 m (39–46 ft) long

HABITAT Deep ocean waters

LOCATION Southern Ocean

DIET Light-emitting fishes and other squid

Sleeve-like skin covers body

Mouth is sharp and beak-like

Fin helps direction control

Gills absorb oxygen from water

Funnel gets rid of waste

THE LARGEST EYE IN THE WORLD

SEEING IN THE DEPTHS

The squid eyeball is as complicated as a human eye, with a large pupil to let in as much light as possible, and a lens to focus it on the retina. A light organ in each eye emits light – like headlights – so that the squid can see in the depths.

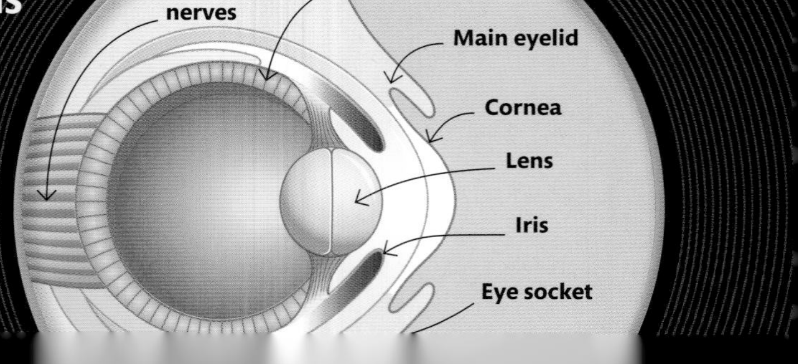

Optic nerves

Retina

Main eyelid

Cornea

Lens

Iris

Eye socket

Muscular arm

FLESH-RIPPING HOOKS

Two long tentacles end in swollen clubs that carry fierce-looking hooks. The hooks can swivel round in a full circle. The eight shorter arms have bigger suckers and non-rotating hooks. Once the squid catches its prey, the suckers and hooks work together to keep a firm grip.

Deep sea monster

This squid is huge – up to 14 m (46 ft) long – and a formidable predator. It has eight arms, each with two rows of strong, clasping suckers. Two longer tentacles have ends that are shaped like massive clubs. These tentacles reach out to capture prey, which is pushed through the sharp, beak-like mouth.

"Its eyes are the size of footballs"

Long tentacles have club-shaped ends

Suckers for gripping

IN THE PINK

No-one has seen a living squid in the depths of the ocean, but as this model shows, its skin is pink – caused by tiny capsules of pigment. We know that other kinds of squid can change colour intensity according to mood – so it's likely that the colossal squid can do the same.

STATS AND FACTS

495 KG
MAXIMUM WEIGHT

The colossal squid is perfectly adapted for life in the deep. It is also one of the smartest of sea creatures, with a doughnut-shaped brain and a complex nervous system.

TIME TO GROW TO 3M

18

EYE

	27 cm (eyeball diameter)
	9 cm (lens diameter)
in	5	10
cm	10	20	30

2.4 cm (human eyeball diameter)

LENGTH

	2 m (tentacles)
1 m (arms)	
ft	3	6	9
m	1	2	3

DEPTH

1,000–2,500 m		
ft	3,000	6,000	9,000
m	1,000	2,000	3,000

RECORD-BREAKERS

Senses help animals negotiate the world around them. Besides vision, hearing, smell, taste, and touch, some animals have additional senses, such as echolocation in bats and heat detection in some snakes. Others have phenomenal powers of smell, or see colours and hear sounds that humans cannot. Senses are also used to communicate. Animals may call to their mates, use scent to mark their territories, or have bright coloration to warn off predators.

HIGHEST FREQUENCY HEARD

● White-beaked dolphin	200 kHz
● American shad	180 kHz
● Wax moth	150 kHz
● Mouse	91 kHz
● Tarsier	91 kHz
● Owl	12 kHz

"An ostrich's eyeball is bigger than its brain"

HIGH-PITCHED HEARING

Animals that use echolocation, such as bats and dolphins, can detect sounds that are well into the ultrasonic range. Africa's short-eared trident bat can detect sound frequencies as high as 212 kHz.

212 kHz

TAWNY OWL

BOTTLENOSE DOLPHIN

MOST TASTE BUDS

The channel catfish has the best sense of taste of any fish. It has 25 taste buds per square millimetre in the barbels around its mouth and others on its body.

NUMBER OF EYES

● Scallop	110 eyes
● Box jellyfish	24 eyes
● Sunflower star	24 eyes
● Tuatara	3 eyes

"Dolphins and orcas have no sense of smell"

ULTRAVIOLET SENSOR

Unlike humans, a scorpion can have up to six pairs of eyes. One pair lies on top of the head, with smaller pairs positioned lower down. Recent evidence suggests that the scorpion's exoskeleton may be able to detect ultraviolet light.

12 EYES

SCORPION

HOWLER MONKEY

GREEN PIT VIPER

WATER BOATMAN

LOUDEST CALLS IN DECIBELS

●	Snapping shrimp	200 dB
●	Blue whale	188 dB
●	Water boatman	105 dB
●	Howler monkey	100 dB
●	Oilbird	100 dB

FLASHY FISH

The deep-sea flashlight fish has organs containing bacteria that produce the brightest light made by any living organism.

OSTRICH

CROAKY CALLER

The world's noisiest amphibian is the Puerto Rican coqui frog. Its name comes from the 100-decibel, two-part call it makes in the breeding season. The "co" warns away other males, and the "qui" attracts females.

100 DECIBELS

BIGGEST EYES

●	Colossal squid	27 cm (10½ in)
●	Blue whale	15 cm (6 in)
●	Ostrich	5 cm (2 in)

EYE CAN SEE YOU

The land mammal with the biggest eyeballs, at 4 cm (1½ in) in diameter, is the horse. The position of the eyes high on the sides of the head gives the horse a wide field of view, which helps it spot approaching danger early and make a speedy getaway.

WANDERING ALBATROSS

SUPER SNIFFER

Birds are not known for their sense of smell, but the wandering albatross can locate food that is up to 20 km (12 miles) away.

PRZEWALSKI'S HORSE

4 CM

SUPERNATURAL SENSES

GLOSSARY

ABDOMEN
In insects, this is the rearmost part of the central body's three sections. In vertebrates, this is the part of the body also known as the belly, which contains the stomach and bowels.

AMPHIBIAN
A cold-blooded vertebrate such as a newt or a frog. Amphibians start life in water as larvae (often called tadpoles), but as adults they breathe air and some live partly on land.

ANTENNA
Long moveable sense organ on the head of animals such as insects and crustaceans – normally in pairs.

ARACHNID
An animal such as a spider or scorpion that has a two-part body and four pairs of walking legs.

ARTHROPOD
An invertebrate animal, such as a fly or crab, that has a segmented body, jointed limbs, and a hard outer skeleton called an exoskeleton.

BLOOD VESSEL
Tube that carries blood around the body. There are three types: arteries, veins, and capillaries. Arteries carry blood away from the heart, and veins carry blood to the heart. Tiny capillaries between the arteries and veins distribute food and oxygen carried by the blood into the body tissues and remove carbon dioxide and other waste products from them.

BLOWHOLE
Breathing hole, or "nostril", on the top of the head of whales, dolphins, and porpoises. It can also be a hole in ice that aquatic animals visit to breathe.

CAMOUFLAGE
Colours and patterns on an animal's skin or fur that help it blend in with its surroundings.

CARAPACE
The hard case covering the upper body of some insects and crustaceans.

CARNIVORE
Any animal that specializes in eating meat.

CHRYSALIS *see* **PUPA**

CLOVEN HOOF
A hoof that is split into two weight-bearing toes, such as in a deer.

CNIDARIAN
A simple water-dwelling animal such as a jellyfish or sea anemone that has stinging cells and tentacles.

COLD-BLOODED
A cold-blooded, or ectothermic, animal's body heats up and cools down with its surroundings – it sunbathes to warm up and cools down in the shade. Reptiles, fishes, amphibians, and invertebrates are all cold-blooded animals.

COLONY
A group of animals living closely together, often relying on each other. Termites, honey bees, and dracula ants live in colonies.

COMPOUND EYE
An eye made up of many small lens units (ommatidia). Many arthropods have compound eyes.

COUNTERSHADED
Darker coloured above and lighter below – for example, a leatherback turtle or a shark. This helps disguise the animal from predators looking up or down at it.

COURTSHIP
Animal behaviour aimed at attracting a mate – for example, dancing, singing, calling, presenting food, or otherwise showing off.

CRUSTACEAN
An animal such as a crab, shrimp, or woodlouse that has a hard outer shell and two pairs of antennae.

DECIBEL
A unit that measures the intensity or loudness of sound to the human ear – almost total silence is 0 decibels (dB) and a car horn measures about 110 decibels.

DIGESTION
The breakdown of food into small particles that can be absorbed and used by an animal's body.

DIURNAL
Animals that are active during the day and sleep at night.

ECHINODERM
A spiny-skinned marine invertebrate such as a star fish or sea urchin.

ECHOLOCATION
The detection of objects by listening for reflected sound waves, or echoes, used by bats and dolphins.

ENDANGERED
An animal or species that is at risk of becoming extinct throughout all or part of its habitat.

EXOSKELETON
The hard outer skeleton that covers, supports, and protects some invertebrates, especially arthropods.

EXTINCT
When a species no longer exists on Earth it is said to be extinct. Some animals are extinct in the wild, which means that the only surviving examples are in captivity.

FLEDGED
A young bird that has large enough wing feathers to be able to fly is said to have fledged.

FLEDGLING
A young bird that has recently left its nest, but does not yet have all of its adult feathers and is still dependent on its parents for food.

FREQUENCY
A measurement of how quickly a sound wave repeats itself, which affects the pitch of a sound. For example, a squeak is a high-frequency sound with close-together waves, compared to a boom, which has low frequency, spread-out waves.

GESTATION
The period of time between fertilization of an egg and the birth of the animal – the gestation time in humans, for example, is 40 weeks.

GILL
An organ used by fishes and other aquatic animals to obtain oxygen from water.

GLAND
An organ that produces and releases certain body chemicals such as milk, sweat, and in some cases, venom.

GRAZER
An animal that feeds on grass and ground-level green plants.

GRUB
The young of various insects, also known as a caterpillar, larva, or maggot.

GUT
The tube that carries food away from the stomach; also known as the intestines.

HABITAT
The natural environment of an animal or plant.

HERBIVORE
An animal that specializes in eating plants.

HERTZ
A unit used to measure frequency of sound waves. One hertz is equal to one cycle per second. A kilohertz (kHz) is 1,000 cycles per second, or 1,000 hertz (Hz). The higher the frequency, the higher pitched the sound. Humans can hear sounds between 20 Hz and 20 kHz whereas a bat's hearing range is 20 Hz to 150 kHz.

INSECTIVORE
An animal that specializes in eating insects.

INTRODUCED
When a species that does not occur naturally in an area has been brought in by humans, by accident or on purpose, from somewhere else.

INVERTEBRATE
An animal without a vertebral column, or backbone.

JUVENILE
A young animal that is not yet able to reproduce.

KERATIN
A tough protein found in hair, feathers, claws, and horns.

KILOHERTZ *see* **HERTZ**

KRILL
Small, shrimp-like oceanic creatures that are eaten by whales and other marine animals.

LARVA
A young stage of an animal that looks very different from the adult form, for example, a grub, maggot, nymph, or tadpole. (Plural is *larvae*.)

LIFE CYCLE
The developmental changes through which every organism passes – from a fertilized egg to its mature adult state, when it is capable of producing another fertilized egg, through to death.

MAGGOT
Legless larva of a fly.

MAMMAL
Warm-blooded, hairy animals that always feed their young on milk from a gland in the female.

MARSUPIAL
An animal, such as a kangaroo, whose young are born at an early stage of development and complete their growth in their mother's pouch, where they feed on her milk.

METAMORPHOSIS
The transformation of young forms of certain animals into a very different adult shape. For example, tadpole to frog, or caterpillar to moth.

MICROBE
A minute organism normally only visible under a microscope.

MIGRATION
The regular, often yearly, return journey that an animal makes in search of feeding areas or breeding grounds to avoid harsh winters.

MOLLUSC
An invertebrate animal with a soft, muscular body and, often, a hard shell. Snails, clams, slugs, and squid are all molluscs.

MOULT
In arthropods, moulting means shedding the entire exoskeleton to allow for growth. In vertebrates, it is the shedding and regrowth of skin, hair, or feathers. Mammals and birds all moult to keep in good condition, adjust to seasonal weather changes, or prepare for breeding.

NECTAR
A sweet liquid produced by flowers that bees and insects feed on.

NERVOUS SYSTEM
A body system that consists of the brain, spinal cord, and special fibres called nerves, which send rapid signals around an animal's body to control all body functions.

NEWTON
A Standard International (SI) unit that measures force. One newton is the amount of force needed to move an object weighing 1 kg (2¼ lb) at a rate of 1 m (39 in) per second.

NOCTURNAL
An animal that is active at night and sleeps during the day.

NUTRITION
Food necessary for the health and growth of animals.

NYMPH
A young insect that has the same body shape it will have as an adult but no wings. This type of insect does not have a larval stage or become a pupa, but moults several times as it grows. Wings only form after the last moult, when it becomes an adult.

OMNIVORE
An animal that eats both meat and plants. Humans are omnivores.

ORGAN
A structure within the body that is designed to carry out a specific task. For example, the heart is made of muscle and nerve tissue and its job is to pump blood around the body.

OXYGEN
A gas found in the atmosphere and dissolved in water. Most living organisms need oxygen for respiration.

PARASITE
An organism that lives on, or in, another one (its host), and from which it gets shelter and food. The presence of a parasite is usually harmful to the host.

PEST
An animal that causes a nuisance to humans – for example, by attacking crops or other animals.

PHEROMONE
A chemical released by one animal to communicate with another of the same species – for example, to mark a trail, attract a mate, or warn off rivals. This method is often used by animals that live on their own, such as moths, tigers, and pandas.

PIGMENT
A chemical substance that produces a colour in skin, hair, scales, and feathers.

PITCH
The high or low quality of a sound.

ABBREVIATIONS USED IN THIS BOOK

/	per – for example, km/h means kilometres per hour
bpm	beats per minute
°C	degrees Centigrade
cal	calories
cm	centimetre
dB	decibel
°F	degrees Fahrenheit
fl oz	fluid ounce
ft	foot
g	gram
ha	hectare
Hz	hertz – see glossary for definition
in	inch
kg	kilogram
kHz	kilohertz – see glossary for definition
km	kilometre
lb	pound
m	metre
min	minute
ml	millilitre
mm	millimetre
mph	miles per hour
N	newton – see glossary for definition
oz	ounce
s or sec	second
sq	square
wbpm	wingbeats per minute

PLANKTON
Tiny (mostly microscopic) organisms, such as algae and the larvae of invertebrates and fishes, which drift in lake and ocean currents.

PREDATOR
An animal that hunts and kills other animals (its prey).

PREHENSILE
The ability to coil around an object and grip it – for example, the tail of a seahorse or a chameleon is prehensile.

PREY
An animal that is killed and eaten by a predator.

PRIMATE
Mammals such as monkeys, apes, and humans. All primates have forward-facing eyes and grasping hands.

PROTEIN
A type of chemical containing carbon and nitrogen that is made in the bodies of living organisms. Some proteins take part in the vital processes in the body, and others form body tissues such as skin, hair, and muscle.

PUPA
Also known as a chrysalis, this is the intermediate, usually immobile, stage in the life cycle of some insects. During the pupal stage, the larva changes into an adult.

PUPIL
The dark circular or slit-like hole at the front of an animal's eye that widens or narrows to control the amount of light entering it.

RAINFOREST
Forest in a warm climate that has a very high annual rainfall.

RECEPTOR
A cell, or group of cells that senses and responds to inputs from the environment, such as heat, touch, light, sound, or chemicals. Receptors are found in the skin and in the sense organs such as ears, eyes, and nose.

REGURGITATE
To bring partially digested food from the stomach back up to the mouth – for example, when a cow brings grass back up for rechewing.

REPRODUCTION
The process of producing young. Reproduction can be sexual (including mating and the mixing of genes from two parents) or asexual (without mating or mixing).

REPTILE
A cold-blooded vertebrate with scaly, waterproof skin such as a snake, lizard, tortoise, or crocodile.

RESPIRATION
Also called breathing, this is the process of taking oxygen into the body and getting rid of carbon dioxide, the waste product of respiration. It also describes the chemical reaction that takes place in every living cell when food molecules are broken down with the help of oxygen to release energy for all of the body's processes.

RETINA
A light-sensitive layer at the back of the eye where receptor cells gather visual information and send it to the brain along the optic nerve.

RODENT
A mammal that has specialized front teeth for gnawing – for example a squirrel, beaver, or capybara

ROOST
To rest or perch, usually above ground level, in a tree.

RUMINATE
To regurgitate plant food and chew it again. Many plant-eating mammals, including cows and goats, have to do this to help break down the tough cells walls and extract the nutrients from leaves and grass.

SALIVA
A liquid produced by glands in the mouth that aids chewing and swallowing. Saliva contains body chemicals that begin digestion. In some animals it also contains a poison that kills or immobilizes prey.

SAVANNA
A grassy plain in tropical and subtropical regions of the world where there are very few trees.

SEPTIC
Infected by pus-forming bacteria.

SKELETON
A framework of bones or other hard parts that supports the body of an animal and provides attachment points for muscles.

SPECIES
A group of animals that look like one another and can reproduce by pairing with each other – animals cannot pair with members of another species.

SUBSOIL
The layer of soil beneath the surface soil, known as topsoil.

TERRITORY
The part of an animal's habitat that it defends from rival animals, usually of the same species.

THORAX
In arthropods this is the central body part to which the legs and wings are attached. In four-limbed vertebrates it is the part of the body between the neck and the abdomen enclosed by the ribcage.

TOXIC
Relating to a poison or toxin. The bite or sting of an animal may have a toxic effect on another animal.

TROPICAL
Climate in the region of the world north and south of the equator that undergoes very little seasonal change in either temperature or rainfall. Tropical areas lie between the Tropic of Capricorn and Tropic of Cancer.

TUNDRA
A flat treeless area between the icecap and the tree line of Arctic regions, where the subsoil is permanently frozen.

TUSK
In elephants this is a modified incisor tooth. The tooth loses its enamel cap soon after it appears, leaving only a bone-like substance, known as ivory, which grows continuously.

ULTRASOUND FREQUENCY
Sound that is too high in pitch to be heard by humans, but which can be heard by many animals. Echolocation sounds are ultrasonic. Bats and dolphins hunt using echolocation.

VEGETARIAN
An animal that eats only plants – for example a giraffe.

VENOM
A poison, or toxin, produced by one animal that is injected into another by a bite or sting. Venom is normally used for hunting prey or in self-defence.

VERTEBRATE
An animal with a vertebral column, or backbone, made of bones called vertebrae. (Single is *vertebra*.)

WARM-BLOODED
A warm-blooded, or endothermic, animal keeps its body temperature within a certain range by means of internal chemical reactions, regardless of whether its surroundings are hot or cold. All mammals and birds are warm-blooded.

WEAN
To accustom a young animal to eat solid food rather than suckle its mother's milk.

ZOOPLANKTON
Plankton that consists of tiny animals, often juveniles of coral, sea anemones, and jellyfishes.

INDEX

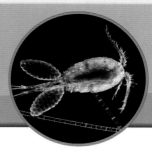

ACKNOWLEDGMENTS

Dorling Kindersley would like to thank: Jackets Development Manager Amanda Lunn; Lili Bryant for proofreading; Amy-Jane Beer for writing the introduction; Clive Munns at Montgomery Veterinary Clinic, Kent and Jane Hopper and Kerry Anderson at the Aspinall Foundation for help with picture research; Sakshi Saluja for additional picture research; Arijit Ganguly, Aanchal Singal, Jacqui Swan, and Duncan Turner for design assistance.

Picture Credits

The publisher would like to thank the following for their kind permission to reproduce their photographs:

(Key: a-above; b-below/bottom; c-centre; f-far; l-left; r-right; t-top)

Alamy Images: Blickwinkel 48, 92cl, John Cancalosi 18tr, cbimages 43br, 165br, Ethan Daniels 167tr, Gallo Images 47bl, Nick Greaves 174cl, Amar and Isabelle Guillen - Guillen Photography 150c, Hawkeye 1b, 146-147b, Hemis 196bl, B Holland 101c, Juniors Bildarchiv 59, 182bl, The Natural History Museum, London 42br, Gerry Pearce 4l, 18-19, 19br, Premaphotos 43cr, RBO Nature 238cl, Malcolm Schuyl 195, Ivan Synieokov 22c, tbkmedia.de 29tr, travelbild.com 47tl, Mike Veitch 166c, Carlos Villoch – MagicSea.com 71tl, 84bl, A & J Visage 152-153, 228bl, Joe Vogan 124cl, Rob Walls 18bc, 42tr, WaterFrame 167, Wildlife 124bc, WoodyStock 185cb; **Ardea:** Brian Bevan 28cr, Jean-Paul Ferrero 111c, 221c, Francois Gohier 65r, 229tl, Tom & Pat Leeson 20, Adrian Warren 62-63; **Nick Athanas/Tropical Birding:** 58b; **Corbis:** All Canada Photos / Glen Bartley 139bl, All Canada Photos / Stephen Krasemann 7cr, Robert McGouey / All Canada Photos 50, Terry A. Parker / All Canada Photos 30-31, Tim Zurowski / All Canada Photos 52-53, Theo Allofs 38c, 48-49, 63c, Caspar Benson 8-9c, Hal Beral 242, Steve Bowman 142c, Siggi Bucher 80, Michael Callan 186cl, Visuals Unlimited / Ken Catania 232l, 232-233, Clouds Hill Imaging Ltd 85cr, Brandon D Cole 156cl, 157tr, Daniel J. Cox 114-115, Tui De Roy 22cr, DLILLC 27c, 118tr, 119bc, 119br, 188-189, 222-223, 231bl, DPA 135c, 186-187, DPA / Bernd Thissen 68b, Richard du Toit 174tr, Nicole Duplaix 220cl, EPA / Sanjeev Gupta 60-61, Jan-Peter Kasper / epa 76-77, Stephen Frink 150-151,

Anthony Bannister / Gallo Images 208tr, Nigel J. Dennis / Gallo Images 127, Farrell Grehan 207, Rose Hartman 125tl, Martin Harvey 9c, 23bl, 66-67, 146c, Jason Isley – Scubazoo 144-145, Andrew Watson / JAI 70cr, M. Philip Kahl 174cb, Frans Lanting 38-39, 54-54, Joe Macdonald 60cl, Steve Maslowski 223tr, 235bc, Joe McDonald 52tl, 52c, 66bl, 138br, Mary Ann McDonald 23cb, MedicalRF.com 118bc, Minden Pictures / Ingo Arndt 35b, Minden Pictures / ZSSD 4r, 185tl, Thomas Marent / Minden Pictures 178, Momatiuk – Eastcott 36c, Arthur Morris 140cl, National Geographic Society / Paul Nicklen 36-37, David A. Northcott 66cl, Richard T. Nowitz 47br, Ocean 8bl, 100-101, 120cl, Robert Pickett 8bc, Radius Images 188tl, Radius Images / F. Lukasseck 124cr, Fritz Rauschenbach 238, Reuters 160, 226-227, 236bc, James Hager / Robert Harding World Imagery 35t, Jeffrey L. Rotman 85tl, Kevin Schafer 20-21, David Scharf / Science Faction 158-159, 239, Norbert Wu / Science Faction 156-157, 166cl, 166cr, 242-244, Anup Shah 113tr, 192-193, Brian J. Skerry / National Geographic Society 145c, Paul Souders 56-57, 190-191, Ron & Valerie Taylor / Steve Parish Publishing 88-89, Jeff Vanuga 15br, Visuals Unlimited 46tl, 80-81, 82-83, 90c, Visuals Unlimited / Alex Wild 208bc, 210-211, 211c, Visuals Unlimited / Andy Murch 84tr, Visuals Unlimited / David Watts 220-221, 221tr, Visuals Unlimited / David Wrobel 156br, 244br, Visuals Unlimited / Eric Tourneret 237cr, Visuals Unlimited / Reinhard Dirscherl 8cr, Wim Van Egmond / Visuals Unlimited 162tr, 212bl, 212r; **Dorling Kindersley:** Steve Gorton / Oxford University of Natural History 12bl, Thomas Marent 14br, Ian Montgomery 249cl; **courtesy of Ismor Fischer, photo by Sara Abozeid:** 64bl; **FLPA:** Ingo Arndt / Minden Pictures 187tr, Reinhard Dirscherl 148-149, Gerard Lacz 26-27, 32-33, Frans Lanting 188cb, Oliver Lucanus 90-91, Hiroya Minakuchi / Minden Pictures 228tr, Konrad Wothe / Minden 142-143, 182cl, Mark Moffett / Minden Pictures 13tr, 96cl, Matthias Breiter / Minden Pictures 9cl, Minden Pictures / Albert Lleal 237bc, Minden Pictures / Grzegorz Lesniewski 186bl, Minden Pictures / Patricio Robles Gil 120-121, Mitsuaki Iwago / Minden Pictures 173tr, 173b, Piotr Naskrecki / Minden Pictures 129cr, Thomas Marent / Minden Pictures

34bl, ZSSD / Minden Pictures 60tr, 61cr, Ariadne Van Zandbergen 104-105; **Getty Images:** Altrendo Nature 99t, Pete Atkinson 102-103, Anthony Bannister 126-127, Jonathan Blair / National Geographic 110-111, Tom Brakefield 172c, Mark Carwardine 123c, Mark Carwardine / Peter Arnold 54c, Mark Conlin 155tl, Stephen Dalton 133bc, Danita Delimont 99br, Carol Farneti-Foster 147tc, 147tr, Kelly Funk 140-141, Karen Gowlett-Holmes 89c, David Haring / DUPC 122-123, Thomas Kitchin & Victoria Hurst 23br, 31, S.J. Krasemann 180c, Rene Krekels 240-241, Jens Kuhfs 199, Laguna Design 213tr, 213l, Frans Lemmens 183tr, Wayne Lynch 222cl, Thomas Marent 241, Mark Miller 15tl, 247t, Michael & Patricia Fogden / Minden Pictures 176-177, Michio Hoshino / MInden Pictures 180-181, Minden Pictures / Kevin Schafer 225cr, Minden Pictures / Richard Herrmann 198-199, Piotr Naskrecki / Minden Pictures 224-225, Eastcott Momatiuk 57, Morales 105, National Geographic / Ed George 65tl, National Geographic / Joel Sartore 172-173, National Geographic / Tim Laman 58tr, 130-131, Oxford Scientific / Steve Turner 18cl, Panoramic Images 208, Andrea Pistolesi 129br, Mary Plage 98c, Jeff Rotman 214cl, Luis Javier Sandoval 86-87, James R. D. Scott 148, Jami Tarris 179cr, Tier Und Naturfotographie J & C Sohns 173tr, David Tipling 230cl, Roy Toft 128c, Damian Turski 147tl, Visuals Unlimited / Alex Wild 95c, Stuart Westmorland 86c, Winfried Wisniewski 191; **Andrea Hallgass:** 94-95; **imagequestmarine.com:** 200, 200-201; **naturepl.com:** Eric Baccega 184bl, Philip Dalton 206-207, Nick Garbutt 130cl, 136cl, Sandesh Kadur 61tr, David Kjaer 50-51, Bence Mate 1t, 146-147, Gavin Maxwell 204-205, 205, Nature Production 160-161, Fred Olivier 189br, Roger Powell 194-195, Roberto Rinaldi 102c, Andy Rouse 134-135, David Shale 83c, Martin H Smith 29b, Kim Taylor 236cl, Nick Upton 176c, Tom Vezo 223cr, Bernard Walton 227cr; **NHPA/ Photoshot:** Anthony Bannister 164bl, Stephen Dalton 147ftr, Gerard Lacz 228-229, Jonathan & Angela Scott 71cr; **Christine Ortlepp:** 156bc; **Press Association Images:** AP Photos / Christopher Austin 75; **Rex Features:** © 2012 Rittmeyer et al. 74-75; **Dario Sanches:** 59t; **Science Photo Library:** David Aubrey 139br, CDC 158, Eye of Science 202cl, 202bl,

202-203, 203tl, Andy Harmer 139t, George Holton 8-9, Rexford Lord 64tl, Andrew J. Martinez 244, William H. Mullins 70bl, Louise Murray 96-97, Nature's Images 203cr, 239tr, Simon D. Pollard 93br, James H. Robinson 245, Paul Zahl 245br; **SeaPics.com:** 44-45, 247br.

Jacket images: *Front:* **Dorling Kindersley:** Twan Leenders br, cl, Paignton Zoo, Devon l; **Dreamstime. com:** Isselee cb, bc, Jagronick c; **Getty Images:** Stone / Art Wolfe cr; **NHPA/ Photoshot:** Stephen Dalton tc; *Back:* **Alamy Images:** H Lansdown cla; **Corbis:** Ocean cra; **Dorling Kindersley:** Peter Minister fclb; **Dreamstime.com:** Amwu br, Jocic tl; **Getty Images:** Karen Gowlett-Holmes cl, Stuart Westmorland cr; **Andrew Kerr/.dotnamestudios:** c; **naturepl. com:** Bence Mate tr; *Spine:* **Dorling Kindersley:** Paignton Zoo, Devon t; **Dreamstime.com:** Olga Bogatyrenko b; *Endpapers:* **Corbis:** Martin Harvey *(front)*; **Science Photo Library:** Chris Sattlberger *(back)*.

All other images © Dorling Kindersley
For further information see: www.dkimages.com